THE POP SIXTIES

THE pop Sixties

A PERSONAL AND IRREVERENT GUIDE

ANDREW J. EDELSTEIN

WORLD ALMANAC PUBLICATIONS
New York, New York

Interior design: Koppel & Scher
Assistant designer: Drew Hodges

First published in 1985.

Distributed in the United States by Ballantine Books,
a division of Random House, Inc.,
and in Canada by Random House of Canada, Ltd.
Library of Congress Catalog Card Number: 85-50961
Newspaper Enterprise Association ISBN: 0-911818-67-7
Ballantine Books ISBN: 0-345-32623-7
Printed in the United States of America.
World Almanac Publications
Newspaper Enterprise Association, Inc.
A Scripps Howard company
200 Park Avenue
New York, New York 10166

10   9   8   7   6   5   4   3   2   1

Photos reproduced with permission from Wide World Photos, Inc. pages: vii (upper left), 4,
19, 26, 27, 29,33, 56, 91, 115, 120, 135, 145, 155, 156, 157, 159, 162, 163, 165, 166, 167, 168, 170,
172, 173, 176, 177, 178, 179, 180, 181 (top), 182 (bottom), 183, 184 (left), 185, 186, 187, 191, 196,
199, 203, 204, 206, 207, 215, 216, 217, 218, 219, 221, 222, 224-225, 229, 230 (top), 239, back cover.

I wish to thank the following:

Jeff Tamarkin, a good buddy since 1967 and a true '60s Mania-c.

Rockin' Howie, whose intense devotion to the 1960s fueled the idea
for this book.

Connie Passalacqua, for moral support.

My editors at World Almanac Publications: Pat Fisher, Rob Fitz
and Daril Bentley for their assistance and encouragement.

My co-workers at United Media Enterprises, for putting up with
me while writing this book and for not arguing with me when I
insisted that "Gilligan's Island" is the greatest sitcom in the
history of the world.

Polly and Al Vonetes of the United Media Enterprises office in
Hopewell, Virginia, for allowing me to roam through their library
of TV photos; Pepper O'Brien for use of her rock photos; Joe
Canale at Wide World Photos for his patience.

Lydia Sherwood and Lisa Berger for their research assistance.
Debby Felder for her copy-editing.

Public relations contacts who helped me arrange interviews or
obtain photos: Bernie Ilson, Rogers and Cowan, Lippin and Grant,
Paul Roberts, Doug Watson of *Old Cars* magazine, John Koenig of
Goldmine, Candace Irving of Mattel.

The New York Public Library for the Performing Arts at Lincoln
Center.

DOES SOCIETY HANG BY A HAIR?

For my parents, Betty and Marvin Edelstein, and my sister, Sally; for their love and support not only in the '60s, but also in the '50s, '70s and '80s.

The '60s - Yours, Mine, and Ours

INTRODUCTION

I entered the '60s as an 8-year-old with a crew cut and a Little League T-shirt and exited them as an 18-year-old with shoulder-length hair and a tie-dyed T-shirt. In between, I was probably influenced by and a participant in nearly every fad and fashion in that decade — everything from eating fast food and TV dinners to rooting for the New York Mets, watching "Batman," dancing the Frug, and hero-worshiping James Bond.

Growing up in an affluent suburb, sheltered from the "real" world, made for an adolescence suffused with pop culture. At the time, I probably wasn't aware of the term or its sociological implications. Because of the key role it played in my day-to-day existence, pop culture just seemed to be a natural aspect of growing up.

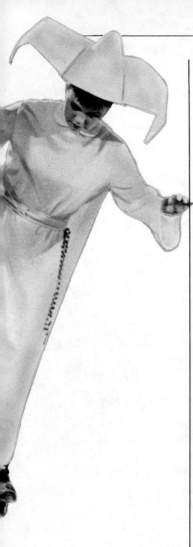

But as I look back from the lofty vantage point of twenty years (!!), I realize what made '60s pop culture seem so special was its sense of being plugged into the spirit of the NOW. Never before had so many elements— books, art, dances, slang, movies, music, and fashion — coalesced in the same exciting mood. It was a pop culture predicated on prosperity, non-durability, and infatuation with youth — three concepts that have taken a beating in the '80s.

It was a boss trip while it lasted. Because one day, the '60s were over. Not exactly on December 31, 1969. Maybe the sixties ended the day Nixon beat McGovern, or the day Nixon resigned. Or maybe it was the day you cut your hair and went for a job interview. But, whatever, they weren't here anymore.

Some say the economy was responsible. During the '60s, it was bouncing as high as a Super Ball. But in the '70s, it was tossed around like the Minnow in that terrible sit-com storm. When we crawled onto the Gilligan's Island that was the post-'60s, here was this brave new world: Granola replaced Lucky Charms; TV got more "relevant"; music became blander; disc jockeys no longer screamed; recycled replaced disposable. In the movies, the king of the beach was a shark, not Frankie Avalon.

You turn on the television and Larry Hagman wears a Stetson, not a space helmet. You notice that kids would rather play video games than electric guitar. Somebody calls the Beatles Paul's old group. You turn 30, 35. When walking into a restaurant, I find it hard to believe that they're talking to me when they say "Can I help you, sir?"

You can't name more than two of the current president's cabinet, but you can remember the name of the butler on "The Addams Family" and what records were in the Top 10 in the summer of '65.

The memories remain. We've learned a lot about the '60s since then — a lot of things we may not like: that John Kennedy was a scheming womanizer when he was portrayed as a family man; that the Beatles were using drugs when they were at the same time being portrayed as lovable moptops; that Marilyn Monroe's death may not have been an accident.

But that's not the purpose of this book. It's meant to be more evocative, than provocative: To fondly recall pop culture — the fun, silly underside to the '60s that was a part of one's daily life — but which has been overlooked in the wake of the more profound social changes of that era.

Pop culture is a tricky thing to define. Eggheads have spilled a lot of ink debating its precise definition. But I happen to be aligned with the school of thought that considers pop culture to be all those elements of life which are not narrowly intellectual or creatively elitist and which are generally disseminated through the mass medium—the spoken and printed words, sounds, objects, pictures, and artifacts. I started talking like that after I grew up.

For the purposes of this book, pop culture encompasses, as it did in the '60s, a wide range of areas not traditionally associated with "culture" per se — TV commercials, ad slogans, pop sports, pop politicians, pop cars. Of course, we'll also look at music, TV films, print, and the fads and fashions that made up the pop culture of the entire decade.

Likewise, for the concept "the '60s,"—ask 100 people what the '60s meant to them and they'll give you a hundred different answers. The reason for such diverse answers is that the '60s, of course, were not a monolithic decade. The years between 1960 and 1969 can be divided into three distict eras:

1960-63: '50s hangover, Camelot
1964-67: The pop '60s

1967-69: The Counterculture '60s

I prefer to consider the decade as a whole. Take your pick: whatever 1960s you want to remember — go-go boots or peasant blouses; Jackie or Jimi— they're here again, if you want them.

A "Pop" Day In The Life—Circa 1966

Nine-thirty on a Saturday morning. Clock-radio alarm rings, set to Fabulous 57! WMCA, the home of the Good Guys, the home of the hits. Check out that new Beatles record. First and exclusive! It's a gas. Too many commercials ("National Shoes ring the bell!" "Palisades Amusement Park— swings all day and after dark").

Too much homework over the weekend. I'll do it tomorrow. Social Studies essay: "The Negro's Quest for Freedom." Two hundred and fifty words. Crib the info from *The World Book*. Current Events quiz: Look at the *Times* tomorrow morning. Why does that guy Shastri look like he should be selling Good Humor?

Chime time! says the radio. Ten A.M. Seventy-six swinging degrees already. Dress cool, and you'll *be* cool. Wear the purple-and-white-striped surfer's shirt. Let that hair fall over your forehead into your eyes. Makes you look boss. Slip into white Levis and chukka boots.

Breakfast. No time for Lucky Charms today. Lemme have a glass of Instant Breakfast. If it's good enough for the Gemini guys, it's good enough for me.

Gotta meet Mark at the slot-car track at eleven. First time I'm riding the new Schwinn with the banana-seat over there. Looks sharp, but doesn't feel just right. Get the old man to fix it tomorrow. In three years, I'll be able to drive.

Slot-car track too crowded. Too many hoods hanging out there anyway. Cosmo Matafari is there. He has a cousin who knows the Rascals' road manager; or so he says. Let's hack around someplace else. Wetson's maybe, but they raised their hamburgers up to eighteen cents. Vinnie's instead? Gotta great jukebox. Pizza tastes like they poured STP on it though.

How about a flick? The new Bond is out. I saw something about it in *Life*. You should see him suck poison out of this chick's foot. Oh yeah? Let's go.

Thunderball not as good as *Goldfinger*. Domino is no Pussy Galore. Ride home for dinner. Mother has left me a Patio frozen Mexican TV dinner. Heat it up as you please. There's Wink in the fridge to wash it down.

Jay's party tonight. Gotta choose between the paisley shirt or the dickey and the velour V-neck. Gonna wear those Beatle boots; bought 'em at Flagg Brothers. Principal says I can't wear them to school, but I *can* wear 'em to the party. Taps make 'em sound real cool and heels make me 3/4" taller. Splash on a little Hai Karate. The ad in *Playboy* says you'll slay the chicks.

Eight P.M. Turn on "Gilligan's Island." Boy! That Ginger is a piece! I'd like to be stranded in the middle of the ocean with her. She's not as hot as Nancy Sinatra, though. Nancy's boots are gonna walk all over me.

Party time. Usual crew. Robin, Linda, Laurie, Debbie, two guys named Jeff, Mark, Jay, me, and some kid from algebra. The minute *Rubber Soul* goes on, the lights go off. More guys than girls. Make wisecracks while the others make out. Stare at the *Shangri-Las* LP cover instead and think of Nancy Sinatra.

Eleven-thirty P.M. Home. "Paint It Black" on radio, appropriately. Put on "Chiller Theatre." Even "Atomic Age Vampire" seems more upbeat than me. Can't hold my interest. How come I don't feel like a teenager in an *Archie* comic book?

THE POP SIXTIES

SHAKE IT UP, BABY!

THE MUSIC SCENE

INTRODUCTION

Back in the '60s...Kenny Rogers sang psychedelic songs, the Bee Gees were imitation Beatles, Cher got thrown out of restaurants, and Linda Ronstadt wore peasant blouses.

At the beginning of the decade, the music was called rock 'n' roll and you could only read about it in 16 Magazine; it was said to cause juvenile deliquency and acne. By the end of the decade, it was called rock and you read about it in the New York Review of Books; it was said to be able to stop war.

In between, the decade spawned about 20 different genres, with the focus of creativity shifting from New York to Detroit to Southern California to Liverpool and back to Northern California. In this chapter, we'll take a look at all these genres.

The Everly Brothers kept the spirit of the '50s alive in the early '60s with their hit singles, "All I Have to Do Is Dream", and "Cathy's Clown."

2

Chubby Checker demonstrates the Twist in 1961.

The Sounds of the Early '60s

U.S. popular music of 1960 was hardly worth discussing seriously. The curse of rock & roll still hung heavily over most of the widely-heard songs, and more than 90 percent of the material could be dismissed as unadulterated trash." — *Encyclopedia Britannica* Yearbook 1961.

How bad was the music scene in 1961? It was so bad that Lawrence Welk had a Number 1 record in 1961, "Calcutta," which actually beat out the Shirelles' "Will You Still Love Me Tomorrow".

Things actually weren't that bad — but even for teenagers, rock 'n' roll undeniably had lost much of its punch. Rock 'n' roll came out of the '50s scarred by its now-familiar litany of troubles. Elvis in the army, Little Richard had found God, Jerry Lee Lewis socially ostracized, Buddy Holly dead, plus payola scandals scaring the industry. At the dawn of the '60s, rock 'n' roll was a bleak landscape dominated by Top 40 novelty singles, one-shot hits, and clean teen idols.

The first two years of the '60s were years of preparation: Berry Gordy was just gearing up his new record company; the Beach Boys were students at Hawthorne High; Bob Zimmerman had just thumbed his way to New York City; the Beatles wore leather jackets, had five members, and were playing in Hamburg. The art crowd and the intellectuals hadn't yet discovered rock 'n' roll.

The most exciting sounds in 1960 and 1961 were made by black artists such as Sam Cooke, Ray Charles and

Jackie Wilson, who were transforming the R&B of the '50s into the soul music of the '60s. The Twist was a dance for teenagers only.

Among the stars hitting the charts in 1960 and 1961:

GARY U.S. BONDS—The first time for this singer, who would be rediscovered by Bruce Springsteen in the 1980s. Recording for a tiny label in Norfolk, Virginia, he produced records like "Quarter to Three," "New Orleans, " and "School Is Out" in a gravelly, off-key voice buried under a dirty mix and Daddy G's sax.

SAM COOKE—The smooth-voiced Prince of Soul ("You Send Me," "Chain Gang," "Twistin' the Night Away," "Shake") was fatally shot in a Los Angeles motel room while on vacation in December, 1964, ending a brilliant career. He was 29.

THE DRIFTERS—Now led by Ben E. King, they put strings on records like "This Magic Moment," "Save the Last Dance for Me," and "Some Kind of Wonderful."

INSTRUMENTALS—From rock 'n' roll guitar bands like the Ventures and Johnny and the Hurricanes to lush movie themes (Ferrante and Teicher: "Exodus," "The Apartment" and Al Caiola: "The Magnificent Seven"), songs without words were a popular chart item.

BEN E. KING—The former lead singer of the Drifters went on his own and breathed life into the Spectoresque "Spanish Harlem."

GENE PITNEY—The electronically-distorted trembly-voiced singer of "Town without Pity," "Every Breath I Take," "The Man Who Shot Liberty Valance," also wrote hits like "He's a Rebel" for the Crystals and "Hello Mary Lou" for Ricky Nelson.

DEL SHANNON—With one of rock's most incredible falsetto voices and that roller-rink organ, Shannon's hits included "Runaway," and "Hats off to Larry."

THE SHIRELLES—This New Jersey quartet, inspired by the Chantels, became the first of the girl groups of the '60s. Their hits included "Soldier Boy," "Dedicated to the One I Love," "Tonight's the Night," and "Will You Still Love Me Tomorrow?"

BOBBY VEE—Bob Dylan allegedly played in his back-up band. He was a shade more substantial than the teen idols with whom he was grouped. A Fargo, North Dakota boy who got his big break taking Buddy Holly's place the night Holly's plane went down. Hits: "Take Good Care of My Baby," "Rubber Ball," and "The Night Has a Thousand Eyes."

JACKIE WILSON—He was a Detroit native whose first record in 1958 was produced by Berry Gordy. He could switch from frantic soul ("I'll Be Satisfied") to mock opera ("Night"). Wilson collapsed on stage during a 1975 performance and died in 1984, never having regained consciousness.

Dion (second from right) with the Belmonts

The Sharkskin Princes: Dion and Frankie Valli

They were the pride of the East, these princes in sharkskin. Dion and Frankie Valli. During the early 1960s, these two Italo-American singers were, to one growing up in the urban and suburban ethnic enclaves of New York, Newark, and Philly, what the Beach Boys were to the youth of Southern California. They were guys that guys dug—not prefab sissies like Fabian or Frankie Avalon—and it was all right. Don't give me any of that homo stuff. We're talking attitude here. These guys taught you how to swagger, how to hang out on the street corner or at the pizzeria window, leaning just right so that the hot oil didn't drip on your pearl gray continentals.

Frankie, leader of the Four Seasons, dispensed the essential advice— the only four words you'll ever need—"Walk Like a Man." At the same time, he told us that it wasn't true that "Big Girls Don't Cry." But we knew that already, thanks to Dion.

Dion knew how to handle girls. Ya love 'em, and then ya leave 'em. 'Cause to him they're just the same. He tussled with tough chicks like "Runaround Sue" and "Donna the Prima Donna", and in one song ("Little Diane") he even alluded to slugging her to keep her in line. His music was the inspiration for the best novel about growing up in the early 1960s, *"The Wanderers"* by Richard Price. He sang using sort of an earnest whine, an adenoidal cross between Wally Cleaver's "Aw, gee mom" and a juvenile deliquent's "Don't bug me, man."

Dion was from the Bronx—Belmont Avenue to be exact. In the late 1950s he had his doo-wop hits with the Belmonts—Freddie Milano, Carlo Mastrangelo, and Angelo D'Aleo— "Teenager in Love" and "I Wonder Why." They split in 1960, and Dion went on his own.

Some people tried linking Dion to the teen-idol school then popular, but in our hearts we knew he could take all those wimps from South Philly to the mat. His first solo disc, "Lonely Teenager," about a runaway 15-year-old, had a provacative theme, leaving much to the imagination. Why was the protagonist on the run? Did he knock up his girlfriend? Did he steal one hubcap too many? Was he caught sniffing glue?

He followed that with his smashes, "Runaround Sue," "The Wanderer," and "Lovers Who Wander." His career faded in 1963; we didn't know it at the time, but the reason for his sudden downturn wasn't the Beatles. Dion had become a junkie. That's not cool, Dion.

After he kicked his monkey, Dion returned to the charts in 1968 with his snappy "Abraham, Martin, and John." He later cashed in on the '50s revival, and tried to become an introspective singer-songwriter type in the mid-'70s with a minor neglected classic called "Lookin' for the Heart of Saturday Night." Then, in the '80s, he became a born-again Christian.

Frankie Valli and the Four Seasons had more staying power. The Four Seasons were from New Jersey and had been knocking around since the mid-'50s. They had been without a hit since 1956 when, calling themselves "The Four Lovers," they scored with something called "Apple of My Eye." In 1962, they struck with "Sherry." Their sound was firmly rooted in the 1950s black doo-wop groups, with the key difference being Frankie Valli's soaring falsetto that gave the group its trademark sound. That, plus classy studio production by "the fifth season" Bob Crewe, who also co-authored "Big Girls Don't Cry" and "Walk Like A Man," were keys to their success.

With Frankie's voice, it was a case of reverse-macho. When you sang with the guys in front of the candy store, were you man enough to hit those high notes as well as Frankie did?

The Seasons were the most on the (East) Coast in 1964—even when those longhaired Limeys got your girl-friends all worked up. It's no surprise that a lot of guys I knew refused even to acknowledge the existence of the Beatles as long as the Four Seasons were still boss. Why do you think Vee-Jay records released an LP in 1964 featuring a battle of the bands between the Beatles and Four Seasons? Who had a Number 1 hit that summer of Beatlemania? Same group, this time with "Rag Doll."

The Four Seasons continued to be favorites through the rest of the '60s ("Working My Way Back to You," "Opus 17," "Let's Hang On"). In the late '60s, they tried becoming vaguely psychedelic, but realized that wasn't the way to go. By 1967, Frankie Valli showed the first hints of his middle-aged taste with his hit ballad "Can't Take My Eyes Off You."

In the '70s, Valli became the middle-of-the-road singer he always wanted to become, a contemporary version of Al Martino or Vic Damone. Temporarily splitting from the Seasons, he had a profitable solo career, successfully riding the disco wave ("My Eyes Adored You," "Grease," "Our Day Will Come," and "Swearin' to God"). The new Four Seasons without Frankie even had a hit on their own ("Who Loves You"), and, together again, they still draw impressive crowds on the Vegas-Atlantic City Golden Oldies circuit.

Predictably, both Dion and Frankie got softer as the years wore on. It's as if they grew flabby like their fans—all those lean young pompadoured men in plain white T-shirts who left the attached houses and walk-up apartments of the city streets for the Cape Cod houses in suburbia. Only now they spill hot pizza oil onto their Sergio Valentes.

DION AND FRANKIE QUIZ

1. What is Dion's last name?

2. Who were the Wonder Who?

3. How did the Four Seasons get their name?

4. What is Frankie Valli's real name?

ANSWERS

1. DiMucci.

2. A pseudonym used by Frankie Valli to record a falsetto-voiced uptempo version of Bob Dylan's "Don't Think Twice, It's Alright," a small hit in 1965.

3. A New Jersey bowling alley—although another school of thought claims it's for the posh Manhattan restaurant.

4. Frank Castelluccio.

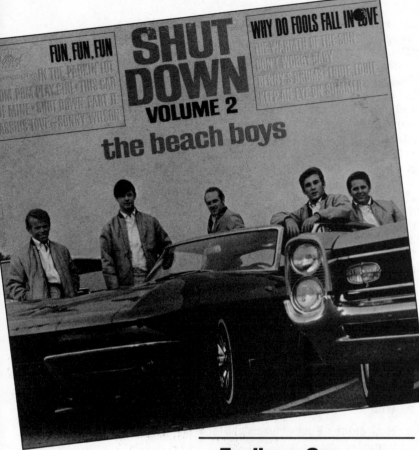

The Beach Boys

Endless Summer–
The Beach Boys and
Surf Music

The Beach Boys were a rock band disguised as shills for the Southern California Chamber of Commerce. The band's music—so full of sun, sand, sex, and surf—earned more free publicity for the good life in California in the early '60s than a dozen Disneylands. And, nowhere was their PR more effective than with us non-Californians.

After all, what did I know about beaches? The beach for me was dirty sand littered with rusty beer cans and diapers; pimply-faced college students selling soggy knishes and dripping creamsicles from huge aluminum crates; every square inch covered by screaming humanity; paunchy men, merchants from the city, promenading on the boardwalk on Saturday nights in their white shoes and seersucker sportcoats. The only bushy bushy blonde hairdos were peroxided bouffants.

So, naturally, I was enticed the first time I heard the Beach Boys urge me to go on a "Surfin' Safari." Once you found out what surfing was, that is. The only boards we found in the ocean were driftwood.

Of course, no one in the band except Dennis Wilson knew how to surf (ironically, accidental drowning would cause his death in 1983). The rest had other interests, from cross-country running (Mike Love) to music (Brian Wilson). They were basically a bunch of suburban kids—three brothers, their cousin, and a family friend—who concocted a winning musical mix, wedding '50s-style vocal harmonies to surf music, which until then had been primarily an instrumental genre.

It was that sound, together with Mike and Brian's lyrics, of course, which trumpeted this mythological lifestyle. Catch a wave. Two girls for every boy. Let's have "Fun, Fun, Fun." Everybody's gone surfing. When surfing cooled, they wrote about cars: "409," "Little Deuce Coupe." For two years they occupied the red-hot center of American rock 'n' roll. They weren't greasy, yet they weren't totally bland. They were wholesome and optimistic in an era when young Americans were still allowed to possess those virtues.

There were hints, however, that something more serious than hedonism lurked beneath the surface. Brian's "In My Room," for example, was moody, introspective, and lyrically sophisticated for 1963.

By 1966, Brian Wilson wanted to be taken seriously. By then, the chubby, reclusive singer had had a nervous breakdown, stopped touring with the band and had begun experimenting with drugs. While his colleagues were still on the road, wearing their silly striped shirts and white duck pants, Brian was in the studio listening to the music playing in his head. The result was *Pet Sounds*, one of the most accomplished and critically praised LPs of the time. Unfortunately, it didn't sell well; the public still wanted surf-and-car songs.

"Good Vibrations," released in October, 1966, changed all that. The tune, featuring a weird electronic instrument, the theramin, which had previously been heard on horror-movie soundtracks, broke through public resistance and became the Beach Boys' biggest record. In the mid-'80s, "Good Vibrations" would be used as the music in an orange-flavored soft-drink commercial. ("California Girls" got the TV-commercial treatment, as well, in a diet spin-off for the same product.)

In the late '60s, the Beach Boys suffered a drop in popularity. In an attempt to grapple one-on-one with the Sgt. Pepper-era Beatles, Brian became obsessed with producing the ultimate rock opus, *Smile*. But the group became impatient with his eccentric behavior. *Smile* was never released. Furthermore, the band's conservative image didn't jibe with the new hypercritical hippie sensibility. When the Beach Boys tried acting hip, they were only patronized. The band would have to wait for the mid-'70s when times changed and being square again became hip. By the '80s, the Beach Boys had become an American institution, seemingly content to play their hits for an audience that now contained the children of their original fans.

The beaches of Southern California may have eroded, but not so the Beach Boys.

BEACH BOYS' TIMELINE

1961

Brothers Brian, Carl, and Dennis Wilson, cousin Mike Love, and family friend, Al Jardine, form a rock 'n' roll combo called the Pendletones.
Brian and Mike write "Surfin'." The group's name is changed to the Beach Boys. December 31: The band plays its first gig, a New Year's Eve dance at the Long Beach Municipal Auditorium.

1962

March 24: "Surfin'" is a local L.A. hit and reaches Number 75 on the national charts.
October: The first Capitol single, "Surfin' Safari," hits Number 14 on the charts.

1963

May: "Surfin' U.S.A.," based on Chuck Berry's "Sweet Little Sixteen," peaks at Number 3.
Brian and his father, Murray, form The Sea of Tunes Production Co.
Summer: Jan and Dean have their first Number 1 hit surf song, "Surf City," written by Brian.

1964

"Fun, Fun, Fun," is released.
July: "I Get Around" becomes the band's first Number 1 song.
December 7: Brian suffers a nervous breakdown while flying from Los

I wish they all could be California Girls.

1966
May 16: *Pet Sounds* is released.
October: "Good Vibrations" is released. It becomes the band's third U.S. Number 1 hit.

1967
July: "Heroes and Villains," the long-awaited follow-up to "Good Vibrations," fails to have the desired impact.
November 20: Co-produced by Paul McCartney, *Smiley Smile* is released in the U.K. and the U.S. The album features the single, "Vegetables." *Smiley Smile* does not make the Top 40 in either country; "Vegetables" fails to make the charts at all.

1968
May 3: The group opens a U.S. tour. The second half of the show features a lecture by the Maharishi Mahesh Yogi. Audience response is poor, and half the tour is canceled.

1969
April 1: The group announces plans to start its own label, Brother Records.

JAN AND DEAN

The Beach Boys' biggest car-and-surf-sound rivals (although in reality they were buddies) were Jan (Berry) and Dean (Torrence). Their hits included "Surf City," "Little Old Lady From Pasadena," and "Drag City." They projected the correct clean-cut, blond image; they liked to ride skateboards, wear striped shirts, and act nutty onstage. Their career came to an abrupt halt in 1966, when Jan was injured in an automobile accident after his Corvette Sting Ray failed to negotiate a tricky curve in Los Angeles. He suffered paralysis for over a year, as well as extensive brain damage, but his condition has steadily improved over the years.

1964
"Fun, Fun, Fun," is released.
July: "I Get Around" becomes the band's first Number 1 song.
December 7: Brian suffers a nervous breakdown while flying from Los Angeles to Houston. He quits touring and decides to concentrate on writing and production.

1965
January: Glen Campbell replaces Brian in stage appearances. Campbell is replaced three months later by Bruce Johnston.
May: "Help Me, Rhonda" hits Number 1.

Girl Groups

The Shangri-Las really knew how to stoke prepubescent fantasies. They were four teenage girls (two sets of sisters, actually) from Queens, New York, who sang of things like motorcycle thugs, broken homes, and sex— not puppy love, not flowery love. "How does he dance?" the lead singer was asked in "Give Him a Great Big Kiss." "Close, very very close," she replied in a voice that sent steam through the tubes of my Motorola.

When all the girls you knew were named Debbie or Laurie or Robyn and wore hair bows, penny loafers, and hidden tissue paper, the Shangri-Las were quite a revelation. They personified forbidden fruit—the bouffanted, gum-chewing, leather-jacketed, mesh-stockinged "bad" girl. The ones you'd stare at out of the corner of your eye when you brushed by them in the junior high corridors, checking out their well-developed, 12-year-old chests as they clung to the arms of their older

The Shangri-Las (1964)

Murray the K goes bowling with the Ronettes.

As Alan Betrock noted in his 1982 book *Girl Groups*: "Their story is not one of females in rock 'n' roll (there were hundreds of female stars who had nothing to do with the girl-group sound), but of a musical setting, lyrical direction, and business organization that added up to the creation of a unique genre—a style that would prove to be as significant, trendsetting and lasting as almost any of rock 'n' roll's many permutations."

Alas, not all girl groups were as erotic as the Shangri-Las. (The Ronettes, who wore slit skirts and projected a vaguely Eurasian sexuality, were one exception.) Most, in fact, sang harmless love pleas that provided teenage girls with the perfect excuse to dial their favorite deejay and ask him to dedicate the record to that "really cute guy in my bio class."

Still, in the pre-Beatle '60s, the girl groups formed the backbone of Top 40 A.M. radio with songs like "Be My Baby," "He's a Rebel," "Soldier Boy," "The Locomotion," and "Chapel of Love." They were simple, catchy songs crafted with precision by some of rock's best producers and songwriters—Phil Spector, Don Kirshner, Carole King, Ellie Greenwich, Barry Mann, and Cynthia Weil—and energetically sung by seemingly interchangeable groups of teenage girls with names like: the Shirelles, the Crystals, the Ronettes, the Jelly Beans, the Bob B. Soxx, the Blue Jeans, the Dixie Cups, and individuals such as Lesley Gore, Dee Dee Sharpe, and Little Eva.

The true artists, however, were the writers, producers, and arrangers, not the musicians. They plucked the singers from obscurity, wrote the lyrics, music, and arrangements, and spun the studio dials. If the follow-up flopped or the producer lost interest, usually the singers' career could also

(15 at least!) boyfriends.

Shangri-Las records were an anthropological experience, letting me eavesdrop on life as it was lived on the other side of the tracks. I learned more about life from listening to Shangri-Las records than from an entire semester of hygiene class. But soon you wouldn't hear sounds like theirs anymore. The Shangri-Las were left behind, when most other groups rode off with the leader of the pack, heading West to San Francisco.

The Shangri-Las' string of hits in 1964 and 1965—"Leader of the Pack," "Remember (Walkin' in the Sand)," and "I Can Never Go Home Anymore"—climaxed one of the most interesting rock genres, the so-called girl groups.

be kissed bye-bye. There'd always be another group of girls singing at a school dance somewhere. Some singers, such as Darlene Love and Ronnie Spector, had powerful voices but were never given enough time to develop their potential.

The nerve center for all this activity was the Brill Building in Manhattan where a coterie of ambitious Brooklyn Jews in their early 20s wearing narrow ties and white shirts ran around pounding pianos and banging tambourines, coming up with *the hook*—all under the furious stewardship of Don Kirshner.

And then in the studio there was Phil Spector. The mysterious "first tycoon of teen," as Tom Wolfe dubbed him, created the most sophisticated pop sound of the early '60s. He took the Brill Building tunes and molded them into mini-pop symphonies, employing his famous "Wall of Sound," created at L.A.'s Gold Star Studios with its special echo chamber. "My records are built like a Wagner opera. They start simply, and they end with dynamic force, meaning and purpose. It's in the mind. I dreamed it up. It's like art movies," Spector once said. The irony is that Spector went through all that production and expense just to be heard out of some six-dollar transistor radio. On today's expensive equipment, however, Spector's stuff sounds even better.

In that interregnum between Elvis Presley's induction into the army and the Beatles' arrival in America, the girl groups were the only truly distinctive genre to fully blossom in the early '60s. The music had more punch than the teen idol stuff, yet lacked the rawness and crudity of such antecedents as the Midnighters and Laverne Baker. And the sound didn't die with the British Invasion; the Shangri-Las had their hits "Remem-ber (Walkin in the Sand)" and "Leader of the Pack" in 1964, and the Dixie Cups' "Chapel of Love" was one of the biggest hits that summer. However, by 1966 the record business was changing. Singer-songwriters were the wave of the future.

Most of the Brill brigade went on to better things. Kirshner became the mastermind behind the Monkees and host of TV's "Midnight Special," while King became the reigning Queen of Mellow on college campuses of the early '70s. Spector worked with the Righteous Brothers, producing their 1964 classic "You've Lost That Lovin' Feelin'" and then retired from the music biz when his masterpiece, the stunning "River Deep—Mountain High," recorded by Ike and Tina Turner, was rejected in 1966 by the record-buying public. He came out of retirement in 1969 to work with the Beatles in their final days and continued working sporadically during the '70s with such groups as the Ramones, but his hand no longer brought forth that same magic.

The groups (or truncated versions thereof) make more money today on the oldies revival circuit than they did twenty years ago. Echoes of their sound can be heard in acts ranging from Bruce Springsteen, Southside Johnny, the Pointer Sisters, and Marshall Crenshaw to today's so-called girl groups such as the Go-Go's and Cyndi Lauper.

The girl groups are all women now, and times have changed, to say the least. One of the Shangri-Las, Marge Ganzer, died in the late '70s of an accidental drug overdose; "Leader of the Pack" has been used in McDonald's commercials; the "Soldier Boy" got blown away in Vietnam; and the "Chapel of Love" has been taken over by the Moonies. But it was a pretty scene while it lasted.

The Supremes with lead singer Diana Ross (foreground) as they appeared on The Ed Sullivan Show in the mid-'60s

The Motown Sound

Motown was the beat that kept America dancing during the mid- and late- '60s. At basement parties, disc jockey hops, and chic discotheques, the turntables shook with "The Sound of Young America." Rolling out of Detroit with assembly-line precision were 45-RPM hits by the Supremes, Marvin Gaye, the Temptations, Martha and the Vandel-las, Stevie Wonder, the Marvelettes, the Miracles, and the Four Tops.

Until 1959, Detroit was strictly an automobile town; its miniscule music scene consisted of several small rhythm-and-blues labels aimed solely at a black audience. What changed all that was the presence of one man: a former prizefighter named Berry Gordy, Jr. Gordy's shrewdness, judgment, and business acumen helped create what would become the most profitable black-owned business in the world.

In January, 1959, Gordy started Tamla Records in a small clapboard villa on Detroit's West Grand Boulevard, which he optimistically called "Hitsville, U.S.A." Legend has it that Gordy, then an $85-a-week assembly-line worker, borrowed $700 to start the label. The story, apparently, is apocryphal. By 1959, Gordy wasn't exactly a music business novice; he had written song hits for R&B great, Jackie Wilson ("To Be Loved," "Reet Petite") and produced the earliest records of Smokey Robinson and the Miracles.

The first release, Marv Johnson's "Come to Me," hit Number 30, had a respectable showing. The seeds of the famed Motown sound—the gospel call-and-response, the heavy use of the tambourine, the pumped-up bass—could be heard in the earliest Gordy discs such as "Money" by Barrett Strong and the Miracles' "Way Over There."

The hits kept coming through 1962 and 1963. By early 1964, Gordy had assembled an impressive roster of musicians, all of whom attested to his unerring knack for picking talent. The Temptations, the Miracles, and the Four Tops had made records for other labels without large-scale success; Marvin Gaye had been an obscure member of the Moonglows; Stevie Wonder, Mary Wells, the Marvelettes, Martha and the Vandellas, and the Supremes had never recorded before being signed by Gordy.

As talented as the singers were, the true stars of Motown operated out of the public's eye. The songwriting-production team of Eddie Holland, Lamont Dozier, and Brian Holland took Gordy's concepts and molded them into the well-recognized Motown sound: lots of tambourine, a watered-down gospel-pop, propelled by sizzling bass and a hissing cymbal. Every record was different, but there was that certain something that marked it as Motown. The departure of Holland-Dozier-Holland in a contractual dispute in 1967 helped hasten Motown's decline. And of course, credit goes to the Motown house band, studio musicians who anonymously supplied the pulsating rhythm that was the secret of the label's success.

Motown succeeded because it reversed Colonel Tom Parker's theory that led him to sign Elvis Presley. In the mid-'50s the canny colonel allegedly said he could make a million dollars if he could find a "white boy who could sing like a Negro." Elvis proved him correct. In essence, Gordy said let me find a Black (or Blacks) who will appeal to whites because they won't sound too black, and I'll make a fortune. He, too, was right.

Motown always downplayed its racial aspect; consequently, its audiences were integrated. Unlike raw-sounding soul music, any harsh elements were filtered out. Gordy followed a deliberate strategy that put the Motown acts into places like the Copacabana and Las Vegas. Even though some people saw Martha and the Vandellas' "Dancing in the Street" as a metaphor for the urban riots that hit Watts in the summer of 1965, there was no overt social message in any of the label's early songs.

The Motown sound hit its chart peak between 1964 and 1967. The Supremes reeled off an incredible streak of hits: fourteen out of fifteen discs by the trio reached the Top 10; five made Number 1. In late 1966, the Four Tops recorded what many consider the greatest Motown single, "Reach Out I'll Be There," driven by the powerful voice of Levi Stubbs.

Then, in the summer of 1967, the city of Detroit burned, and eight months later Martin Luther King was killed. Motown's bouncy ditties lost their audience. They were too simple for the white hippies, not hip enough to be played on the new underground FM rock stations, and too fluffy for the new militant black mood. By the late '60s, the shape of black music itself was changing. Motown was being left behind by the innovations of performers such as Sly and the Family Stone. Gordy tried upgrading the sound, blatantly borrowing Sly's techniques for the Temptations' "Cloud Nine." The Supremes went through a brief period of relevance with "Love Child" and "I'm Living in Shame."

Before the decade was out, Motown had two last shining moments. In 1968, Marvin Gaye recorded "I Heard It Through the Grapevine," a song that had been a Motown hit a year earlier for Gladys Knight and the Pips. It became the label's biggest seller. In 1969, Motown introduced its first successful new act in several years, The Jackson Five, five young brothers from Gary, Indiana, who were discovered by Diana Ross. The youngest of the five, Michael, was cuter as a 10-year-old than as the king of rock video he'd become in the '80s.

In the '70s, Motown's downward spiral continued. Most of the major stars eventually jumped ship for more lucrative pacts with other labels. In 1972, the label itself abandoned Detroit for Los Angeles, and the Philadelphia sound replaced the Motown sound as the preeminent form of black pop. Today, however, Motown records from the '60s are as popular as ever. Every year brings a new batch of cover records; its beat has been borrowed by many of the English syntho-pop bands, and those old 45s are still heard mixed in with contemporary music at rock clubs.

But Motown's most enduring legacy was, and is, the fact that it moved black music into the pop mainstream for the first time.

AN INTERVIEW WITH MELVIN FRANKLIN OF THE TEMPTATIONS

The Temptations—David Ruffin, Eddie Kendricks, Paul Williams, Otis Miles, and Melvin Franklin—were Motown's most consistent male hitmakers, with a stage show known for its smooth-stepping choreography. The Detroit group started in the early '60s, aided by the production wizardry of Smokey Robinson. The group's hits included "My Girl," "The Way You Do the Things You Do," and "Beauty Is Only Skin Deep." Franklin, the bass singer of the tall, debonair, temptin' Temptations, was the youngest member when the group formed in the early '60s, and he's still a Temptation after more than twenty years.

Q: What was Detroit like in the early '60s?

Franklin: Detroit was the kind of town where if you wanted to make it, you'd have to leave that town. Motown represented a place we could go to in our hometown with growth potential. It gave every indication that it would grow.

Q: Why?

Franklin: Because of Berry Gordy. It was the man and his approach. He was a go-getter. He is a go-getter. A person who knows how to work with people. Yes always meant yes; he always kept his word. He never committed himself to something he could not do. He helped you believe in yourself the same way he believed.

Q: In the early days, the Temptations put out records like "In a Mellow Mood," which featured old-fashioned ballads and very un-rhythm-and-blues-like material. Why?

Franklin: In those days, we were seeking exposure in all areas. We knew we could sing any kind of thing, not just R&B. We were opening the door up to the whole world, to let them know that black people sang *songs* not just oogie-boogie songs. It was a way of growing, a way of showing our abilities and becoming acceptable to America that we weren't R&B artists, but artists in the truest sense of the word.

That's why we were able to work the Copacabana, Bob Hope specials, Ed Sullivan. You had to have something to offer, something to sell the people; you had more than just met the eye.

Q: How did Berry Gordy polish your image?

Franklin: He had a school for artist development where they taught charm, poise, stage presence, hygiene, everything. Everybody don't get it at home—some people are vagabonds, come from broken homes. I was lucky. I came from a special background; I was a minister's son. You had to learn how to check into hotels. I mean you had kids who had never been exposed to the world. Detroit is a city that's geared to making automobiles, not singing on Broadway.

Q: How did the band develop its sense of choreography?

Franklin: We had seen road shows with the Teenagers and the Cadillacs, and their choreography was a quantum leap from what we were doing. We were inspired. In Cleveland, the first big show we were on was at a place called the Keith 105 Theatre. Gladys and the Pips were on, and they had choreography. They blew our minds.

After signing with Motown, we went 1,200 miles away from Detroit, up in the Michigan woods to a place called Muskegon, Michigan, and we stayed up there for six weeks to two months. We never left and worked at the club day and night. We sang in the evening. Paul Williams really helped us with the choreography.

MELVIN FRANKLIN'S FIVE FAVORITE TEMPTATIONS SONGS

1. "My Girl"
2. "Since I Lost My Baby"
3. "Papa Was a Rolling Stone"
4. "Cloud Nine"
5. "Just My Imagination"

Folk Music

The folk-music boom of the early '60s produced a mixed bag of modern-day minstrels. Among those strumming acoustic guitars with varying degrees of success were a singing nun, a Jewish TV comedy writer, a score of crew-cut fraternity brothers, and a scraggly, gravelly-voiced appliance store owner's son from Minnesota. You'd hear the music from coffee houses to college campuses to camp fires, from the stages of sweaty nightclubs to the shoulders of dusty Mississippi highways.

Let's make the campus scene first, which was where folk music first boomed during the late '50s and early '60s. So you thought all fraternity brothers in the early '60s were like the gross-out gang in *Animal House?* Not a chance. That's why John Belushi smashed folksinger Stephen Bishop's guitar over his head during the memorable toga party. Ol' Bluto was jealous of the tunesmith's talent. Yep, the heppest frat rats on campus were busy being folksingers, strumming guitars, and singing old Negro spirituals and ancient ballads.

Some of these groovy Greeks hit the big time. The Brothers Four (A quartet of University of Washington Phi Gamma Deltas: a medical student and a prospective electrical engineer, TV director, and diplomat) scored with "Green Fields" in 1961; the Highwaymen (from Wesleyan University) took the old spiritual "Michael Row the Boat Ashore" to the top of the pop charts in the fall of 1961.

On any campus, you'd find cleancut, earnest-looking young men with guitars, banjos, and bass fiddles, and soulful girls with waist-length straight hair parted in the middle, all wielding acoustic guitars. Anyone for a hootenanny?

The Kingston Trio were the role models for this campus crusade. The trio—Dave Guard, Bob Shane, and Nick Reynolds—were musical Dobie Gillises with crew cuts, striped jackets, and lusty voices. They got their start at the Cracker Pot in Palo Alto, California, and, between 1959 and 1962, had such hits as "Tom Dooley," "MTA," "Scotch and Soda," and "Where Have All the Flowers Gone?" The latter song has been done to death as the title of contemporary articles wondering about the fate of '60s youth.

With their slyly witty songs, the Kingston Trio slowly helped to nudge the lid off the silent '50s, before it eventually became the pressure cooker of the '60s. They inspired such other acts as the Limeliters and the Chad Mitchell Trio (John Denver was

a member in its later years), whose biggest hit immortalized accused axe-murderer, Lizzie Borden.

The Kingston Trio engendered a big split in the folk-music community. The purists—especially those on campuses whose nascent political consciousnesses were being raised—considered the trio to be the epitome of commercialism, which they felt had tainted folk music. Perhaps they were jealous of the $30,000 the group was supposedly earning each week.

What you heard on college campuses, however, was basically simple, fun, and clean. You could sing these songs around a fire at summer camp. The most sanitized version of the folk boom was ABC's "Hootenanny," which picked up on the do-it-yourself folk trend about three years after it actually peaked. "Hootenanny," a folk-variety show that traveled from campus to campus, was hosted by the decidedly non-radical Jack Linkletter, son of Art. Students felt shocked; the show wouldn't allow certain performers on such as Pete Seeger, because of his alleged Communist connections, and many of the top performers, such as Peter, Paul, and Mary, Joan Baez, and Bob Dylan, refused to appear.

By 1962, the folk scene was shifting off campus to coffee houses where serious people in beards, berets, and turtlenecks sipped espresso while sitting at tables that had been made from doors, and lit by candles inserted into Chianti bottles. These dens of iniquity were not only found in Bohemian quarters like New York's Greenwich Village or Cambridge, Massachusetts, but also in such unlikely spots as Joliet, Illinois, where people hung out at a "folk cave" called the Know Where, and in Omaha, where cornfed beatniks made The Crooked Ear the place to be.

Folk music always carried political, moral, and social overtones, and, by 1961 and 1962, as events such as the Freedom Rides and the Cuban missile crisis began politicizing students, the protest side of folk music again became more prevalent. Inspired by the topical songs of the '30s, by the songs of Pete Seeger and Woody Guthrie, a new generation looked around and discovered the world was a rotten place.

Greenwich Village was the creative crucible where many of this generation of singer-songwriters held sway. Walk down MacDougal Street in 1962, and you'd hear pre-electric Bob Dylan singing about such subjects as racial injustice and the bomb. Or you'd find Texas-bred, New York resident Phil Ochs, whose topical songs made him, in effect, a singing journalist (his first LP was entitled *All the News that's Fit to Sing)*, or the barbed wit of Tom Paxton.

We heard songs that came from the headlines: fallout, medicare, direct-digit dialing. But not since the labor songs of the '30s had a movement inspired such a rash of grass-roots music as did the civil rights movement of the '60s. In the forefront was Joan Baez. She was first heard in 1960 as a 20-year-old, whose pure, sweet voice was a change from her nasal-sounding counterparts (although she had never formally studied singing).

At first, she made her mark singing traditional tunes like "House of the Rising Sun" and "Silver Dagger," that suggested a purist's approach. Her long, raven-colored hair and lack of makeup inspired thousands of young women to affect a similar look. She also became the first mass-marketed folksinger. By the end of 1962, she had three chart albums and had been the subject of a *Time* cover story. She is also known as the person who first

introduced Dylan to a large audience when she asked him to join her onstage. She was active in the civil rights and antiwar movements, inspiring cartoonist Al Capp to create a not-so-flattering character named Joanie Phonie.

Scoring folk hits in 1963 were the Singing Nun ("Dominique") and comedy writer Allan Sherman, who parodied the phenomenon with his Jewish-American humor on *My Son, the Folksinger.* Peter, Paul, and Mary, whom rock writer Lillian Roxon

Peter, Paul and Mary — with Paul Stookey (at left) — brought Bob Dylan's music to the masses with their hit version of his "Blowin' in the Wind" (1963).

called a "Kingston Trio with sex appeal," made the "message" song commercial. Their 1963 version of Dylan's "Blowin' in the Wind" was, at the time, the fastest-selling single in the history of Warner Brothers.

Peter, Paul, and Mary's performances today, as they have been for more than twenty years, are full of good humor, tight harmonies, and robust singing. Today they also pursue separate solo careers and are all still politically active, working on behalf of such causes as the nuclear freeze and El Salvador. Says Peter Yarrow: "We have a very balanced existence—something very few artists have. We have a limited performing schedule, so we have a lot of time for other careers—being parents, producing TV and records, which I do, or spending a lot of time organizing in the political arena.

"If you go to our concerts, there is no sense of it being a nostalgia piece. There's a very powerful sense of continuity with the past. It's no more nostalgic than seeing Pete Seeger perform. You don't say, 'Boy, remember the '50s when Pete Seeger was performing.' It's different than being a part of a style of music that's in and then goes out. I think it's a little tougher for Chubby Checker."

By 1965, the folk boom was fading. The Byrds and their hybrid folk rock arrived, and Dylan went electric. Folk rock put the pure folkies on the defensive, and many experimented with the hybrid form; they either went electric or retreated to the coffee-house circuit.

During the rest of the '60s, folk music didn't disappear, it just slipped out of the mainstream. Amidst the noise of acid rock in the late '60s, you could still hear the strumming of Arlo Guthrie, Woody's son, and his lengthy, memorable talking song "Alice's Restaurant." His second most memorable rap can be heard on the Woodstock soundtrack ("Whew...far out..lot of freaks here...the New York State Thruway is closed, man!").

By the late '60s, folk music was no longer the dominant sound on college campuses, but it still pulled weight. LPs by Joni Mitchell and Judy Collins were absolutely essential for the collection of any co-ed—to get you through those depressing nights in the dormitory. (Sexist confession: It was also a good way to meet sensitive chicks; tell 'em you, like, really, dug where Joni was coming from.)

In the '70s came the bastard grandchild of folk music, the so-called "mellow sound": Dan Fogelberg, Jackson Brown, James Taylor—corporo-folkies. But that's another decade.

Today one reads about a popular New York City group called the Washington Squares who are nostalgic for the Greenwich Village of Folk City, the Kettle of Fish, and the Bitter End. They wear turtlenecks, leotards, shades, bangs, bongos, and play acoustic folk music. They may just be the next thing.

FOLKIE FACTS

- Did you know that Maureen Reagan, then 21, daughter of Ronald Reagan, made her screen debut in 1963 in something called *Hootenanny Hoot?*

- In the summer of 1963, *Time* reported that a college girl shouted out to a performer at an Ogunquit, Maine cocktail lounge, "sing something about integration."

- 400,000 guitars were sold in the United States in 1961.

- "There's never been a good Republican folksinger."—Joan Baez, 1961.

- *Joan Baez played in coffee houses, but she didn't drink coffee.

BOB DYLAN

Here's the dope on Bob Dylan—the man of whom no less an authority than *Modern Screen* magazine said in 1965: "He's the hottest thing since the Beatles, the coolest cat since Elvis. He's a one-man Tin Pan Alley who composes his own music, writes his lyrics—in free verse, no less, for the backs of his record albums."

Real Name: Robert Allen Zimmerman
Place of Birth: Duluth, Minnesota
Date of Birth: May 24, 1941
Father's occupation: Appliance dealer
Religion: Jewish, Christian, Atheist

A DYLAN TIMELINE

1947:
The Zimmerman family moves to Hibbing, Minnesota.

1951:
Young Robert Zimmerman learns to play the guitar.

1956:
Young Robert learns to play the harmonica, autoharp, and piano.

1951–1959:
Zimmerman runs away from home seven times.

1959:
Zimmerman drops out of the University of Minnesota and bums around country, heading East to see his idol, Woody Guthrie, who is hospitalized in New Jersey.

1961:
Zimmerman establishes residencè in Greenwich Village and changes his name to Bob Dylan in honor of the poet Dylan Thomas. He plays hootenanny clubs, gets noticed by the press (he's described by a *New York Times* writer as looking like "a cross between a choir boy and a beatnik"), and is signed to a Columbia record contract.

1962:
Bob Dylan releases his first LP, *Bob Dylan.*

1963:
Peter, Paul, and Mary have a hit record with the Dylan tune "Blowin' in the Wind."

1965:
Dylan goes electric at the Newport Folk Festival and gets booed by folkies, but he hangs tough.

Dylan the folk-rocker has two Top 10 hits, "Like a Rolling Stone" and "Positively Fourth Street."

November 22: Dylan marries former model, Sara Lowndes.

1966:
Dylan releases his masterpiece LP, *Blonde on Blonde* and writes a novel, *Tarantula.*

1967:
Injured in motorcycle accident near Woodstock, New York, Dylan becomes a near-recluse, which magnifies his myth.

1968:
Dylan resurfaces with a simple, country-influenced LP, *John Wesley Harding,* his signal that rock has gotten too excessive.

1969:
Dylan goes country all the way with the *Nashville Skyline* LP and sings a duet with Johnny Cash on TV.

MEMORABLE DYLAN
QUOTE

"I just can't make it with any organization."—explaining why he refused to join any civil rights and social-action groups during the '60s.

The British Invasion

If you ask a school kid today what the British Invasion refers to, you can lay good odds that he'll say the Beatles-Stones-Dave Clark Five onslaught of 1964-65 and not the events of 1776 or 1812. Despite the efforts of newsweekly hypesters, some rock journalists, and record companies to promote other British musical invasions, there has never been one in rock 'n' roll's thirty-year history that captured the public's fancy like the nineteen months framed by the Beatles' arrival at Kennedy Airport in February, 1964 and the release of "Yesterday" by the same group in September, 1965. Later, when the Beatles started using strings on their records, you knew the fun was slipping out of rock 'n' roll.

This event was truly an invasion because, until 1964, rock 'n' roll had always been considered a distinctly American commodity. England was regarded by most young Americans as somewhat of an exotic locale known more for its political scandals than for its music. Prior to 1964, the major British contribution to the collective American teenage consciousness was probably Ian Fleming's James Bond. The British music that had infiltrated the American charts usually consisted of such oddball numbers as Lonnie Donegan's 1961 skiffle tune, "Does Your Chewing Gum Lose Its Flavor (on the Bedpost Overnight)?" or Kenny Ball's 1962 traditional jazz instrumental, "Midnight in Moscow."

But during the early '60s, hundreds of young Brits, fueled by their passion for American rock 'n' roll, blues, and R&B, were coming out of art schools and working-class neighborhoods into dank cellar pubs where they would enrapture audiences with their interpretations of the sounds that turned them on. However, word of these efforts, which would eventually become the substance of the British Invasion, never reached American ears. American rock fans, probably because of their insularity, would rather have been reading *Hit Parader* or *16* than *Melody Maker*. Even word of European and British Beatlemania in early 1963 was slow to get to the States.

There are those observers who claim that the assassination of President Kennedy in November, 1963 was responsible for creating the conditions that fostered Beatlemania and the British Invasion. These pundits say that American youngsters needed new heroes to replace their martyred president, but this theory is overrated. Lee Harvey Oswald didn't serve as an unwitting cultural tastemaker; if America was ever ready for a musical invasion, it would have been from late 1963 to early 1964.

When you are an adolescent, the assassination of a president, as shocking as that might have been, is still not as crucial to you as trying to establish your own sense of identity. And by 1964, an entire sub-generation was coming of age who knew of Elvis Presley, rock 'n' roll's first mass idol, only through second-hand association—as a purveyor of oldies but goodies and as an actor in amusing, shlocky films. American youth needed a style of its own; it would clearly not be modeled on such hitmakers as Paul and Paula or Bobby Vinton. The Beach Boys were too wholesome; Motown was too black.

The Beatles filled the vacuum on the strength of their music (snappier and more guitar-oriented than American rock, although their lyrics were no more sophisticated than "It's My

Party"), their novel physical appearance (so-called long hair which drove adults into apoplexy), and their nationality (British—how exotic!). American teens, primed by watching newscasts of their European peers swooning and fainting at the sight of the band, acted the same way when the Beatles arrived here.

The Beatles' success spurred U.S. record companies to purchase discs by other British bands, many of which had been hits in England more than two years earlier, and to throw them at the American public—who lapped them up. The British Invasion began in earnest. Many of the bands who followed the Beatles had only one or two hits and then faded. Others became prime shapers of rock.

The first British bands to have hit records here were those that either also came from Liverpool or had some association with the Beatles. Brian Epstein, the Beatles' manager, also guided Billy J. Kramer and the Dakotas, who had three hits—"Little Children," "From a Window," and "Bad to Me," the latter two written by John Lennon and Paul McCartney—as well as Gerry and the Pacemakers (a Liverpool band who had been together since 1959 and whose first American release was a ballad called "Don't Let the Sun Catch You Crying"). Both bands made pleasant records that are recalled pleasurably today, but in the long run they were flyweight outfits who had minimal impact.

The strongest of the original Liverpool outifts were the Searchers. They were a quartet who had mined American R&B for their hits (the Drifters' "Sweets for My Sweet" and the Clovers' "Love Potion No. 9"), but they also had tight harmonies and great pop sensibilities (notably, their classic "Needles and Pins," a tune written by Sonny Bono). The Searchers rate a second listening today.

Then there were the dynamic duos. Peter (Asher) and Gordon (Waller) had hits in the spring and summer of 1964 with the Lennon-McCartney tunes "A World Without Love" (the first British act after the Beatles to have a U.S. Number 1 song) and "Nobody I Know." The duo's success was, no doubt, aided by the fact that Peter's sister, Jane, was dating Paul McCartney at the time and was often rumored to be married to the Beatle. P&G hung around till the mid-'60s with a couple of novelty tunes ("Lady Godiva" and "Knight in Rusty Armour"). Asher gained new respectability when he emerged in the mid-'70s as the crafty producer behind glossy but bland LPs by James Taylor and Linda Ronstadt.

On the other hand, Chad (Stuart) and Jeremy's (Clyde) music owed more to American folk groups like the Kingston Trio than to the Mersey sound. But because anything English sold in America in 1964, this duo had

The Dave Clark 5: Kings of the top 10.

two pleasant, folksy hits ("Yesterday's Gone" and "A Summer Song"). If the truth were to be known, these two ditties still surpass most of the so-called "mellow" music foisted on the public during the '70s.

My faves were the Dave Clark Five, former members of a British soccer team. They were the first band to displace the Beatles from the top of the British charts. They rocked harder than the Beatles, often using a saxophone, a staple of '50s rock 'n' roll, on their cuts. For those who thought the Liverpool sound was too light, the DC5 were an effective counterweight. They were the prototypical British singles band—reeling off a string of fifteen Top 10 tunes in a row. But, when singles went out of style, so did the DC5. Their *Greatest Hits* LP is one of the best ever of that genre.

If the Dave Clark Five presented a tougher, rockier side of the British Invasion, then the Animals, a quintet led by an acne-scarred singer named Eric Burdon, introduced the darker, bluesier aspect. The band's name was designed deliberately to shock audiences as much as the Sex Pistols would twelve years later. Their first American release, a remake of an American blues classic, "House of the Rising Sun," in the late summer of 1964, became the first by a British band other than the Beatles to become Number 1 in America.

For a brief time, the Dave Clark Five had the position that the Rolling Stones would eventually occupy—the nightmare opposite to the Beatles, or the world's ugliest rock 'n' roll band. Ultimately, Mick Jagger's lips and hips proved more popular than Burdon's acne and growls. The Animals faded when the Stones ascended. Burdon formed a new Animals and fell in love with the hippie scene. His paean to the Summer of Love, "San Francisco Nights," ranks among rock's most pretentious songs. The Animals reformed in 1983 to catch a whiff of the '60s revival and found large, enthusiastic audiences wherever they played.

The Rolling Stones' first records in the States weren't huge hits ("Not Fade Away," and "Tell Me"), but "Time Is on My Side" in late 1964 and "Satisfaction" in the summer of 1965 jolted them to the top.

A second wave of records by British Invasion bands hit these shores in the fall of 1964—including the Zombies ("She's Not There" and "Tell Her No"); Manfred Mann (whose "Doo Wah Diddy," a remake of an obscure 1961 Exciters tune, became the second non-Beatle British Number 1 tune); and the Honeycombs (who featured a female drummer and had one monster hit "Have I the Right?").

Of course, who can forget Herman's Hermits—the lightest of the lightweights—led by 16-year-old Peter Noone, who sang in the most pronounced Cockney accent yet heard here. The guys couldn't decipher it, but the little girls understood, and they kept buying the Hermits' string of hits, "Mrs. Brown," "I'm into Something Good," and "I'm Henry the 8th, I Am." As a grown-up, Noone ("Don't call me Herman.") pursued a stage career (Pirates of Penzance) and then surfaced again in 1980 with a band called the Tremblers, refusing to play any of the old Hermits hits. Talk about gratitude.

More significantly, the fall of 1964 marked the American debut of the Kinks. Their bonecrunching "You Really Got Me" was the loudest record of the British Invasion. Leader Ray Davies would develop into one of rock's wittiest songwriters, but for some inexplicable reason, they never have been considered up there with the British Holy Trinity—the Stones, Beatles, and the Who. They're still playing today and are just as good as ever.

Into 1965, more British groups kept hitting America: Wayne Fontana and the Mindbenders ("Game of Love"), the Moody Blues ("Go Now!"), Freddie and the Dreamers ("I'm Telling You Now" and "Do the Freddie"), the Fortunes ("You've Got Your Troubles"), and the Yardbirds (one of the most influential, blues-based bands, much more innovative compared to the other pop bands). By the summer of 1965, much of the excitement had paled. British bands were no longer a novelty—American bands such as the Byrds had shown that they could create their own style of British-flavored music. The Stones' "Satisfaction" effectively wiped out the cutesy-poo overtones of the British bands, and in September, when the Beatles released "Yesterday," which featured Paul McCartney singing alone accompanied by a cello, it signaled that the Beatles were no longer going to be content with simple melodies and lyrics.

Eventually, the Beatles, Stones, Who, and Kinks matured and grew, while others faded. Others tried to mature (i.e., the Moody Blues) and sounded pretentious. Of course, more British groups kept coming (the Who and the Hollies didn't really hit here until 1966) and a spate of blues bands that followed in the Cream's wake in 1967-68 hinted at another British invasion, as did the Sex Pistols-Clash punk rock movement a decade later and the rush of Culture Club, Duran Duran, and the syntho-pop bands of the '80s. But all it means is a catchy term without any cultural context to support it. Let the issue hereby be sealed: There was, and forever will be, only one true British invasion.

BritQuiz

1. According to the "Game of Love," what is the purpose of a man?
2. What was the House of the Rising Sun? Where was it located?
3. What song was recorded both by the Beatles and the Stones?
4. Who played the harmonica solo on Millie Small's "My Boy Lollipop"?
5. How do you do the Freddie?
6. What was the name of the feature film starring the Dave Clark Five?
7. What is Manfred Mann's real name?
8. In "I'm Henry VIII, I Am," what were the names of the men not picked by the woman, each of whose husband was named Henry?
9. What is the plot of "Little Children" by Billy J. Kramer and the Dakotas?
10. What is a bird?

Answers

1. To love a woman
2. A brothel in New Orleans
3. "I Wanna Be Your Man"
4. Rod Stewart
5. Throw your arms in the air wildly and kick up one leg
6. *Having a Wild Weekend*
7. Michael Leibowitz
8. Willie or Sam
9. A plea from a young man to a group of neighborhood kids who love snooping around while he's kissing one of their older sisters, imploring them not to tattle to the girl's mother
10. British slang for girl

Anyone who was old enough remembers where they were on February 9, 1964 when Ed Sullivan introduced the Beatles to the world.

The Beatles

Everyone who grew up in the '60s had a story about Beatlemania. This is mine:

"You won't believe this," said Mr. Johnson, my sixth-grade teacher, a lanky, crew-cut guy who looked like John Glenn and made us call him sir. "On Huntley and Brinkley last night they had a report about this strange new music that's sweeping England. You won't believe what these guys look like. In fact, they don't look like guys, they look like girls."

"Get ready," he said, laughing. "It's probably going to happen here as well."

Now, Mr. Johnson wasn't any friend of rock 'n' roll, so I had to take his pronouncement with several grains of Tang. After all, here was a guy who, just a few weeks earlier, had given us an English assignment to change rock 'n' roll lyrics so that they were grammatically correct.

Well, hey, I could use a laugh as much as the next kid. JFK's been in the ground for six weeks; the Giants lost to the the Bears; we're selling wheat to the Russians; some M.D. says smoking causes cancer; and DeGaulle's gonna recognize Red China. This had *better* be funny.

But England? Christine Keeler and Mandy Rice-Davies, a dour prime minister named MacMillan and a queen whose photo I collected on postage stamps—that's England. Rock 'n' roll was American. I didn't even think Limeys *knew* about rock 'n' roll.

Guys who looked like girls? Strange new music? Even though I was a faithful listener of Top 40, I had never heard of these "Beatles." So, during the next few weeks, I paid special attention, straining to hear this "strange new music" that had the power to make my teacher laugh. The first time I heard "Surfin' Bird" by the Trashmen I assumed that this must be what he was talking about. It certainly had a strange new sound, a lot weirder than anything by Bobby Vinton or Paul and Paula.

But I quickly learned that the Bird wasn't the Word, and that bird was a word that meant girl. Because within a couple of days you couldn't avoid hearing disc jockeys talking all about the Beatles and their new groovy fab gear language. The Beatles were about to invade America. Some kid came to school with a "The Beatles Are Coming" bumper sticker that his father had brought home from the radio station where he worked (later, of course, we would learn that this was part of Capitol Records' $50,000 crash publicity program to hype the band).

The first time I heard "I Want to Hold Your Hand" I was disappointed because this strange new music wasn't all that different from the stuff I'd been hearing for years on Murray the K's oldies but goodies show. It sounded like speeded-up Everly Brothers with a pinch of Buddy Holly, but mostly like a bunch of white kids trying to sound black by hiding their accents.

Soon you couldn't avoid hearing them. Radio went crazy. One local station became "W-A-Beatle-C." Disc jockeys competed for the right to play Beatle records (YOU HEARD IT FIRST!! RIGHT HERE!). "Three more days until they're here!" screamed the Deejays. On February 7: "It is 6:30 A.M., Beatle time. They left London thirty minutes ago. They're out over the Atlantic Ocean heading for New York." Record stores were stripped quickly of *Meet the Beatles* LPs. Kids began trying to speak in English accents. One nerd I knew became Mr. Popularity with the

chicks when he told them he had a cousin who had actually visited England.

I really couldn't understand what the screaming was all about. I was a 12-year-old with a Butch Wax pompadour, who desperately wanted to be Italian. My loyalties lay with the urban-macho sound of Dion and the Four Seasons. Naturally, I was suspicious of these new guys who, frankly, with their collarless suits (What, no sharkskin?) and hairstyle (What, no Vitalis?) looked like fruits.

They did have cool boots, though, and a cool attitude. ("What about the movement in Detroit to stamp out Beatles?" asked a reporter at their airport reception. "We have a campaign to stamp out Detroit," replied John.) Despite their accents, they were bigger wisenheimers than Eddie Haskell. Score one point in their favor.

When Pan Am Flight 101 landed at JFK, I was pouring over *My Weekly Reader* and trying to figure out the New Math, deliberately ignoring the commotion that was occurring not more than twelve miles from my

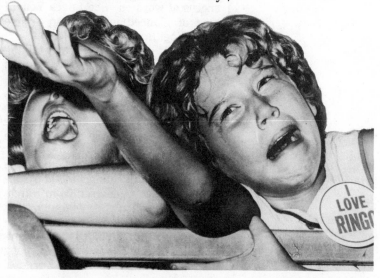

Scenes like this were repeated everywhere the Beatles appeared. This particularly desperate fan pleads her case behind police barricades in Indianapolis during the Fab Four's September 1964 concert at the Indiana State Fair.

school. The Beatles' arrival in America was a mildly curious diversion—something for the girls. And, as we knew (as the president of the He-man Woman Hater's Club on the "Little Rascals" had proclaimed), "Girls are silly." Even the Sullivan show had little effect.

On that Sunday night, per custom, the clan Edelstein gathered around the old Admiral in the living room, armed behind our defenses: I with *The Sporting News*, my father with the *Sunday Times* crossword puzzle; my sister buried in an *Archie* comic book; my mother toting a tray of Jeno's pizza rolls.

But that night we weren't there to watch Sophie Tucker or Jackie Mason or Myron Cohen. That night Ed had shum-thing for the youngshters. Old Ed read a telegram from Elvis and introduced the band. They appeared: four matching suits and haircuts.

My sister looked up and appeared mesmerized. My father looked up briefly, winced and intoned, "At least they aren't greasy like Elvis Presley. How can you hear them with all those girls hollering?" He went back to the crossword puzzle before the second chorus of woos on "She Loves You." I kind of glanced up from an article about Yogi Berra and scowled.

The next day, *everyone* was talking about the Sullivan show. Mr. Johnson asked for a show of hands and all thirty hands went up. I sulked in a corner, muttering about wimps and pansies and commies. Then it dawned on me that I was copping the same attitude as my old man and my teacher.

That's when my feelings about the Beatles began to change, aided by this elaborate theory, devised from watching teenagers on TV: Namely, that anyone who could get a negative reaction from an adult had to, by definition, be cool. Since we were too young for Elvis, and I was on the verge of

teendom, we had to have something typically teenage to bug the adults with. How could you be a true teenager, I reasoned, if you had the same heroes—JFK and John Glenn—that your parents did?

I also discovered girls at the same time. And if you didn't like the Beatles, I quickly discovered, then girls wouldn't like you. I looked into these "Beatles" a little more. So, it was time to shape up. Reluctantly, I found myself humming their tunes, but only the "tougher" ones like "I Saw Her Standing There" and "Roll Over Beethoven." (I still couldn't stomach their wimpy ballads like "All My Loving" and "P.S. I Love You.") Eventually I found that it was possible to divide one's loyalties between the Beatles and the Four Seasons and to equally enjoy both sides of *The Beatles* vs. *The Four Seasons* LP. And on May 29, 1965, for the first time ever, I combed out the Butch Wax and let my hair spill over my forehead. It took a year and three months, but the Beatles had won me over.

"When people ask to recreate the mood of the '60s, they will play Beatles music." No less a musical authority than composer Aaron Copland said that in *Look* magazine in 1968—a time when even those of Copland's generation were coming around to the view that the Beatles were OK. His prediction has come to be remarkably accurate.

Would the '60s be the upper-case SIXTIES without the Beatles? Well, we would still have been in Vietnam (someone else might have told us to give peace a chance) and there still would have been a youth movement (someone else would have been there to tell us that all you need is love) and there would be the specter of mind-altering drugs (someone else would have said relax your mind and float downstream).

During the '60s, rock critics endlessly debated whether the Beatles' impact was primarily sociological or musical. The debate no longer seems as important now as it did then. Musically, their work, except for "Sgt. Pepper," was not earth shattering. That's not the issue; the quality of their music needn't be analyzed, and, as Aaron Copland predicted, Beatle music is used to recreate the mood of the '60s. But sociologically, their influence is incalculable. My decisions to play in a rock band, wear wire-rimmed glasses, degrease my hair, grow a moustache, and take drugs, were all influenced by the Beatles.

At first they were to be gawked at like four Elvises who were expected to have the longevity of hula hoops. Let the kids have some fun. No one expected them to turn out the way they did.

Merits of their music aside, the Beatles did change the course of rock music. They brought the singer-songwriter and self-contained groups to the forefront. Before the Beatles, rock 'n' rollers were never considered artists. Rock musicians weren't expected to grow—except in directions toward Vegas or oblivion. They made the LP the primary form of rock expression, especially after *Sgt. Pepper* was released. Whether it was a curse or blessing, the Beatles made rock 'n' roll respectable.

But what a dull time it would have been without the Fab Four, the lovable lads from Liverpool, the merry moptops. Other musicians may have been more daring (the Stones wrote nastier lyrics, had longer hair, and were more upfront about their drug use), or critical of authority (Dylan took more risks), or even better musicians, but only the Beatles had the correct chemistry and authority to alter the shape of pop culture. The Beatles, above all other pop culture phenomena, set the style for attitude, dress, and haircuts for my generation; only the Beatles had the ability to make the avant-garde safe for mass consumption.

The Beatles were our FDR, a source of inspiration, style, and moral leadership, guiding us through a time as stormy and calamitous as the Depression and World War II had been to our parents. If you grew up in the '60s, chances are you marked events in your life by when a certain Beatles LP was released. Beatle records were the soundtrack—the music playing in our heads as "Lady Madonna" proclaimed—for most of my generation. Just as a rebroadcast today of one of FDR's fireside chats gets our parents misty-eyed, hearing a Beatle song now causes a similar reaction in many under 35.

Of the 18,000 fans who crammed the Hollywood Bowl to see the Beatles in August, 1964, 17,999 enjoyed the concert.

Pete Best
(left) as a mem-
ber of the Sil-
ver Beatles

PETE BEST—
THE FORGOTTEN
BEATLE

I f you asked a teenage girl in Liverpool in 1962 who her favorite Beatle was, chances are her answer wouldn't be John, George, Paul, or Ringo.

Her answer would be Pete.

Pete—as in Pete Best—was the Beatles' first drummer and was considered by chroniclers of the group's formative years as its most popular member. But in August, 1962, he was sacked from the group without warning—only eight weeks before the band, with its new drummer, Ringo Starr, had its first Number 1 record, "Love Me Do," the first volley in the cultural assault that came to be known as Beatlemania.

Instead of being part of the most famous group in rock history, Best ended up as a footnote. He insists he's not bitter.

"It caused me a lot of hardship, grief, and financial embarrassment. I was of strong enough character to stick it out and say well, OK, let's get on with life," says Best, who has worked for the past fourteen years as an employment counselor in Liverpool.

Best, now 44 years old (1985 years), is a soft-spoken man with a moustache and alert blue eyes who wears his wavy, brown hair swept back from his forehead, a style not much different from the one he sported in the early '60s as a Beatle. Casually dressed in a tan pullover shirt, jeans, and cowboy boots, he sits in a Manhattan hotel room, as he recalls his first meeting with John Lennon, George Harrison, and Paul McCartney.

It was 1959, and the three, who then called themselves the Quarrymen, were the house band at the Casbah, a club located in the basement of the Best residence in Liverpool. Pete's mother had converted the room into a rock 'n' roll club for neighborhood teens.

According to Best, John Lennon was the "typical arty type, white jeans, black shirt, swept-back hair, longer sideboards [sideburns] than the others, the laugh-a-minute wit." George Harrison was "very much the youngster, tight trousers, winklepicker boots, spiky hair, very much into his guitar work." Paul McCartney "wasn't ashamed to let others know he had a good voice. He was easily egged on by John. John would start a practical joke, and Paul would follow suit."

Best had originally wanted to be a teacher, but, after becoming infatuated by American rock 'n' roll, he learned how to play drums. In August, 1960, the Beatles, who never previously had a steady drummer, asked him to join them for their first tour of Hamburg, West Germany. The Beatles, who then included a fifth member, bassist Stu Sutcliffe (Sutcliffe died in 1962 of a brain hemorrhage), became regulars at the Kaiserkeller, a seedy club where the band's interpretations of American R&B classics competed with nightly razor fights and beer-and-blood-splattered brawls.

By 1962, they had built a loyal following, both in England and Germany. When they played their home base, Liverpool's Cavern Club, or their home away from home, the Star Club in Hamburg, lines would stretch around the block; while inside, girls would scream and sometimes faint—scenes that would be repeated on an international scale two years later.

But on August 16, 1962, Best was summoned to manager Brian Epstein's office. He was told that he was being replaced by Ringo Starr, then drummer for Rory Storm and the Hurricanes. Why he was sacked, Best claims, remains a mystery to this day. The other Beatles were not present when he was told, and he has not spoken to any of them since.

"They didn't give me any time to defend myself, what might have instigated it, how I possibly could have known about it beforehand. But they didn't have the decency to do it."

Best doesn't buy the often-suggested theories that he was sacked because the others considered him a loner because of his shy, taciturn personality, or because of his unwillingness to change his hairstyle. He attributes the former to his having to frequently leave to go into Hamburg to replace drum parts and the latter simply to the Beatles' having never asked him to change the style. The most likely reason was that the other three were jealous of Best, whose dark, moody presence had attracted much of the fan's adulation.

The extent of Best's popularity may be seen by the reaction when word of his sacking leaked out. When the Beatles next played the Cavern, they were heckled by fans shouting "Pete forever, Ringo never." A night-long vigil was kept outside the Best home. The local newspaper received petitions asking for the group to take Best back. George Harrison, who, some of Best's fans thought, was most responsible for causing their hero's removal, received a black eye from an irate Best supporter during a punch-up prior to a Cavern Club show.

"It suddenly dawned on me that I was as popular as people had made me out to be. Although these fans didn't like what had happened to me, in my own heart of hearts, I knew it was futile. I was out. There was no way that what had happened could be changed."

After he left the Beatles, Best played with another Liverpool band, Lee Curtis and the All-Stars, and then formed his own group, which toured North America in the mid-'60s, but his band never really caught much attention. He retired from music in 1968, took a job as a baker in Liverpool, and then finally got his current civil service job.

He says he's content to be with his wife and two teenage daughters and to play rugby for the Collegiate Old Boys of Liverpool. But when asked whether he'd join another band, he paused and then allowed himself a weak smile. "I'd have to give it a lot of consideration. I guess it would depend on the proposition."

SOME BEATLE QUOTES YOU MAY NOT REMEMBER

"The Communists have contrived an elaborate, calculating, and scientific technique directed at rendering a generation of American youth useless through nerve-jarring mental deterioration and retardation."—Dean Noebel, of the Christian Crusade, on the "Communist-Beatle" pact.

"In 1976, the Beatles could be as

old-fashioned as Frankie Laine is today."—*Melody Maker*, British music publication, 1966.

"It was fab, a gear, a gas. The most! By which I mean it was the best job in the world!"—singer Jackie DeShannon, who spent a month touring with the "Liverpool Larks" in 1965.

"Men are allowing themselves to look too much like women. I love the Beatles, but they've ruined our men. They're more like dandies."—Eva Gabor, actress.

"There's one thing we should do with the Beatles—spray 'em."—Alan King, comedian.

"I'm afraid I'm on a different wave length than the Beatles. I don't dig them. I hope when they get older, they will get a haircut."—Reverend Billy Graham.

BEATLES
TIMELINE

1956
John Lennon and Paul McCartney meet and form a partnership; Paul performs with John's "shuffle" band, the Quarry Men.

1957
George Harrison joins the group.

1959
The group changes its name to the Silver Beatles, adds John Lennon's Art college friend, Stu Sutcliffe, as bassist.

1960–1961
Now known as the Beatles, the band, with its first full-time drummer, Pete Best, travels to Hamburg to back up singer Tony Sheridan. They build a loyal following in Hamburg.

1961
Record salesman Brian Epstein keeps getting requests for a disc his store doesn't stock—"My Bonnie" by the Beatles, a group he's never heard. He tracks the group down to the Cavern Club in Liverpool, where they have become the most popular attraction in the city. He becomes their manager and orders an image change: Out go leather jackets, in come matching suits.

1962
Sutcliffe dies of a brain hemorrhage. Epstein fires drummer Best, hires Ringo Starr from Rory Storm and the Hurricanes.

The Beatles' first single, "Love Me Do," is released and makes the Top 20.

1963
Beatlemania sweeps the rest of England and then Europe. The Fab Four play a royal command performance for Princess Margaret.

The *Please Please Me* LP is Number 1 on charts for six months.

1964
Beatlemania hits the United States. The Beatles appear on the Ed Sullivan Show and are watched by seventy million people.

February to May: The group has four Number 1 singles ("I Want to Hold Your Hand," "She Loves You," "Can't Buy Me Love," "Love Me Do").

August: *A Hard Day's Night* comes out, and film critics liken the Beatles to the Marx Brothers.

1965
A single, "Yesterday" (Paul McCartney singing solo accompanied by a string quartet) and an LP, *Rubber Soul,* (showing Dylanesque, folk, and raga influences), are released. Suddenly, the Beatles no longer sound so simple.

The group's second movie, *Help,* is released.

The Beatles receive an OBE for helping the British balance of trade.

1966

Revolver (which includes the haunting "Eleanor Rigby" and acid-drenched "Tomorrow Never Knows") sounds like nothing the group has ever done before. Conservative fans yearn for the moptops of yore; others applaud the group's growth.

The Beatles tour as a group for the last time.

John Lennon's opinion about the Beatles' value vis-a-vis Jesus results in many records burned, banned, and in public censure. ("Some subjects must not be dealt with profanely, not even in the world of beatniks," says *Osservatore Romano*, the Vatican newspaper.)

1967

The Beatles grow moustaches and expand their musical horizons with "Penny Lane" and "Strawberry Fields Forever." But the single is only a dress rehearsal for *Sgt. Pepper's Lonely Hearts Club Band*, which is released in the summer. It is the most ambitious rock LP ever released, and adults and intellectuals (who wouldn't have bought a rock 'n' roll single even as a gag) spill pages of ink extolling its virtues. The Beatles begin to take themselves seriously.

The group admits using LSD and tells the world "all you need is love."

August: Brian Epstein dies.

1968

Out goes LSD, in comes the Maharishi Mahesh Yogi. Out goes *Sgt. Pepper's* symphonic complexity, in comes the '50s-flavored "Lady Madonna."

November: *The Beatles* (the "white album"), a pastiche of two dozen musical styles is released, inspiring Charles Manson and later Joan Didion.

The group starts their own record label, Apple.

Yellow Submarine, the Beatles' feature-length animated movie, is released.

1967: The Beatles travel to Bangor, Wales to spend a weekend with their Indian guru, the Maharishi Mahesh Yogi.

Lennon takes up with Japanese artist Yoko Ono; the pair pose naked on the cover of the *Two Virgins* LP.

1969

The "Get Back" single and the *Abbey Road* LP are released.

The "Paul Is Dead" hoax sweeps the country.

March 12: Paul McCartney marries photographer Linda Eastman in London.

March 20: John marries Yoko. Rumors continue to circulate that the band will break up.

1970

The release of *Let It Be* confirms increasing dissension in the group.

Paul McCartney leaves the group.

The Beatles disband.

The Rolling Stones (c. 1965)

The Rolling Stones

The Rolling Stones were the second most famous band to emerge from the British Invasion. Their music, except for a brief foray into psychedelic excess, was always bluesier and tougher than the Beatles; their image more threatening. After more than twenty years, the Stones are still together, although they increasingly resemble parodies of themselves. They still have the gall to call themselves "the world's greatest rock 'n' roll band," a sobriquet first applied during the '70s when the Stones filled the vacuum left by the Beatles' breakup. To his credit, Mick Jagger is still as thin at 42 as he was at 22.

If Mick Jagger is the heart of the Rolling Stones, then lead guitarist Keith Richards is certainly its soul. He's considered the musician's musician of the Stones, as well as one of rock's best guitarists, period. But he's also the one whose controversial behavior, including a decade-long bout with heroin addiction, has fixed him in the public's eye as the bad boy of the Rolling Stones. But in the past couple of years, Keith has cleaned up his act. He claims to have kicked the smack habit and in public he appears considerably more hale and robust than he has in the past.

Here are excerpts from an interview I conducted with Richards in January, 1983, at the Plaza Hotel in New York.

Question: Among the many controversies the Stones were involved in during the '60s was the uproar in 1967 when Ed Sullivan made Mick Jagger change the lyrics of "Let's Spend the Night Together" to "Let's Spend Some

Time Together." What was your reaction?

Richards: The rest of the band wasn't singing so we didn't give a damn whether you changed a lyric—we didn't consider it to be an incredibly moral stand that we'd be selling out if we did it. But, by telling us to do this, those people actually in fact enhanced the thing they were trying to avoid. That was typical of self-imposed censorship by the networks. By trying to avoid somebody, they end up tripping up everybody.

I always remember when we'd do the Sullivan shows, there'd be these hushed, reverent tones the minute he walked into the studio. And he'd say "the Bible Belt, the Bible Belt." It's the one phrase that sticks in my mind—"Sorry, boys, we can't do it. We have to consider the Bible Belt."

Question: You have a reputation as a fanatic record collector. Could you name the five favorite R&B songs from the '60s in your collection?

Richards: That's a tough one. Bob and Earl's "Harlem Shuffle"; Wilson Pickett's "Midnight Hour"; any one of the first four or five Otis Redding singles. It's hard to pick five actual titles because those people were producing so much great stuff.

Question: What do you think of all the bands—both in the mid-'60s and more recently—who have modeled themselves after the 1965 Stones?

Richards: Now we're used to it, but there was a time when we used to say let's spot the Mick Jagger and the Keith Richards character in that group. In a way, we feel a mixture of cynicism and flattery. In a way, you're kind of pleased about it; it's always great to know you've influenced so many people. It's also that you realize that what you were doing then didn't come out exactly as you wanted it.

It's strange when you see these influences because it doesn't seem that we've been around that long. Sometimes it seems like a few days. When we actually started to cut our first record, we had the feeling that this is really the beginning of the end—because in the early '60s, even if you were a success, 99 percent of all recording acts lasted eighteen months to two years. We felt that it would be over before we really got going, so it was very strange that we just kept on going.

Question: Does it bother you when people say "How can you be over 40 and still be playing rock 'n' roll?"

Richards: No. It hasn't bothered Muddy Waters or Chuck Berry very much. I'd like to be playing as well as them at 60—and no doubt people will be asking me the same thing then. But as long as I can play well and improve in my own life, then dammit, I'll be playing.

Question: What are the most satisfying Stones albums to you?

Richards: In retrospect I suppose *Exile on Main St.*, *Beggars Banquet*, *Some Girls*, *Let It Bleed*. In the '60s, *Aftermath* was particularly satisfying to me at the time. I don't like *Goats Head Soup* and *It's Only Rock 'N' Roll* because that was such a stormy period for us, uprooted from England; Mick Taylor left the group; it took us awhile to settle down to a new nomadic way of living. A lot of energies were used up in different things during that period.

Question: In retrospect, what do you think of the *Satanic Majesties* LP?

Richards: It's grown on me. It was the one Stones album that I never listened to for years and years, and then a few years ago I put it back on the turntable, and it was a lot more interesting than I thought it was.

James Brown

Soul

DO YOU LIKE SOUL MUSIC? THAT SWEET SOUL MUSIC? When singer Arthur Conley asked that question on one of 1967's biggest hit records, soul music—a gritty, emotionally-charged style of black music that mixed the earthiness of the storefront church with the sensuality of rhythm and blues—was at its peak.

Singers like Otis Redding (who died later that year in an airplane crash), Wilson Pickett, James Brown, Sam and Dave, and Aretha Franklin churned out hit after memorable hit ("In the Midnight Hour," "I'm a Soul Man," "Respect") and performed to standing room only crowds in the United States and Europe.

Ray Charles pioneered soul in 1959, using the gospel form to express secular thoughts in his smash "What'd I Say," and Sam Cooke helped refine the sound in the early '60s. Soul hit its stride in 1965 when James Brown announced that "Papa's Got a Brand New Bag!", and people paid attention.

Stax-Volt Records in Memphis, whose roster included Otis Redding, Sam and Dave, Eddie Floyd, and Johnny Taylor, was soul music's nerve center. Unlike Motown, Stax never sought to blanch the sensuality of black music. Its performers were more heartfelt and spontaneous, the production less calculated.

But by the late '60s, sweet soul music had turned sour. The civil rights movement—with whose optimistic spirit soul was inextricably linked—took on a harsher tone following the murder of Martin Luther King and the advent of black power. Then, in the '70s, the rise of the lushly-orchestrated disco music helped remove much of the soul stars from the public eye.

A GALAXY OF SOUL STARS

JAMES BROWN—For 350 nights a year, this Georgia sharecropper's son lived up to his numerous sobriquets: Soul Brother Number One; Mr. Dynamite; The Godfather of Soul; The Hardest Working Man in Show Business. "I got soul...and I'm superbad!" he squealed, and to this day, the 50-year-old singer remains the embodiment of soul.

Brown always closed his shows with his histrionic rendering of "Please, Please, Please," which was his first hit back in 1956. The scenario: as the band hits the final note, he drops to the knees, sobbing, sweating, feigning a nervous breakdown. An aide rushes out, drapes a purple, silk cape over Brown's limp body and tries to hustle him offstage. Suddenly, James breaks free, tosses the cape and aide aside and starts to sing again as his band picks up precisely where they left off.

OTIS REDDING—The Crown Prince of Soul started as a Little Richard imitator in the late 1950s. His own style emerged about 1965—a hoarse, rapturous voice that could shift easily between ballads ("I've Been Loving You Too Long") and uptempo numbers ("Respect"). His performance at the 1967 Monterey Pop Festival blew the flower children's minds. His biggest hit, "(Sittin' on) The Dock of the Bay," was posthumous. He was only 26 when he died; most people thought he seemed much older.

WILSON PICKETT—He called himself the Midnight Mover, and his tunes conveyed a coarse, bold sexuality that was the essence of soul. Hear him work out on "In the Midnight Hour," "Mustang Sally," and "Land of 1,000 Dances."

ARETHA FRANKLIN—This piano-playing preacher's daughter was passed off by her first label as the new Sarah Vaughan. She switched to Atlantic where she began testifyin', soon earning the title "Lady Soul." Her hits include Otis' "Respect," "Chain of Fools," "Baby I Love You," and "Natural Woman."

PERCY SLEDGE—Most people only heard his gospel-pure tenor on his one hit, which topped the pop charts and is considered by many to be among the greatest soul records of all time: 1966's "When A Man Loves a Woman." His other, compelling ballads, "Take Time to Know Her" and "Out of Left Field," were limited to the boss-soul radio stations.

THE IMPRESSIONS—Chicago's greatest vocal group featured tight, gospel harmonies behind the haunting falsetto and sharp songwriting of Curtis Mayfield. Three of their best hits were "People Get Ready," "Amen," and "Gypsy Woman."

SAM AND DAVE—High-energy Memphis duo with palm-slappin' dynamic stage presence. In real life, they didn't talk to each other offstage for years. Interest was renewed in them when the Blues Brothers covered their biggest hit, "Soul Man."

POST-SOUL MORTEM

Wilson Pickett is especially bitter about the decline of soul music. He blames radio in the '70s for rushing into playing nothing but disco.

"You don't throw away a lifetime of music just because another trend comes in," Pickett says. "You don't bury one format of music to make another one work. Just because someone says R&B doesn't fit in someone's format shouldn't have meant you weren't gonna get played for the next ten years. We worked hard all those years to create what we did, and then all of a sudden our music was trampled on by radio. One time, I thought about getting into the dump-truck business—but I knew I could do better than that."

Pickett acknowledges many of the soul performers were shortchanged during their heyday, getting paid perhaps $750 or $1,000 a night. "We did more than play soul music. We helped integrate the South. We helped Martin Luther King and all those cats. We were the ones who were starving on those damn buses. Promoters wouldn't pay us." Alluding to renewed interest in soul music in the '80s: "I know this time I want to be paid up front. We're ready to make money. We're not gonna be kicked back no more."

WHAT IS SOUL?

Curtis Mayfield: "It's a matter of communication. If you can say something and get a response from another person's heart, and you feel that response comes back to you, that might be projected as something soulful."

Jerry Butler ("The Iceman"): "Soul is what God gives to a human being to communicate to all the members of the human race. That's as close as I come to a definition. Sometimes it's beauty, sometimes it's a voice, sometimes it's the way a person does a thing, the way a person sees or feels a thing."

Don Covay, singer-songwriter of "Have Mercy Baby" and "Chain of Fools": "Soul is spontaneously creating an experience—an ability to feel where the audience is really at."

Radio Rocks On

In the early '60s, there was no MTV, no huge ghetto blasters blaring prerecorded cassettes, no Walkmans, no portable FM stereos. Besides, who listened to FM, anyway? FM radios were usually just pieces of furniture that collected dust in the living room and was listened to by squares (i.e., your parents). The chance of hearing the Four Seasons on FM radio in 1962 was about as good as the Mets winning the World Series that year. No, if you wanted to be where the action was, you tuned to AM. AM was where the boss jocks or the Good Guys or the All Americans held sway, creating a now-classic radio style that was meant to be heard on the car radio or the pocket transistor.

The deejays of the early '60s built on the frantic style pioneered by the first rock 'n' roll and R&B spinners such as Alan Freed and Jocko ("The Rockin' Ace from Outer Space").

And what a style it was! If you flipped around the dial, you'd hear a series of sound effects, sirens, shrieks, bells, and echoes, all wrapped around the half-Borscht Belt, half-beatnik patter of frantic disc jockeys ("This song goes out to Mary at Central High from Tony at Lincoln. He says he loves ya, baby.") Oh yeah, they also played records, mostly spinning two-and-a-half-minute singles by the Beach Boys, the Miracles, the Ronettes, or Dion. Radio became a Pop-Art phenomenon.

Every city had its Number 1 disc jockey hero—a slick-talking character with razor-cut hair who knew Ringo Starr like he was his own brother, who hosted record hops and tried to sell you with earnest sincerity the virtues of Tackle Pimple Gel. Radio stations exerted enormous influence on their listeners; personality cults formed around particular deejays.

Believe it or not, one of the more raging debates among New York area teens twenty-three years ago was which deejay was better. In New York that meant WABC's Cousin Brucie, WMCA's B. Mitchell Reed, and WINS' Murray the K. This wasn't an argument to be taken lightly. I once wore a WMCA Good Guy sweatshirt while passing by a candy store where kids were hanging out listening to WINS. They chased me.

Around 1966, however, some hippies on the Coast realized that AM radio wasn't the place to hear Bob Dylan's 12-minute songs or any of this new weird-sounding music. Soon, FM became the home to a new breed of radio, leaving AM to the teeny-boppers. Instead of singles, the new progressive FM stations played albums; instead of pimple cream, deejays peddled rolling paper; instead of spieling at 100 words a minute and reading dedications, the disc jockeys (pardon me, man, radio personalities) "rapped" and read Kahlil Gibran. At the same time, a new breed of radio programmers fine-tuned AM, leeching whatever life was left in it. The one-two punch of progressive FM radio and the tightening of AM playlists helped KO the concept of radio-as-Pop Art.

In the early '80s, however, a new version of Top 40 radio, known as Contemporary Hit Radio, began becoming popular. Disc jockeys began talking faster, and three-minute singles again were the norm. But there just ain't no way that Prince is going to replace Dion, and Madonna's a poor substitute for Lesley Gore.

Murray the K

MURRAY THE K

Murray the K (for Kaufman) was the maestro of the mile-a-minute mouths and probably America's best-known disc jockey. His nightly "Swinging Soiree" on New York's WINS raised the mid-'60s style of radio to its zenith. He created a world of his own that drew in his audiences, featuring his own language ("Meussurray talk," actually derived from carnival lingo) and hip phrases (blast from the past, golden gasser, submarine race-watching music, and "It's what's happening, baby.")

Murray's true moment of glory, however, came with the arrival of the Beatles in 1964. At the group's first press conference, he dominated the proceedings so much that a TV cameraman cried out, "Tell Murray the K to cut that crap out." Ringo drolly repeated the line, cracking up the audience (except for the miffed cameraman), and, from then on, the group and Murray became close friends. Murray escorted the Beatles on their first U.S. tour, broadcast live from their hotel rooms, constantly denying rumors of Paul's marriage to Jane Asher. George Harrison eventually gave Murray the sobriquet, the Fifth Beatle.

But a year later, Murray was off WINS after he protested the restriction of its playlist. Two months later, the station converted to an all-news format. By 1965, rock 'n' roll itself was changing, and AM radio wasn't the proper outlet for a new breed of musicians who were no longer content with two-minute singles and snappy lyrics. Sensitive to these changes, Murray returned to the air in the fall of 1966, programming WOR-FM, one of the first "progressive stations" to play album cuts. For the first time in his career, Murray spoke slowly. He quit the station on the air in a programming dispute and then spent the '70s in decline and bankruptcy. In the mid-'70s he contracted cancer, and, despite his efforts to combat his illness, he died in 1982.

We spoke during the summer of 1981, two weeks before he was supposed to appear at a Madison Square Garden benefit concert in his honor. His illness forced the cancellation of the show, however.

Question: Why were you so popular with kids?

M the K: Everyone picked on the kids. Parents and teachers were always putting down their music. I recognized and fought for their unalienable rights, understood the frustration the kids felt. Jack O' Brian [a conservative columnist in a New York daily] called me "Murray Decay" and the music "rot 'n' roll." I had to fight it on my own behalf and the kids' behalf as well. I stood by them, championed

their causes, without ever telling them I was just there. I really understood because a part of me never grew up.

Question: How did you see the function of radio?

M the K: AM radio was the "alternative press" of its day. What made WINS tick was the "chemistry" I created between myself and the listener. I respected the teenagers as people, as individuals, and I knew they knew a lot more than I did. I was trying to satisfy them.

Radio was fun because what I would try to do each night was to entertain myself. I was an only child and had to do a lot to entertain myself, making up games and such. So when it came time for me to have the opportunity to do the show, I had a lot of guts and wasn't afraid of trying to do something new. I was fortunate in that most of the things I tried just caught on.

I wasn't trying to emulate them. I wasn't trying to be hip. I was myself and the kids picked up on me, and the reason they did was that I had a chance to be completely honest.

Question: What do you think of radio today?

M the K: No imagination, that's what's so scary. These people in these monolithic corporations don't even try to be creative. People buy on computer readouts, the ultimate cop-out. All they tell you is how many people are listening—how many men, how many women between 18 and 49—so what? That's all bullshit. It's insulting to those who remember the fun stuff.

I cried a lot over some of the pitfalls that have happened to radio stations that were great, where the people who were running it didn't realize that they had a great station that was part of history. Most program directors are assholes.

The Monkees were America's first made-for–TV rock band: (front, l-r) Mike Nesmith, Davy Jones, and Peter Tork; on drums, Mickey Dolenz.

The Monkees

"This isn't a rock and roll group: it's an act."—Davy Jones (*Newsweek*).

"We're advertisers. We're selling a product. We're selling Monkees. It's gotta be that way."—Mickey Dolenz.

"From an adult point of view, the Monkees may only be a roadshow version of the Beatles. But from the kids-eye view of the world, any version of the Beatles is an imitation to be desired. If so, this show is heading for hitsville because the Monkees are almost replicas of the Beatles except cut down to the dimensions of the TV screen."—*Variety*.

One of the best things about the '80s is that much of the polarization among youth that was present in the '60s, especially regarding musical tastes, has been diminished. It's OK to like the Monkees now. "I'm a Believer" and "Last Train to Clarksville" are good songs to sing along and to dance to—just like you knew when you were 14, but were too embarrassed to admit because liking some acid-rock speed-freak guitarist was cooler. There's nothing to be ashamed of anymore; you can give an intellectual patina to your newly-admitted passion. Just lean back, arch your brows and intone with great sincerity about the Monkees being the first rock-video band.

We hepcats weren't so flippant back in '66 when the Monkees first came on

success of *A Hard Days Night* and *Help!*, they conceptualized the idea of a TV show based on a rock band that would capture the zaniness and unpretentiousness of the early Beatles.

In the fall of 1965, they placed an ad in *Daily Variety* which read: "MADNESS! AUDITIONS—Folk & Rock 'n' Roll Musicians-Singers—Running parts for four insane boys, ages 17 to 21, with the courage to work." The goal, said Rafelson, was "not to find four actors to *play* the Monkees, but to *find* the Monkees."

Spontaneity was valued above all. An applicant would walk in and Bob and Bert would be playing with blocks. Another time, they might toss a cup of coffee at the applicant just to check his reaction. The new group was originally going to be called the Turtles and then the Inevitables. Rafelson and Schneider sifted through 437 would-be rock-star hopefuls before they chose the final four, a quartet of disparate personalities.

David Jones, 21, the youngest, was from Manchester, England. The 5-foot, 3-inch singer had been an apprentice jockey (he rode twenty-six winners in three months, made thousands, and lost most of it betting), did some acting on BBC-TV and eventually was in stage productions of *Oliver* and *Pickwick*. The shows were seen here and helped get him a contract with Columbia Pictures. In fact, he was the only one not cast from the *Daily Variety* ad.

Peter Tork (Peter Thorkelson), 24, son of a college professor, and a Washington, D.C. native, was the oldest. A college dropout (twice) who played New York's pass-the-hat coffee-house circuit, he moved to L.A. when that scene fizzled out, where he worked as busboy and part-time musician. He originally resisted answering the ad, but since he had grown his hair

the scene. Hip types smelled a plastic rat when they looked at this multimedia quartet, constructed by slick-talking Hollywood types to tap into the lucrative youth market created by Beatlemania.

THE EVOLUTION OF THE MONKEES

The idea for the Monkees originated in the minds of two men in their early 30s, TV producer Bob Rafelson and Bert Schneider (son of the president of Columbia Pictures). Spurred by the

long while in New York, he figured he was right for the part.

Michael Nesmith, a brooding 24-year-old Texan who had served in the Air Force and was a college dropout, had received his first guitar when he was 19. When he read the ad, he was playing L.A. folk coffee houses (calling himself Mike Blessing) and singing his own compositions. The man with the wool hat was the only married Monkee.

Californian Mickey Dolenz, 21, was described by a critic as the only one of the Monkees who had to learn to be a hipster. He was the son of an actor, George Braddock, and was then known as Mickey Braddock. As a child actor, he had appeared in the '50s TV series "Circus Boy." When he saw the ad, he was lead singer in a California group called the Missing Links.

The four were given an intensive six-week course in improvisation. Now there was a group, but no sound. That half of the deal was created by Don Kirshner, a legendary Brill Building fixture. Kirshner, president of Colgems, a new subsidiary of Screen Gems music division, felt the boys weren't musically talented enough to present the sound he wanted, so he set about creating it, using studio musicians. The sound he created was like the 1964 Beatles—catering to those who yearned for that simpler era two years ago, before the Beatles got so complex.

Then he poured on the hype. Six thousand disc jockeys received Monkee preview records and hundreds of thousands of bumper stickers saying "Monkee Business Is Big Business." Three weeks before their TV debut, a single, "Last Train to Clarksville," written by Tommy Boyce and Bobby Hart, with Mickey singing lead, was released. It hit Number 1 on Oct. 29, 1966. The debut LP also hit Number 1.

The TV show made its debut on Sept. 13, 1966. It featured sight gags, stop action, and out-of-focus underlit and overlit scenes—techniques liberally borrowed from TV commercials and film director, Richard Lester. It holds up well on MTV today. The boys didn't act as much as they romped, said the director.

The TV show received encouraging reviews. *The New York Times* reviewer noted "that the producers may wish to make a voluntary contribution to support of the British pound...but it's quite funny. Best of all, the Monkees were kept on a tight chain away from oppressive histrionics." *Newsweek*: "It may be directed to the skateboard set, but if it can keep up its fast lunatic pace, the show may command a lot of attention."

Even so, several rural NBC affiliates refused to carry the show. "There's giant resistance to long hair," Rafelson explained. Part of the problem was a ruckus caused by the group during an affiliates luncheon at Chasen's the previous June. This conservative group, who had the usual mid-'60s antipathy to long-haired musicians, was stunned when the Monkees, instead of sticking to light patter, performed such stunts as playing volleyball with a stuffed peacock and turning off the light switch.

Still, the potent combination of TV, radio, and records made the Monkees every teenybopper's dream—especially for the young girls who had missed Beatlemania three years earlier. But when word leaked that the boys didn't play their own instruments on their own hits, the Monkees began losing credibility, especially with the respect of hip press who were distrustful of Hollywood types anyway and saw the Monkees as plastic personified.

The Monkees eventually became

proficient enough to play concert dates, which were best known for screaming fans and for unveiling to a shocked subteen audience a crazed opening act named the Jimi Hendrix Experience.

By January, 1967, much of the band's cuteness was wearing thin. Nesmith, who admitted to production and composing aspirations, was becoming more demanding about the group being taken seriously. He was tired of being told what the group could and couldn't do. At a powwow with Kirshner, Nesmith threatened to quit and when Kirshner shrugged him off, he smashed his fist through the wall of Kirshner's $150-a-day bungalow suite at the Beverly Hills Hotel. But less than a month later, the rest of the band followed Mike's lead.

Kirshner was out, but not before he slapped Screen Gems and Columbia Pictures with a $35.5 million lawsuit (that's what he claimed the abrogaton of his contract was worth). The first "true" Monkees LP *Headquarters* came out and was received surprisingly well, even by the rock press.

After it was announced in December, 1967 that the show wouldn't be renewed for the fall, 1968 season, the Monkees began working on their first feature film, *Head* (originally titled *Changes*). Rafelson directed this bizarre effort, which one critic described as "a hybrid between a Godard film and 'Laugh-In.'" It featured not only the band but a young Jack Nicholson and cameos by Frank Zappa, Annette Funicello, and Sonny Liston. Underrated when it was released, today *Head* has become something of a cult classic.

The group made two more TV specials and several mediocre LPs before Dolenz and Jones, the final survivors (Nesmith and Tork had already left), finally called it quits in 1970.

THE FATE OF THE MONKEES

After he left the band, Nesmith produced a $70,000 rock symphony "Wichita Train Whistle" and had a minor country and pop hit in 1970 with "Joanne." He went on to become a respected video producer (his "Elephant Parts" won a video award) and nascent film producer. (His first feature film, *Timerider*, about a motorcyclist who time-warps his way, courtesy of NASA, back to the Wild West, didn't really succeed.)

Dolenz, who prefers to be called Michael now, moved to England in the late '70s "craving anonymity." There, he became a respected TV director and he also directed a musical based on the kiddie gangster film *Bugsy Malone*. He won the Banff Festival Award for a children's series he produced and directed for London Weekend Television.

Tork was reported during the mid-'70s to be living in a tent outside San Francisco and was jailed for drug charges in 1972. He resurfaced in 1982 with a new band called the Peter Tork Project which lasted only a year.

Jones opened a store called Zilch in Greenwich Village, joined with Dolenz and Boyce and Hart in the mid-'70s in a kind of psuedo-Monkees revival and attempted to revive his theatrical career.

Today, the Monkees have lost much of the stigma once attached to them. And out of context—expecially now that people have gotten used to hype and the machinations of the record biz—the Monkee media manipulation seems tame. Without all the hipper-than-thou criticism, their music stands up well, sounding fresh and still enjoyable.

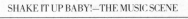

The San Francisco Sound

Tony Bennett may have left his heart in San Francisco, but a whole bunch of people left their heads there, specifically at the intersection of Haight and Ashbury Streets. Here was the locus of what for two years was a genuine counterculture, where people dressed differently, had different attitudes, and above all, played different music. Music was crucial to the hippie lifestyle, much more so than jazz had been to the Beats, their immediate Bohemian predecessors.

Was there really a genuine San Francisco sound? Not really. The groups played a musical stew, combining such ingredients as folk rock, jazz, blues, Eastern, and even classical music, much of it amplified beyond distortion level and accompanied by sense-shattering light shows, which sought to recreate the psychedelic experience. Live performance was crucial—the music was spontaneous, free-flowing; 30 to 40-minute jams were not uncommon.

The Grateful Dead (c. 1967). Jerry Garcia (third from left) had not yet grown his beard.

Drugs, especially LSD, were inalterably linked to the new sound. Musicians played under the influence of it, and songs praised it, usually in quasi-mystical lyrics which one needed a codebook to decipher. The media called this new music "acid rock," one of those terms that are dated and embarrassing almost as soon as they are coined.

The most important aspect of the San Francisco sound, such as it was, may not have been musical but sociological—the communal relationship between performer and audience. The music scene had developed long before record company executives had found their way out of the L.A. smog to venture north to see what all the fuss was about. San Francisco was the home of the first modern rock dance concert (1965), the first underground FM station (KMPX, 1967), and, if not the first, then the most influential of the rock journals, *Rolling Stone* (1967). When you wanted a band for a be-in, love-in, trips festival, bar mitzvah, they were always there—and more often than not would play for free.

But most of this had been going on away from the media spotlight. The Monterey Pop Festival in June, 1967 helped alert the world to what was happening in San Francisco. That summer, the now-clichéd Summer of Love, every transistor radio heard the plaintive voice of ex-folkie Scott McKenzie urging young people to wear some flowers in their hair. San Francisco was called the "New Liverpool."

Psychedelia sold. Soon the world beat a flower-strewn path to the Bay Area. By summer, it was said that 1,500 rock bands were playing in and around the city. Just as three years earlier, every American kid wanted to sound English and wear bangs, in 1967, groups who had been wearing polka-dot shirts and pointy boots the year before, threw them away and donned fringed jackets, flowing paisley shirts and sandals, and began getting awfully mystical. This spread to England where bands like Pink Floyd took up the psychedelic cudgel.

Most of this type of material is enjoyed only as high camp today. Another by-product was the short-lived "flower power" sound — sort of the flip side of the hard-edged acid rock, which encompassed everything from the soft rock of Harper's Bizarre and Spanky and Our Gang to the pretentious musings of Donovan, who only a year earlier had been hailed as the "Scottish Dylan."

But on October 6, 1967, Haight-Ashbury residents, demoralized by tourists, commercialization, bad drugs, and bad vibes, held a "Death of Hippie" ceremony. This may have been true in S.F., but elsewhere, reports of hippie death were premature. It was just starting to spread to the rest of the country.

Ironically, it wasn't until after the "Death of Hippie" that most of the San Francisco bands first began making their impacts on the record charts. They included:

BIG BROTHER AND THE HOLDING COMPANY—"Four gentlemen—and one great, great broad" was how they were introduced at the live concert heard on *Cheap Thrills*. The "great, great broad" was Janis Joplin, ex-Texas beatnik. Seeking refuge in S.F. after being kicked out of her narrow-minded hometown, she became perhaps the greatest white female blues singer ever. Recommended: *Cheap Thrills* (1968).

COUNTRY JOE AND THE FISH— Actually from Berkeley, this quintet was the most politically radical of the Bay Area bands—usually expressing their views humorously. Who can forget their anti-war classic "I-Feel-Like-I'm-Fixin'-to-Die Rag." ("Be the first one on your block," Joe urged, "to have your boy come home in a box.") They copped the song's music from an old jugband tune. Recommended: *Electric Music for the Mind and Body* (1967) and *I-Feel-Like-I'm-Fixin'-to-Die* (1967).

CREEDENCE CLEARWATER REVIVAL—Refusing to bow to psychedelia, John Fogerty's quartet was considered a Bay Area band only because they came from El Cerrito. One of the few '60s bands to be played on both AM and FM radio, CCR kept the rock 'n' roll flame burning during that decade. Recommended: *Bayou Country*, (1969), *Green River* (1969), and *Cosmo's Factory* (1970).

GRATEFUL DEAD—Jerry Garcia and his band of aging acidheads still keep the spirit of 1967 alive to audiences too young to remember. America's longest-running roadshow will always occupy a place in the hearts of all hippies, past and present. Recommended LPs: *Grateful Dead* (1967), *Live Dead* (1970), and *Workingman's Dead* (1970).

JEFFERSON AIRPLANE—The first S.F. band to sign a record contract and have a hit ("Somebody to Love"), had folky roots and featured the complex, soaring harmonies of Grace Slick and Marty Balin. By 1969 they were wealthy capitalists hyping revolution on record, while living in mansions. Today's remnants, the Jefferson Starship, are the Airplane on one engine. Recommended: *Surrealistic Pillow* (1967) and *Volunteers* (1969).

MOBY GRAPE—This intelligent, eclectic band with three lead guitarists was killed by record company hype—their label released five of their singles simultaneously. No one knew what to do with them and consequently this Grape died on the vine. Recommended: *Moby Grape* (1967).

STEVE MILLER BAND—The Texas Space Cowboy played the blues pretty well for a white boy and sounded British to boot. He became a bigger hit-maker in the '70s and '80s than in the '60s. This is the band that spawned Boz Scaggs. Recommended: *Children of the Future* (1968) and *Brave New World* (1969).

Yeah, but what about the Peanut Butter Conspiracy? Honest, all these groups actually played in San Francisco during the late '60s. (Source: Ralph Gleason's excellent book, *The Jefferson Airplane and the San Francisco Sound*.)

Amplified Ohm

Ballpoint Banana

Black Shit Puppy Farm

Clestial Hysteria

CIA

Cleanliness and Godliness Skiffle Band

Colossal Pomegranate

Evergreen Tangerine

Fifty-Foot Hose

Freudian Slips

Gotham City Crimefighters

Great Pumpkin

The LBJs

William Penn and His Pals

Psycle

Shiva's Headband

Truman Coyote

Melvin Q. Watchpocket

STEREO
ANDY EDELSTEIN

reprise 6261

Courtesy of Warner Brothers Records Inc.

Guitar Heroes

Back around the early part of the decade, kids in the neighborhood would have this debate: Who was the better ballplayer, Mickey Mantle or Willie Mays? Mickey's stronger. Yeah, but Willie's faster. Mickey hits more homers. Yeah, but Willie has more RBI's. You'd argue this while riding bikes, playing wiffle ball, waiting on line for the Saturday matinee 'til you were blue in the face. But there'd really be no winner. And always, some wiseacre would put his

thoughts in: Yeah, but what about Hank Aaron?

About five years later the same kids—this time wearing fringed jackets instead of Little League uniforms—would still be arguing. But this time the debate was who's better—Jimi Hendrix or Eric Clapton? Guitars had replaced baseball bats as primary objects of male adulation. Like the Willie vs. Mickey argument, the Jimi vs. Eric debate could be discussed endlessly without resolution.

Hendrix is quick, yeah, but Clapton's tighter. Clapton is all technique, yeah, man, but Hendrix is all flash. You'd argue sitting on the floor in a circle, passing the pipe; tossing a Frisbee; waiting on line at the Fillmore. Then someone would chime in from outside the circle: Yeah, but what about Jimmy Page?

Led by Jimi and Eric, lead guitarists were the true heroes of rock 'n' roll in the late '60s. True, the guitar had been a rock staple since the days of Elvis Presley, but in the late '60s, aided by increased technical sophistication, the guitar became more amplified than ever, pushing the big beat to its limit, aided by gadgets and gimmicks such as wah-wah, echo, reverb, and fuzz.

As rock shifted emphasis from singles to LPs, the guitar solo became the major form of musical expression. Instead of just a one-minute bridge between choruses, guitarists, taking their cues from Clapton, now essayed for twenty minutes, thirty minutes, an hour, bending notes into all kinds of serpentine turns, throwing flats and sharps off into the Twilight Zone, whipping in and out of the maelstrom of bass and drums. Audiences sat entranced, usually because they were stoned out of their gourds. But it all sounded sooo gooood, man.

The electric guitar became a sacrificial icon—to be burned, splintered, crushed, and then tossed to the audience. Instead of standing in front of candy stores harmonizing, imitating the Four Seasons, kids stood in front of head shops flailing their arms and twiddling their fingers, imitating Hendrix or Clapton.

Lots of it *was* flash and jive, but a lot was technically proficient and musically stimulating. The best rock guitarists, like Clapton, built on basic, simple blues structures and embellished and improvised upon them until they became an entire new musical entity. The worst corrupted the power-trio concept and ended up with what would be called heavy metal.

The guitar heroes of the '60s include:

ERIC CLAPTON—Cream was the first of so-called rock "supergroups," bringing together three of the best musicians (the Cream, as it were) of the British blues scene—Clapton, bassist Jack Bruce, and drummer Ginger Baker. Graffiti declaring "Clapton Is God" was common on '60s walls. Cream was almost singlehandedly responsible for the great blues revival of 1967 through 1968 and were almost always appreciated best live. They broke up in 1968, at the height of their fame.

JIMI HENDRIX—The "psychedelic superspade," as some hip writers called him, was a crazed black man from Seattle, discovered in Greenwich Village dives. Hendrix first found fame in England before returning and conquering his native country with his band, the Jimi Hendrix Experience (Jimi and two Brits, Noel Redding, bass, and Mitch Mitchell, drums). As revolutionary with the guitar as Charlie Parker and John Col-

J im Morrison—lead singer of the Doors

Photo by Joel Brodsky

trane had been earlier with the sax, he played behind his back, with his teeth, with his tongue, upside down, made love to his guitar, made hate to it. He made feedback and distortion a part of the music, not just a gimmicky sideshow. No one since has been able to duplicate just quite that sound. He was unquestionably the sexiest rock performer of the '60s. Essential listening includes his first three LPs: *Are You Experienced, Axis: Bold as Love, Electric Ladyland.*

One can only guess where he would have headed if he hadn't checked out inadvertently in September, 1970, choking on his own vomit while sleeping.

MIKE BLOOMFIELD—No American guitarist could bend a blue note better than this nice Jewish boy who loved to hang out with the schvarzes in Chicago. First with the Butterfield Band, then with his own Electric Flag, he was doing in the U.S. what Clapton was doing to the blues in England but with less commercial success. Check out his playing on the Butterfield Blues Band's *East-West* LP. He died under mysterious circumstances in 1981.

ALVIN LEE AND 10 YEARS AFTER—The leader of this British quartet was pure speed and flash. He made Clapton seem as slow as Blind Lemon Jefferson. Critics didn't like them, but the American public loved them—especially at Woodstock.

JIMMY PAGE—First with the Yardbirds, then with his own Led Zeppelin, Page helped create what would become heavy metal—crude, blues-based sludge with lots of yowling vocals and howling guitars. Led Zeppelin would become the most popular rock band in the world during the '70s. Their "Whole Lotta Love" (1969) from *Led Zeppelin II* still remains the quintessential '60s stereo headphone experience.

And oh, yes, our neighborhood kids are all grown up now. But they're still debating. Now it's What's a better investment, pork belly futures or a money-market fund?

THE 7 COOLEST GUITAR SOLOS

1. "Journey to the Center of Your Mind" (Amboy Dukes)
2. "Moonlight Drive" (Doors)
3. "SWALBR" (Cream)
4. "I'm Going Home" (10 Years After)
5. "Whole Lotta Love" (Led Zeppelin)
6. "Purple Haze" (Jimi Hendrix Experience)
7. "Summertime Blues" (Blue Cheer)

WORST ABUSES OF A GUITAR DURING THE '60S

"In-a-Gadda-Da-Vida" (Iron Butterfly)
"Fried Hockey Boogie" (Canned Heat)

Woodstock

This was recently discovered in an underground newspaper's archive when the building was renovated for a pasta-and-croissant shop in New York's East Village. Apparently the newspaper went out of business before the article could appear.

THE TRUTH ABOUT WOODSTOCK

In the summer of 1969, twenty-five days after man first walked on the moon, the youth of America began behaving strangely. As if propelled by some unknown alien force—believed to be linked to atmospheric disturbances caused by the flight of *Apollo XI*—about half a million young people suddenly, inexplicably found themselves heading, zombie-like for a huge alfalfa field on the fringes of New York's Borscht Belt.

Under the spell of this lunar-inspired behavior, these flower of American youth would spend the next seventy-two hours twitching madly while listening to eardrum-shattering, atonal music, wallow contentedly in mud, take off their clothes in public, and ingest all kinds of foreign substances. Things they would never do at home.

But just as quickly as it started, it was over. American youth returned to their suburban split-levels. Returned, in body, yes. But the damage had been done. For, like the pod people of *Invasion of the Body Snatchers*, they had surrendered their souls to alien forces. All other youth—especially those who hadn't attended the "Woodstock Music and Art Fair," the code name given this circumstance by the coverup media—would soon be infected after coming in contact with any of the chosen half-million.

The youth of America may never be the same again. President Nixon has ordered an investigation.

THE GREAT WOODSTOCK QUIZ

1. What was something to avoid at Woodstock?
   a. Brown acid
   b. Brown rice
   c. Acid rain
2. What was meant by the phrase "I'm a Farmer"?
   a. The title of a song by Crosby, Stills, Nash and Young
   b. Introduction of a speech by Max Yasgur
   c. Introduction by a merchant selling wares on "Groovy Way"
3. What was meant by Wavy Gravy?
   a. A band that never showed up
   b. Alias of a hippie commune leader
   c. A nickname for one covered by the mud at Woodstock
4. How many people attended Woodstock?
   a. 450,000
   b. 750,000
   c. Like who cares, man. Numbers are irrelevant. We are everywhere.
5. Which newspaper headline is authentic?
   a. "Music, love outasite at Woodstock"
   b. "Hippies let it all hang out"
   c. "Traffic uptight at hippie fest"

ANSWERS

1. A
2. B
3. B
4. A
5. C

Tubegazing

'60S TELEVISION

INTRODUCTION

I am a member of the generation for whom TV has always been a part of the household. I assumed that that huge squat box called the Admiral had always been sitting in my parents' living room. So that quintessential early-'50s experience, the thrill of being "the first one on your block," is alien to my experience. Shows such as "Milton Berle," "Your Show of Shows," and "Playhouse 90" are not in my memory bank.

I am a child of '60s TV; the '60s were my Golden Age. The '60s was a time when "54" meant a police car in the Bronx, not a disco in Manhattan—a time when, until the middle of the decade, most programs were still aired in black-and-white.

No one told me that TV was supposed to be bad for you, so we watched and watched the parade of doctors, hillbillies, monsters, secret agents, caped crusaders, spies, funny Nazis, and flying nuns who popped up each year on the 19-inch screen.

TV was something to talk about the next day in school. There were certain shows everybody watched: "Get Smart," "The Man from U.N.C.L.E.," "Laugh-In," "The Monkees," "Batman." If you were doing your algebra while these shows were airing, you'd find yourself ostracized.

This chapter will take a look back, genre-by-genre, at the best of '60s TV. Consider it a nostalgic cruise—on the *Minnow*, not the Love Boat.

Batman

BAT-SCENES:

Batman enters the What-a-Way-to-Go-Go Discotheque where go-go girls in birdcages are dancing the Batusi. Robin is under age so he has to stay outside in the parked Batmobile.

Head waiter: Would you like a ring-side seat, Caped Crusader?

Batman: No thank you. I don't want to be conspicuous.

Batman walks to the bar and orders a tall, refreshing glass of orange juice.—From "Hi Diddle Riddle," the debut episode of "Batman," 7:30 P.M., January 12, 1966.

"Batman" was the quintessential flowering of the pop '60s, in which many diverse elements of '60s pop culture—comic books, camp, Pop Art, television, and super heroes—came together in a dazzling melange that nearly drove the U.S.A. bats in the spring of '66.

Batmania included a discotheque in Sunnyvale, California called Wayne Manor (named for the stately home of Batman's alter ego, millionaire playboy Bruce Wayne), where the ushers dressed like Batman, the maitre d' was the Joker, and the Dynamic Duo were painted in throbbing, electric colors on the wall. There was also a new style invented by a Detroit hairdresser—the Bat cut—in which women's eyebrows were shaved off, and the hairline was shaped to imitate Batman's cowl.

"Batman's" debut was aired as part of ABC's "second season," a ploy by the then perennial also-ran network to lure more viewers on Wednesday and Thursday nights. At the time, citizens of the Great Society were entranced by the concept of camp—or something that's so bad or corny that it's good—and one of those elements was venerating old-time comic heroes. "Batman" took camp to the bank. Has there ever been a more doggedly strait-laced advocate of righteousness than Batman as interpreted by an ex-surfer, ex-bit actor named Adam West?

West's Batman embodied all the principles of the Boy Scout Code—and more. The deadpan acting of West and Burt Ward, who played Robin, was just one aspect of the show's success. Remember the cliffhanger endings? The comic Pop Art "splats" and "biffs" that punctuated fights between Batman and his enemies?

All those gimmicks were created by William Dozier, "Batman's" executive producer, who previously had been a CBS programming honcho responsible for shows ranging from "Playhouse 90" to "Dennis the Menace." Even today, Dozier says he still can't put his finger on just why "Batman" was so incredibly popular. "I think the mood of the country was just ready for something wild and crazy—there's really no other expla-

TV's Dynamic Duo—Batman (Adam West) and Robin (Burt Ward), the quintessential '60s pop culture phenomenon

nation for it," says Dozier, now in his 70s. He's semi-retired due to cataracts and lives in Beverly Hills.

Under normal circumstances, Dozier explains, "Batman" should never have even made it to television in the first place. He relates the show's genesis as follows: Back in 1965, ABC wanted to create a new series on comic book characters for the important 7:30 time slot (following the theory that viewers' innate laziness would keep their sets tuned to ABC all evening). Five characters were chosen, their order of popularity determined by a market research firm—Dick Tracy, Superman, Batman, the Green Hornet, and Little Orphan Annie. The rights to the first two were unavailable so ABC decided to go with the third choice, which was Batman.

After ABC secured the rights to the character from National Periodicals, network executives contacted Dozier about his interest in working on the proposed series. "Frankly, I never heard of Batman. I didn't read comic books when I was a kid. I had never even seen a comic book," Dozier says. Nevertheless, he was intrigued by the idea and purchased several comic books while on a business trip to New York. He read them furtively on the plane trip back to Hollywood—to avoid his own embarrassment as well as to conceal hints of ABC's planned blockbuster.

Shortly after he returned to California, Dozier finally came upon the idea that would ultimately make "Batman" as successful as it turned out to be. "I decided to exaggerate seriousness—to make the show so serious that I thought it was funny. I used to have one admonition which I'd tell everyone in connection with the program—'you've got to treat the show as if you were dropping the bomb on Hiroshima.'"

With that concept in mind, Dozier flew to the Ritz Hotel in Madrid where he hatched the show's plot with a zany writer named Lorenzo Semple over lunch and two bottles of red wine. Casting was next. Dozier's first choice, cowboy star Ty Hardin, was unavailable, so he followed up an agent's lead and contacted Adam West, whose only claim to fame were minor roles in "The Detective" series.

"After we talked, I realized right away that Adam understood what we were trying to do. I told him that 'you're not going to be Cary Grant; you're going to come off like a small idiot, but that's what's going to be funny.' I told him about the Hiroshima concept, and Adam grasped it right away," Dozier recalls. Meanwhile, Burt Ward, a karate expert who had no previous acting experience and was "living off pop bottle deposits" was chosen to play Robin because the "minute he walked into the room and opened his mouth, I knew he was the boy I was looking for."

When the pilot was completed (cost: $300,000—expensive by '66 standards), it was shown to a test audience, the type that twists dials to register their reactions. This particular group, however, didn't understand at all the campiness behind Batman and emitted nary a titter. By all rights, the show should have been sent to the final cutting room, but ABC was desperate. They disregarded the test results and ordered the pilot be aired as the debut program.

And what an episode it was. To this day, Dozier says he considers it his favorite. Veteran character actor Frank Gorshin played the "special guest villain," The Riddler—a wily fellow whose caramel-colored long johns were emblazoned with question marks. Jill St. John (who later was to be romantically linked with Henry Kissinger), played the Riddler's moll who fell in love with Batman. But she also became the only character ever to die in a "Batman" episode; after she had sneaked into the ultra-top secret Bat Cave, she slipped and was French fried to death in the atomic-powered Bat-generator.

Choosing the special guest villains and villainesses was a chore that Dozier always relished. Gorshin and Burgess Meredith, who played the Penguin, had always been Dozier's first choices to play their respective roles—but the Joker, the baddest of the bad, was originally designed for Jose Ferrer. He couldn't make it and was replaced by Cesar Romero.

As the show's popularity increased, competition to play the archfiends increased. Dozier recalls being besieged by requests from agents eager to place their clients as nemeses of the Dynamic Duo. In fact, Otto Preminger, who had not acted in seventeen years, once called Dozier and pleaded with him: "Bill, if I don't do a Batman, I can't go home; my children won't let me into the house." Dozier says he couldn't resist and cast Preminger as the second Mr. Freeze (the first incarnation was supplied by George Sanders).

Many special guest villains took their tasks seriously. Liberace, who played the nefarious Fingers, used his own concert grand piano during the filming of his episode—spending more money transporting the piece across Los Angeles than the $2,500 fee the villains received.

Dozier maintains that "Batman's" success was due to its special blending of adult and children's audiences, a feat which has been rarely duplicated on television since then. "We found that at about age 3, kids started to watch the show because they enjoyed the adventure and seriousness. But at about 12, they stopped watching altogether because they thought it was sil-

The Batcurl was one hair-style inspired by the Dynamic Duo in 1966.

ly and childish," says Dozier. "But then again, at about age 17, when they were old enough to enjoy the humor, they started watching again. But there was a very large gap between the ages of 12 and 17."

Eventually, however, the show's novelty faded, and children became the primary audience, making the show too risky and expensive to deliver to sponsors at that hour. "Batman" was cut back to one night a week, and the Caped Crusader and Boy Wonder took their final trip in the Batmobile in 1968.

"Adam was and is a very decent, sensible guy," says Dozier. "He was marvelous with the kids who'd visit the set—talking to them, signing autographs, keeping them quiet while filming was on. Burt, on the other hand, was most uncooperative. He was cocky, arrogant—all that success went to his head, and he didn't get along with too many people."

Adam West today does regional theater, occasional TV appearances in series and TV-movies—and still, of course, makes public appearances as Batman, the role with which he has been identified for nearly twenty years. He is angered that he is not going to be considered for the lead in the proposed "Batman" movie. The studio says that West, 56, is too old for the part.

I asked West about the show:

Question: Why did "Batman" succeed?

West: Some people refer to the '60s as a kind of mindless period. That kind of fantasy escape was what people were seeking at that time. I just feel it was simpler. The main reason we hit so hard was that the show was well-promoted, well-done, and it was a first on TV. It was different; it was unusual, something people could look forward to, laugh at, laugh with, criticize, yell at.

ABC and Fox really beat the drums. For a long time we had really interesting and delightful scripts. Then when the producers wanted to go into reruns, they figured, well we're losing a lot of money now, let's see if we can play prime time two or three seasons, get enough product, and then we're ready to go into reruns, and we can recoup our losses and make a lot of money.

They started cutting back costs, and there was a certain sameness after a while. For example, the comic balloons used to be superimposed over the action. You didn't cut to a separate card and block and interrupt the fight in progress. In the second or third season, because the cost of superimposition was high, they'd just cut to cards instead of "supering" it over the action, which was a lot classier. It was a way of saving a little money. That's just a small example. So, indeed, they got enough product to go into reruns. I got kind of unhappy with the shows in the last year because I felt the quality was diminishing. It's the same old story with actors who care. But we had some really good segments, didn't we?

Question: What are your favorites?

West: I love the segment with George Sanders as Mr. Freeze in which the set was agonizingly, carefully lit so that anytime he was around, it was glacial blue—his native surroundings. Another, when Catwoman put me under the love spell, was so much fun.

Question: Who were your favorite villains?

West: That's difficult to say. But I am really very fond of Penguin because he was so irascible—parading around saying "wap wap," always putting cigarette smoke up my nose. Cesar Romero, with the white makeup painted over his moustache, had great energy as the Joker.

Question: Even watching the show today as an adult, I find that the satire really holds up well.

West: More and more people are talking that way. But not enough—they will someday. While we were doing the show we made a very serious effort to do that. The show is really comedic—comedy is a very serious business. To get to that point takes an effort and at the same time make the show legible to children, where they can enjoy the fantasy and get involved and find it affecting. We had to walk a tightwire.

Question: Let's talk about the Batmobile—that was a state-of-the-art vehicle for 1966.

West: Thank you for defending the Batmobile. Many people criticize it when they see it in person, when it is leased out around the country to auto shows. It appears more awesome on film—when it's doing its thing, when it's well lit. But when it's not maintained, cosmetically, and it's not doing its thing and the lighting isn't effective, it just doesn't look that good or awesome. After all, it was just a Lincoln that was altered.

Back then nuclear energy was seen as the coming thing, a positive force. Today people would probably say, don't let that thing come near my kids.

Question: Did you drive it?

West: I drove it most of the time, but sometimes a stunt double drove it in the format shots, coming in and out of the Bat Cave.

Question: How would you do "Batman" today?

West: For the big screen I'd try and retain a lot of the Bondian wit. Some of the things done in "Superman," for example, especially the first movie, before it got out of hand. I would

make it more serious; the presentation wouldn't be camp—I hate that word—not a put-on. Any superhero who jumps around in a costume—I don't care what anyone says—anyone who dresses up like a beaver, this is a send-up. But you can do it, if you're artful enough, so it's believable. If it's done with mystery, the world's greatest detective, the dark night, solving some gigantic crime, most telling with his action technology.

I have no idea whether I'll do the movie. I know there are certain people associated with the movie who have expressed negative things about it, and, since they've done that, I've had more fan mail since prime time saying they'll boycott it. But I don't want to go through a Lone Ranger kind of campaign.

I think I have two or three Batman features in me—if they want me or if I can get the backing.

What we had was wonderful on the tube for its time, and it will go on and on. But for the big-screen, you've got to retain some of the flavor at the same time you've got to give them some wonderful adventures and technology. I'd like to see Batman and/or Bruce Wayne become more romantic. Doesn't have to be sticky.

Question: You played it pretty close to the vest, romantically speaking, except for Catwoman.

West: That's right. And he kind of had curious mixed feelings in his utility belt for her.

BAT-VILLAINS

Said Dozier (from the *New York Times,* May 1, 1966) on what makes a Bat villain: "He must be flamboyant, humorous, bigger than life, bizarre. He must convince us that he is a potential killer. He must suggest humor, but he must not be a comedian."

Frank Gorshin, who played the Riddler, says he developed his patented laugh at Hollywood parties. "I listened to myself laugh and discovered that the funniest jokes brought out the high-pitched giggle I used on the show. With further study, I came to realize that it wasn't so much how I laughed as what I laughed at that created a sense of menace."

Here's a complete list of Bat-Villains.

ART CARNEY, The Archer

TALLULAH BANKHEAD, Black Widow

RODDY MCDOWALL, The Bookworm

IDA LUPINO, Cassandra

EARTHA KITT, Catwoman

JULIE NEWMAR, Catwoman

LEE MERIWETHER, Catwoman

LIBERACE, Chandell

ROGER C. CARMEL, Colonel Gumm

VINCENT PRICE, Egghead

MALACHI THRONE, False Face

CESAR ROMERO, The Joker

VICTOR BUONO, King Tut

RUDY VALLEE, Lord Phogg

MILTON BERLE, Louie the Lilac

SHELLEY WINTERS, Ma Parker

DAVID WAYNE, The Mad Hatter

CAROLYN JONES, Marsha, Queen of Diamonds

ZSA ZSA GABOR, Minerva

VAN JOHNSON, The Minstrel

OTTO PREMINGER, Mr. Freeze

GEORGE SANDERS, Mr. Freeze

ELI WALLACH, Mr. Freeze

BURGESS MEREDITH, The Penguin

MAURICE EVANS, Puzzler

JOHN ASTIN, The Riddler

FRANK GORSHIN, The Riddler

MICHAEL RENNIE, Sandman

CLIFF ROBERTSON, Shame

JOAN COLLINS, The Siren

ANNE BAXTER, Zelda the Great

BAT-QUOTES

Michael Arlen, *The New Yorker*: "It's a zippy program, surefooted, full of nifty gadgets and ridiculous costumes, and with at least a couple of lines that could pass for wit on a foggy night."

Pravda: "Batman brainwashed Americans into becoming willing murderers in the Vietnam jungle."

Dr. David Singer, a Duke University psychology professor, trying to explain the show's popularity among adults: "The superhuman hero they once adored in the 1940s is now a little ridiculous, and the giggles come from having mastered the insecurities and needs of childhood."

OFFICIAL LIST OF BAT-NOISES

AARGH!
CLASH! CRUNCH! KLONK! POW!
SPLATT! AIREE!
CLUNK! EEE-YOW! OOOF! POWIE!
SWOOSH! BIFF!
CONCK! FRLBB! OUCH! QUNKK!
THUNK! BOFF!
CRANK! KAPOW! OWW! RAKK!
THWAPP! CLANK!
CRASH! KAYO! PAM! RIP! TOUCHE!
UGGH!
ZAM! ZOWIE! URKK!
ZAP! ZWAPP! WHAMM!
ZGURPP! WHAP!
ZLONKK! ZAK! ZOK!

"The Beverly Hillbillies"

The Beverly Hillbillies was a watershed, of sorts, in TV programming. Not only was the show critically maligned but publicly adored, it was also the first time living people played cartoon characters. It offered a TV family quite unlike any other in the first two decades of TV.

Viewers who may have identified with Robert Young's or Danny Thomas' TV families, or even the family on the "Real McCoys" (the rural sitcom that presaged the arrival of the "BH"), might have found it difficult to relate to this brood. The Clampett family consisted of:

Elly May (Donna Douglas), the bubble-headed, chesty daughter, who was always trying to get hitched.

Jethro (Max Baer, Jr.), the thick-skulled, ox-like nephew. In real life, Baer had a minor in philosophy from the University of Santa Clara.

Granny (Irene Ryan), the crotchety, moonshine-making grandmother. She was also a part-time doctor. Granny's remedies for "city germs," an ailment that struck Jed, Mr. Drysdale, and the doctor in quick succession, included stump water, dried beetles, and lizard eggs. She was TV's first prime time holistic doctor. One shudders when one thinks about what she would have done if she had known acupuncture.

Jed Clampett, the simple (but good-natured) widowed father. He was played by Buddy Ebsen, a veteran character actor.

The show's reference points weren't Manhattan or some imaginary suburb, as in most previous sitcoms, but two extremes of the American Dream: the

Ozarks and Beverly Hills. The characters spoke a kind of fractured English, which, had they been black, would have had the NAACP raising hell.

But the only people who raised hell were the critics, who threw verbal firestorms at the show. The "Hillbillies" were cited as the absolutely worst example of just how low TV would stoop for laughs. Wailed the *New York Times* reviewer Jack Gould: "Their assorted adventures don't merely strain credulity, they crush it." Quoth *Variety*: "It's strictly out of Dogpatch and Lil Abner, minus the virtues of the Al Cappisms. At no time does it give the viewer credit for even a smattering of intelligence." As the show's popularity increased, TV talk show host David Susskind urged his listeners to write Congress protesting the program.

Who had the last laugh, however? Five weeks after the show debuted on September 26, 1962, it became Number 1 in the Nielsen ratings and it stayed there or in the Top 10 for most of its nine-year run. Its February 26, 1964 episode attracted 20 million viewers and is still among the top 20 most popular programs in TV history.

When the series was beamed to England in 1964, it received the highest rating of any American series ever aired in London, the Midlands, and Northern England. Six million homes were said to watch regularly. In 1963, airing on Nihon TV in Japan, it racked up a 14.6 rating, claimed to be the highest ever scored in Japan by an American comedy series.

The debut episode, in which the basic storyline (a rural family becomes obscenely wealthy and moves to California after oil is discovered on their property) was laid out, also contained all the ingredients that would dazzle and confound friends and foes.

—Pan-fried misunderstandings: When Jed was asked by his cousin Pearl (Bea Benaderet) how much money he had received from the oil company, he replied "$25." Pearl, the most worldly of the crew, is dumbfounded at this meager payment. So is Jed—but for a different reason. He explains that he was going to be paid in some new kind of dollars that he'd never heard of—something called "million" dollars.

—Vintage vaudeville gags: After Jethro crashes the family jalopy into a wall, Jed chastises his nephew, saying he should have disposed of its worn-out brakes. Replies Jethro: "That's jes what ah did...that's why we have no brakes."

—The clash between rural and urban lifestyles: Arriving at their new home, the Clampetts think the huge mansion is actually a prison, a fear compounded by the sight of the fatigue-clad gardeners. Assuming them to be escaped prisoners, the shotgun-toting Clampetts hold the astonished laborers at bay until the police arrive—who promptly arrest the clan and throw them in a real pokey.

And David Susskind didn't think this was funny?

The show finally went off the air in CBS's great rural purge of 1971. Other wealthy oilmen like J.R. Ewing eventually came along to take Jed's place. Ebsen himself went on to success as a detective on "Barnaby Jones," Irene Ryan died in 1973, Donna Douglas retired from show biz in favor of a real-estate career, and Max Baer became an independent Hollywood producer (his films include *Macon County Line* and *Ode to Billy Joe*).

In 1981, the show returned with a TV movie centering on a search for the secret of Granny's moonshine to be used as an alternative energy source. "A stupid, insipid, insulting two hours" is what one reviewer said about the show.

Some things never change.

The Beverly Hillbillies—Jethro keeps an eye out as his family members Jed, Elly May and Granny scurry for cover.

AN INTERVIEW WITH PAUL HENNING, THE SHOW'S CREATOR AND PRODUCER

Henning, a native of Independence, Missouri, was working as a soda jerk in his hometown when he was warned by one of his customers, a local haberdasher named Harry S. Truman, against seeking a career in Hollywood. Ignoring the future president's advice, Henning trekked west and eventually began writing such classic radio comedies as "Fibber McGee and Molly" and "The Burns and Allen Show" (which he also adapted to TV in the '50s). Henning also authored the screenplay of *Lover Come Back*, the early '60s romantic comedy starring Doris Day and Rock Hudson.

Question: How did you get the idea for "The Beverly Hillbillies?"

Henning: I have always been a fan of hillbilly humor. Bob Burns was a radio favorite of mine. The idea occurred to me during a motor trip during the Midwest and South in 1959.

After visiting Abraham Lincoln's cabin in Kentucky and some of the Civil War battlefields, I wondered how Lincoln or a contemporary of his would react to being in the car with me a century later speeding along an interstate highway and seeing a modern city. This led to the idea of transplanting a family of hillbillies who had lived in almost total isolation to a modern city. In order to do this, I had to make them suddenly wealthy. Discovering oil on their land accomplished this.

Question: How did you feel about the critics' extremely negative reaction?

Henning: Frankly, I was too busy writing and producing the series and watching it become first in the ratings in record time to respond to the criticism.

Question: Did you anticipate such negative reaction?

Henning: No.

Question: Max Baer, Jr. was once quoted as saying the show had positive values, including upholding family life, respect for elders, and obedience to authority. Do you agree with his assessment?

Henning: I think Max Baer's observation was very astute.

Question: Do you think the Hillbillies have improved with age, especially when compared to today's sitcoms?

Henning: No comment.

"BEVERLY HILLBILLIES" QUOTE-UNQUOTE

"We love your show. Anytime we get a chance to look at it, we do."—President Richard Nixon to Irene Ryan when she visited the White House in 1970.

"The public is hungry for what we offer—honest humor. We're friendly people but some of our humor has a biting comment. If the show has any overtones, any message, it's that people have more than they need in the material world. Our social comment is that people should live simpler, not necessarily like the Clampetts, but simpler."—Buddy Ebsen, 1963.

"They were humble, God-fearing folk; they weren't trying to impress anyone."—Mr. T of "The A Team," telling *People* magazine why "The Beverly Hillbillies" was his favorite TV show.

"Jethro was a village idiot. His lines were stupid, and I hated doing the show. The only reason I took the part in the first place was money."—

Green Acres—"Fresh Air!" declared Oliver (Eddie Albert); "Times Square!" countered his wife Lisa (Eva Gabor).

Max Baer, Jr., now an independent Hollywood producer.

"BEVERLY HILLBILLIES"
TRIVIA QUIZ

1. Who was Duke?
2. Who sang the show's theme song?
3. What was the ce-ment pond?
4. What served as the Clampetts' dining-room table?
5. Bonus: The Clampett mansion was not actually in Beverly Hills. Do you know where it was?

ANSWERS

1. Elly May's dog
2. Lester Flatt and Earl Scruggs
3. The Clampett's swimming pool
4. A billiards table
5. Bel Air

"Green Acres"

Green Acres (1965-71) runs neck-and-neck with "Gilligan's Island" and "The Beverly Hillbillies" as among the dumbest, hence coolest, sitcoms of the '60s. Personally, it's my favorite.

"Green Acres" did a 180 on "The Beverly Hillbillies." Take a sophisticated urban couple—attorney Oliver Wendell Douglas (Eddie Albert) and his socialite wife, Lisa (Eva Gabor)—and plop them down in the middle of the sticks. (Not surprisingly, Paul Henning helped develop this one.)

The Douglases were actually ahead of the times. Several years before the hippies pronounced it cool to get back to the land, these Park Avenue swells shucked the rat race and headed for...Hooterville. Yes, scenic Hooter-

ville, just around the bend from the Shady Rest Hotel, home of the first successful rubetube spinoff, "Petticoat Junction."

There was so much about the show to love: The unabashed unreality of Oliver riding his tractor or pitching hay in his Brooks Brothers suit; Lisa in her furs and pearls addressing the Hooterville Women's Every Other Wednesday Club; the theme song ("Fresh air! Times Square! The chores! The Stores! Darling I love you, but give me Park Avenue"); the tacky backdrops; the spaced-out supporting players led by Pat Buttram as the fast-talking con man, Mr. Haney, and Alvy Moore as dimwitted, double-speaking county agent, Hank Kimball.

The coolest of them all was Arnold the Pig, the Ziffel's "son," who watched television and engaged in other human pastimes. He was a two-time Patsy winner, for best animal actor on TV, and had fan clubs at colleges across the U.S. There seemed to have been some jealousy concerning Arnold. An angry Eddie Albert told *TV Guide*: "I'm not Eddie Albert, I'm that fellow on TV with the pig."

Jay Sommers, the show's creator, said it was based on a radio show called "Granby's Green Acres." He took the idea to Henning, who then sold the show to CBS without a pilot. Even though "The Beverly Hillbillies" had been successful, many stations refused to pick up "Green Acres" immediately on only hearsay. Despite the shaky start, the show lasted until 1971.

Eddie Albert wasn't the first choice to play Oliver. Don Ameche was. But the producers couldn't pry him away from "Circus." So when it was offered to Albert, he bit. He said of the role: "Swell, that's me. Everyone gets tired of the rat race. Everyone would like to chuck it all and grow some carrots...I knew it would be success-

ful; it had to be. It's about the atavistic urge, and people have been getting a charge out of that ever since Aristophanes wrote about the plebes and the city folk. In a sense, Thoreau is the real author of 'Green Acres'."

The role of Lisa had been proposed for such all-American types as Marsha Hunt and Janet Blair, before it was given to Miss Gabor. At first the network objected to her because she had an accent, until it was pointed out that Desi Arnaz had done quite well in a sit-com with his accent.

Most memorable episode: Try the one in which the Hooterville Repertory Company wants to put on a play. They choose their favorite piece of culture— "The Beverly Hillbillies." Yep. The tattered gingham curtain goes up, and we have Oliver playing Jethro, Lisa as Granny, and Sam Drucker as Jed. This was a double dose of unreality that was even more unbelievable than a government press release about Vietnam.

There was gold in them thar hills, or in the "rubetube," as some critics called it. Here's the background on the others.

"The Andy Griffith Show"

From 1960 to 1968 Andy Griffith played widower Andy Taylor, the patient, philosophical sheriff of Mayberry, North Carolina. Mayberry was hardly law-and-order territory, so most of the episodes concerned the domestic relationships between Andy, his young son Opie (Ron Howard), and Aunt Bee (Frances Bavier), with whom they lived. Also highlighted were the misadventures of two of the show's regulars: Gomer Pyle (Jim Nabors), the bumbling attendant at

Wally's filling station, and Deputy Sheriff Barney Fife (Don Knotts). Both men left the series to go on to other shows—"Gomer Pyle, USMC" and "The Don Knotts Show."

Griffith left the show in 1968, but before he did, he wed schoolteacher Helen Crump, which provided the material for the first episode of "Mayberry RFD," the show's spinoff. The couple moved away, and that show was left to carry on by itself, with Ken Berry in the lead.

"Petticoat Junction"

The first "Beverly Hillbillies" spin-off was "Petticoat Junction," which ran from 1963 to 1970. Cousin Pearl (Bea Benaderet), the only member of the Clampett clan who appeared to have gone beyond the fourth grade, moved to Hooterville where she became Kate Bradley, proprietress of the Shady Rest Hotel. A widow, she ran the hotel with the aid of her three attractive daughters—Billie Jo, Bobbie Jo, and Betty Jo—and Uncle Joe (Edgar Buchanan), the white man's Stepin Fetchit. This show also came from Paul Henning, whose daughter, professionally known as Linda Kaye, played Betty Jo.

RUBETUBE TRIVIA QUIZ

1. What was the name of the train that stopped at Hooterville on "Petticoat Junction"?
2. What were the names of the train's engineers?
3. What was the name of the Douglas' handyman on "Green Acres"?

4. What was the name of "The Andy Griffith Show" after it went into syndication?

ANSWERS

1. The Hooterville Cannonball
2. Charlie and Floyd
3. Eb
4. "Andy of Mayberry"

"Gilligan's Island"

Long after the merits of LBJ or the single-bullet theory have ceased being proper subjects for discussion, there's still one unresolved '60s issue that's guaranteed to start an argument at a cocktail party filled with yuppies who grew up during that debate-filled era. These are the same

Gilligan is amazed once again on Gilligan's Island.

people who can be sold on all means of lunacy—from running marathons to eating raw fish—but still won't accept the validity of this argument: "Gilligan's Island" should be considered as one of the funniest programs in TV history.

Even now I can see the Perrier bottles cracking as they shatter against walls covered by no-nuke posters. Say this, and you'll get stares like you wouldn't believe. You might as well say, yes, Spiro Agnew was right, there *is* an effete corps of impudent snobs.

But I'll stick by this assertion. Here was a show that captured perfectly the zeitgeist of mid-'60s TV lunacy—and lunacy, in general. A world where, as the Beatles said in another context, nothing is real, and there's nothing to get hung about. Reality wasn't to be trifled with. "Gilligan" offered an LSD experience without drugs. It is possible that as the world grows madder, the insanity of "Gilligan's Island" makes increasingly more sense.

Well, if the truth were to be told, "Gilligan's Island" is still one of the most successful shows in syndication. Because it ran only two seasons, more episodes have actually been seen than any other TV show in reruns (let's not forget that "I Love Lucy" ran for a much longer time). That's a nice coconut-sized lump on the head to the critics who ladled out as much if not more abuse on "Gilligan's Island" than they had two years earlier on "The Beverly Hillbillies."

To recap the story, if you're one of those who never watched (or will still not admit to watching) an episode: Seven souls—the skipper (fat, jolly Alan Hale, Jr.), his dimwitted first mate (Bob Denver, trading in Maynard G. Krebs' beret for a sailor's cap), the millionaire (Jim Backus) and his wife (Natalie Schafer), the movie star (Tina Louise), the professor (Russell Johnson), and the naive farm girl Mary Ann (Dawn Wells)—set sail one day on a three-hour tour on the *Minnow*, a dinky, but funky, tour boat.

A storm (possibly a white tornado?) came along and tossed the *Minnow* about as if it was a pair of tights in your mother's Maytag. When the weather cleared, the ship washed up on the shores of an uncharted desert isle.

Here, the magnificent seven built their new civilization and they ended up having more comforts than they left behind. Little has been heard from this crew since 1967 except for two high-rated specials in 1979 and 1980 which kept us up to date.

Since then, the Love Boat stopped by in 1981 to refuel, and Ginger ran off with Captain Stubing. And in October, 1983, Tatoo got lost and went to the other side of Fantasy Island where he saw the castaways. Upon his return, he cried out to Mr. Roarke: "Boss, da Gilligan, da Gilligan!" Ricardo Montalban didn't believe his story and banished him forever from the program. Even now as I write, Mr. Howell and Gilligan are deep in negotiations with officials from Club Med about opening a branch on the island. The antidote to civilization? You bet.

AN INTERVIEW WITH SHERWOOD SCHWARTZ— THE MAN RESPONSIBLE FOR "GILLIGAN'S ISLAND"

Schwartz, a veteran television writer and producer, had worked on such shows as "I Married Joan," "Red Skelton," and "My Favorite Martian." He also created "The Brady Bunch," the last bastion of family programming.

Question: I heard you got the name Gilligan out of the L.A. phone book.

Schwartz: I took it from a phone book, but I don't remember which one. I spent several weeks literally looking for names which, when connected with the word island, would automatically sound like it's a comedy rather than a dramatic show. I didn't want to make it sound too bizarre—you know, you could make up any cockamamie name.

I like hard letters. I just kept looking through phone books for a name—not like Jackson's Island, which would be too dramatic or McGillicuddy's Island, which would sound phony. I came across the name Gilligan and it sounded just right.

Question: What's the course of the show's development?

Schwartz: I developed the concept in 1963 after rereading *Robinson Crusoe*, one of my favorite childhood books. My own agent didn't want to handle it. He had been my agent for eighteen years, and he said "this is ridiculous—who's gonna watch these same seven people on the same island every week?" And I said OK, fine, and I got a different agent. I spent one dime for one phone call and sold the show...so go figure.

Three different actors were in the pilot, but were never on the show...I won't say who they were except that they would have played the professor and the two girls.

Jim Aubrey, president of CBS, OK'd the idea of the show, but disagreed with the way I should do it. Aubrey loved the idea of Gilligan and the skipper, loved the idea of a little charter boat, but he wanted it so that on successive episodes there would be other people on different charters. I said that might be a good show, but that's not my show. We had a running battle about it. The way we resolved it was to let the audience determine whether they get tired of it. The minute the audience seems to say enough of those seven same people on the island, we'll fix the boat and go on to the next charter. That finally solved my difficulty with Aubrey.

Aubrey created "The Baileys of Balboa" to show me I was wrong. This is the way things should be done, with a different charter every week, and he copied the characters. John Dehner playing the Jim Backus role, Sterling Holloway as Gilligan, and Paul Ford was the skipper. Characters were just translated. That show was not successful. It did not have magic.

Jerry Van Dyke was my original choice to play Gilligan. He had a choice to do a pilot called "Goggles," which his agent chose over my pilot. My next choice, Bob Denver, was based on information. I knew Jerry; he was a friend of mine. When I lost Jerry, I had heard so much about Bob, I had one meeting with him; that's all it took.

The most difficult role to cast was the skipper. It's difficult to cast a great big guy in authority browbeating a young skinny inferior who works for him. In order to make sure we had the right guy, I deliberately wrote a scene where he rips him to shreds. I felt that if the actor could survive that scene, he was lovable no matter what he did, lovable under most adverse conditions. Alan Hale proved to be the only choice.

The other characters were meant to be a social microcosm with cardboard characters. Rich is Rich. Beautiful is Beautiful. Stupid is Stupid. These were supposed to be almost cartoon characters so I could say with the story what I wanted to say without having the audience wonder how did this guy get this way.

I toyed around with many other types. The Professor was originally a writer, then an archaeologist; Ginger varied from a sardonic, flip character like Eve Arden. Didn't work with Tina. So we went with a different kind of a movie star, somewhat reminiscent of Marilyn Monroe.

Question: What about the reaction?

Schwartz: Very few shows were villified more than "Gilligan's Island." I think "My Mother the Car" and "The Beverly Hillbillies" were pummeled worse, but Gilligan was right up there.

The surprising thing is that even though big-city critics absolutely crucified it, when I went through clippings looking back, there were a number of critics in smaller cities who thought it was a breath of fresh air and happy-go-lucky fun. I'd forgotten that. I thought the show had been universally panned.

Do you know that "Gilligan's Island" is the most frequently seen show in the history of TV? That's because "Gilligan's Island" only had 100 episodes, while Lucy had about 300, so "Gilligan" turns over more frequently. It has been rerun more than any other show.

Its success in syndication has been phenomenal because there's a little something there for everybody. Older people love it; kids love it. I know people who watch it who just like to see the dialogue between Jim and Natalie; obviously kids love to see coconuts falling on Gilligan. But there's lots of stuff on GI that people weren't aware of.

Question: Like what?

Schwartz: The sociological aspect. Nobody recognized that what I was trying to say with that show was that all the nations of the world have to learn to get along with each other because that's all there is. Those seven very diverse people had to learn to get together with each other. I still believe that's the toughest problem facing the world today. We would get letters from psychologists and educators praising this aspect. Theses have been written about "Gilligan's Island."

The show has many different levels. Sure, it was slapstick, but the basic theme was very serious; it was a social microcosm. Not one critic ever really wrote about it from that standpoint.

Question: But the biggest question of all is: How come the Howells always had all their luggage and possessions with them, considering they were only going on a three-hour tour?

Schwartz: That was my own personal statement. In my opinion, the rich have it good, no matter where they go; that's what I was saying. With rich people in the most terrible circumstances, somebody will be waiting on them, and they will have what they need. That's the only way I can explain it.

FIVE GUEST STARS WHO VISITED "GILLIGAN'S ISLAND"

The castaways didn't spend all their time alone on "Gilligan's Island." Among those who were washed ashore were:

1. Hans Conried as an old-time aviator named Wrong Way Feldman
2. A fake-Beatle rock band, the Wellingtons, who called themselves the Mosquitoes
3. Phil Silvers as movie producer, Harold Hecuba, on a talent search
4. John McGiver as a British butterfly collector and
5. Nehemiah Persoff as an exiled Latin American dictator.

Fantasy Sit-Coms

The great escape of mid-'60s TV showed itself in horses and cars that talked, witches who winked, nuns who flew, genies who popped out of bottles, ghosts who haunted, monsters and Martians who tried to prove they were as normal as you and I. These characters were mostly bombed by the critics, but adored by the viewers.

Why did these shows become so popular? The great escape was one reason; the nation in 1964 still hadn't recovered from JFK's death. TV also began aiming their programming at younger audiences who could appreciate the fact that improved TV technology could make people disappear and do other wacky sleight-of-hand tricks.

Who were these happy haunters and fantasy figures?

In the fall of 1964, two shows about bizarre families went head to head: ABC's "The Addams Family" and CBS's "The Munsters."

"THE ADDAMS FAMILY" (1964-66)—This show, based on the macabre *New Yorker* cartoons of Charles Addams, was wittier and better written than "The Munsters." For starters, this eccentric family looked almost normal (well, at least compared to the Munsters). Shifty-eyed Gomez (John Astin) was a loving husband and father who would go into paroxysms of passion whenever his raven-tressed wife, Morticia (Carolyn Jones), spoke French to him. While other men his age were out on the links, Gomez preferred indoor sports like blowing up electric trains.

Shaven-headed Uncle Fester (the funniest chrome dome on TV since Curly of the Three Stooges), played by former child star Jackie Coogan, was a one-man solution to the energy crisis, lighting electric bulbs by placing them in his mouth.

Morticia and Gomez had two children—Pugsley (Ken Weatherwax) and Wednesday (Lisa Loring)—whose toys included a headless doll (she) and a two-headed turtle (he). Miss Loring, by the way, is now a star on soap operas, where characters are becoming almost as bizarre as those found on her former show.

At the family's beck and call was Lurch (Ted Cassidy), the six-foot, nine-inch, harpsichord-playing butler with one of the best basso profundos on TV ("You rannnngg?") By the way, did you know that Cassidy's only other role before winning the Lurch spot was as Jesus in a syndicated-TV version of "The Last Supper"?

Also on the scene, but more in the background, was Grandmama (Blossom Rock), a witch. Three-foot high Cousin Itt, TV's first longhair, looked like a cross between a yak and a fireplug, and hung around the Addams manse making weird squeals.

The Addams Family—Former child star Jackie Coogan in a characteristic pose as Uncle Fester

"THE MUNSTERS" (1964-66) The members of this family all looked like modified versions of classic movie monsters. The show took two characters from the well-loved "Car 54, Where Are You?" and covered them with twenty pounds of makeup (but you couldn't tell that Herman's skin was green because the show was filmed in black and white).

Leo Schnauzer (Al Lewis) became Grandpa Munster, who resembled Dracula. He was TV's original batman, changing himself into one of those beady-eyed flying mammals when the mood struck him.

Six-foot, seven-inch Fred Gwynne, who used to bump his head on patrol cars as Officer Francis Muldoon, now had plenty of headroom in the huge, musty Munster home. As paterfamilias Herman Munster, who looked like Frankenstein, he presided over a brood that included son, Eddie (who made pointed ears stylish two years before Mr. Spock), wife Yvonne DeCarlo (who shopped and was coiffed at the same shops as Morticia), and the blonde sheep of the family, pretty (to us) niece, Marilyn (Beverly Owen, later Pat Priest).

The stories were livened up by the presence of two of the koolest '60s kustom kars: a $20,000 Munstermobile (from George Barris, who created the Batmobile), a hepped-up 1927 touring car, and Grandpa's 160-mph coffin on wheels that was called the "Dragula."

Cognoscenti prefer "The Addams Family" to "The Munsters," but both monster families sank back into the swamps by the time the 1966 season began.

"I DREAM OF JEANNIE" (1965-70)— The true '60s pop culture aficionado is one who thinks Larry Hagman was cooler as Tony Nelson, the straight-arrow astronaut and master of Jeannie, than he was as ice water-veined J.R. Ewing on "Dallas." The show was created by Sidney Sheldon, who would go on to fame and megabucks in the '70s with his steamy novels, *The Other Side of Midnight* and *Bloodlines*.

Prim NBC censors wouldn't allow Miss Eden's navel to be seen, so her skirt always covered it. She had lived in the bottle from 64 B.C. until 1965, when astronaut Nelson crash-landed on a desert island. He spied the bottle, and, when he opened it, a geyser of pink smoke came out and so did Jeannie. Jeannie's digs inside the bottle were furnished like a motel off Route 66. It got to be a bit claustrophobic, but she was summoned only when her master beckoned. Jeannie wanted to settle down in a no-deposit, no-return bottle of her own. She was finally able to convince her boss, and she and Nelson were wed in December, 1969.

One of the coolest IDOJ episodes featured appearances by members of the "Laugh-In" cast who wanted to spotlight Jeannie on the show as an exotic princess-starlet being touted by Major Healey. The second coolest is

The Munsters— Grandpa (Al Lewis) and Herman (Fred Gwynne) try to convince the fire chief (guest star Charlie Ruggles) that they are as normal as anyone.

the "Mod party" episode. In the latter-day Jeannie, Ted Cassidy, having finished his Lurch role, came to IDOJ as Habib, master of Jeannie II, the original Jeannie's sister (also played by Miss Eden).

"MY FAVORITE MARTIAN" (1963-66)—This sit-com was the original ET of sorts. A lovable adult visitor (Ray Walston) from the red planet, is discovered by Tim O'Hara (Bill Bixby), an amiable newspaper reporter who witnesses "Uncle Martin's" spaceship crash-landing on Earth. No one ever asked Uncle Martin to phone home, however. Martin was friendly—not like the aliens in '50s sci-fi flicks. He could do magic, read minds; he could fly, but was finicky. How did his antennae work, you ask? Well, Walston kept a transistor device in his collar; he would push a button on a small gadget he held in his hand and the twin wires would shoot out of the transistor. Push the button again and they'd recede.

"BEWITCHED" (1964-72)—It was probably the most popular and highest-rated of the supernatural fantasies. Samantha Stephens (Elizabeth Montgomery) didn't look odd; she resembled any other suburban housewife, but all she had to do was twitch her nose and strange things happened. She was a witch—probably the most attractive one since the Good Witch in *The Wizard of Oz*. Sam was married to Darrin (Dick York, later Dick Sargent), the latest in the long line of inept, befuddled TV husbands. The shenanigans of his wife and mother-in-law, Endora, gave Darrin even more reason to be befuddled than Ozzie Nelson.

"MY MOTHER THE CAR" (1965-66)—Some pundits claimed this was the worst TV show ever made. I disagree. It told the story of lawyer Dave Crabtree who heard his late mother's voice emanating from a 1928 Porter. She was just like any other mother—nagging, badgering, and asking him if he had eaten his chicken soup.

The show wasn't bad; it was merely ahead of its time. If this was such a stupid idea, why did NBC copy it fifteen years later with its popular "Knight Rider" series, which also had a car that talked? Besides, what's so weird about talking cars anyway? I mean, have you been in some of those cars lately that talk to you when your door is open? At least Mrs. Crabtree had a personality.

"MR. ED" (1961-65)—He was a talking horse. A semi-talking horse, actually, because only his master, architect Wilbur Post (Alan Young) could hear him. Ed's voice, by the way, was provided by former Western star, Allan "Rocky" Lane. Ed was probably smarter than his owner—he loved Leonard Bernstein and insisted that his stall be furnished in Chinese Modern. In the years after the show was canceled, he went on promotional tours across the nation. Mr. Ed, the horse, died on February 28, 1979.

I Dream of Jeannie—Jeannie (Barbara Eden) wants her master (Larry Hagman) to fight a 7-foot, 2-inch giant (Richard Kiel) who insulted her. Jeannie went to "Harper Valley PTA," her master to "Dallas," and the Giant appeared as Jaws in two James Bond movies.

"THE FLYING NUN" (1967-70)—In between "Gidget" and *Norma Rae*, Sally Field took a leaf from *Mary Poppins* (flight) and *The Sound of Music* (a nun) and—*voilá*—the Flying Nun was created. Sister Bertrille wasn't as graceful as Superman— once she was almost shot down by enemy aircraft, and she was often dunked in the ocean. Some religious orders actually praised the show because it "humanized" nuns and their work.

The Flying Nun—After "Gidget" and before "Norma Rae," Sally Field did her thing for organized religion.

SUPERNATURAL SIT-COM QUIZ

1. Who (or what) was Thing?
2. Who supplied the voice of "My Mother the Car"?
3. What was the name of the advertising agency where Darrin Stephens worked?
4. What was the Munsters' address?
5. Where did Morticia and Gomez go on their honeymoon?
6. Where was the Flying Nun's convent located?

ANSWERS

1. A servant—a right hand on "The Addams Family" which lived in a golden, nail-studded box that seemed to be at the beck and call of any family member
2. Ann Sothern
3. McMann and Tate
4. 1313 Mockingbird Lane, Mockingbird Heights
5. A cave in Death Valley
6. Puerto Rico

The Family Scene

The family—as in Mom, Dad, Butch, and Sis—has been a staple of TV comedy from the beginning.

In the '50s and early '60s, it seemed as if some fathers *did* know best. Dad's word was law. Dad always wore a suit and tie to the dinner table (or a cardigan sweater and tie if he wanted to project a more casual image). This father was a stern, but loving figure who came to us in the guise of Hugh Beaumont's Ward Cleaver on "Leave it to Beaver" or Robert Young's Jim Anderson on "Father Knows Best." Ward and Jim were the role models that kids hoped their dads would emulate. We were disappointed when the reality proved to be something different.

These Dads were biblical figures combining the wisdom of Solomon, the authority of David, and the patience of Job. You called them "sir" and meant it. If you had a problem, Dad was always there to solve it. Of course, these were not earth-shattering issues we're talking about. Back then, the strongest drug a kid took was probably children's aspirin.

On the flip side of the know-it-all, dads were the bumbler fathers such as Ozzie Nelson on "The Adventures of Ozzie and Harriet." They were weak, comical figures who were perpetually victimized and continually upstaged by their wives and children.

Some sociologists have said that by watching these bumbling fathers, an entire generation of kids lost respect for authority figures—the same generation that would make rioting a required course at universities a decade later.

Nevertheless, men wore the pants. Mom stayed at home, and Dad worked, but we rarely saw dads at their workplace. They left each morning to go to "the office" to work for "the boss," who sometimes came to dinner. That was that. Just what *did* Ozzie Nelson do?

During the '60s, the traditional depiction of the TV dad was still pretty much the way it had been during the '50s. The '60s, it seemed, was a decade that stressed relevance everywhere except on television. Even the wacko fathers of mid-'60s sit-coms were conventional TV dads. Herman Munster was nothing more than Ward Cleaver with green skin.

One TV dad who stuck out from the pack in the '60s could be found on the extremely popular and well-written "Dick Van Dyke Show" (1961-66). Van Dyke's portrayal of TV writer Rob Petrie fell in between the bumbler and the patriarch. This dad had a stimulating job *and* a family, both of which were sources of trouble and amusement.

Of course, the show was aided by a clever, colorful supporting cast of characters such as Morey Amsterdam, Richard Deacon, Rose Marie, and Carl Reiner (who created the show). Meanwhile, Laura Petrie (Mary Tyler Moore), not yet having reached her heroine status she would achieve in the '70s, began a subtle transformation of the TV sit-com mom. She wore pants, for one thing. You could also sense that she had more on the ball than June Cleaver. At least, she didn't wear pearls while she was vacuuming.

And what of the kids? Teenagers were a breed apart who combed their hair in pompadours, hung out at malt shops, borrowed the family car for dates, and were always being lectured good-naturedly by Dad after they did something stupid like smashing up the family car. Some kids were goody-goodies, others were inveterate wise guys. Let's drink a Yoo-Hoo toast to Patty and Cathy Lane, Dobie Gillis and Maynard G. Krebs, and Wally and Beaver Cleaver—with a special tip of the Beaver's baseball cap to Eddie Haskell.

TV was obviously wedded to the idea of the nuclear family and eschewed the concept of divorce. Divorce was still too messy an issue, morally speaking. For real-life proof, one should recall Nelson Rockefeller's aborted presidential candidacy in 1964. The widower or "single father," however, has always been a time-honored TV figure. One of the most memorable single fathers of '60s TV was Fred MacMurray, who played widower Steve Douglas on the long-running "My Three Sons" (1960-72).

The Dick Van Dyke Show—America's first family of comedy, the Petries: Laura (Mary Tyler Moore), Rob (Dick Van Dyke) and Ritchie (Larry Mitchell)

MacMurray was trying to raise three growing kids. He was aided in this task by another "helpless man," his father-in-law, Bub (William Frawley) and later by Uncle Charlie (William Demarest). Watching a man—especially these two tough old grizzled birds—trying to cook dinner or clean the house guaranteed laugh tracks would work overtime. But despite the absence of a woman in the house (until Steve finally married), the household managed to survive with minimal trauma. All three sons even got married, eventually.

There were other widows and widowers: "Family Affair"; "Governor and J.J."; "Julia"; "The Lucy Show"; "The Doris Day Show"; "The Ghost and Mrs. Muir"; "Accidental Family"; "To Rome with Love"; and "The Courtship of Eddie's Father." "Julia" was special because, for the first time, a black woman (Diahann Carroll), who wasn't a maid, was featured in the title role.

Shows about single people were also unusual: "That Girl" was the first. Marlo Thomas' Ann Marie was almost the first "Mary." The late '60s featured the pseudo-swingin' singles on "Love, American Style," who looked like they'd sink under the weight of all those medallions they wore around their necks.

The decade ended with one last gasp of wholesomeness—"The Brady Bunch," about a happy, healthy family formed by the union of a widow who had three daughters and a widower with three sons. It sounded not unlike a late '60s movie called *Yours, Mine, and Ours* with Henry Fonda and Lucille Ball.

On TV today, it looks like it's the kids who know best. Ward Cleaver probably wouldn't fare too well in the TV land of the '80s, where it seems the nuclear family has self-destructed. Almost no one calls his dad "sir" anymore.

TV FAMILY QUIZ

1. What was the name of the TV show for which Rob Petrie was headwriter?
2. What was Buddy's wife's name?
3. Name the two children on "The Donna Reed Show."
4. What was the butler's name on "Family Affair"?
5. What was the housekeeper's name on "The Brady Bunch"?
6. What was Lumpy Rutherford's real first name?
7. What were the ages of the boys on "My Three Sons" when the series went on the air in 1960?

ANSWERS

1. "The Alan Brady Show"
2. Pickles
3. Mary Stone and Jeff Stone
4. Mr. French
5. Alice Nelson
6. Clarence
7. Mike was 18; Robbie was 14; Chip was 7.

A BRIEF TALK WITH
DICK VAN DYKE

Question: The show started off slowly the first year, but CBS let you stay on. Do you think the show would have the same chance today?

Van Dyke: We wouldn't have had a chance today. We were left on for a whole season and then canceled. It was only because Sheldon Leonard went in and fought for us that we managed to stay on and develop any

FAMILY SCENES MIX-MATCH

Match the families with where they lived.

1. The Mitchells ("Dennis the Menace")   **a.** New Rochelle
2. The Lanes ("The Patty Duke Show")   **b.** Hillsdale
3. The Cleavers ("Leave it to Beaver")   **c.** Springfield
4. The Petries ("The Dick Van Dyke Show")   **d.** Hilldale
5. The Stones ("The Donna Reed Show")   **e.** Mayfield
6. The Andersons ("Father Knows Best")   **f.** Brooklyn Heights

ANSWERS

1. b; 2. f; 3. e; 4. a; 5. d; 6. c

sort of audience.

I recognize that today it's so expensive that they cannot afford production on the show if it's not bringing ratings points because they're losing money. I'd have to be really in love with something to have to go and try it again.

Back then they'd give a show a season. In those days a show cost $60,000 an episode, where they cost about a half-million per today. Some stars are getting $60,000 a week salary.

Question: What is the show's continuing appeal?

Van Dyke: The only specific reason I can think of is that Carl Reiner never allowed us to use slang jargon of the day; in that way the show hasn't become dated. A lot of old shows of the same vintage use the slang, and it is dated and stale. You don't laugh. We also had solid scripts, and Carl's production was solid, and the chemistry between the five of us was something I'd love to experience again in my life.

Question: Has a reunion been discussed?

Van Dyke: Oh, I've heard it talked about several times, but I don't know if it's a good idea. Just because I'd have to let everybody see how we've all aged. Ritchie Petrie is now 25 and has black hair and a beard and in no way resembles Ritchie.

Question: What do you think would have happened to "The Alan Brady Show"?

Van Dyke: Well, considering what's happened to TV, I'm sure it would have gone the way of all the hour variety shows, like Gleason and Burnett. The hour variety show just doesn't work anymore. I think the talk shows have taken over.

AN INTERVIEW WITH TONY DOW OF "LEAVE IT TO BEAVER"

Leave it to Beaver—Then and now: Tony Dow and Jerry Mathers as Wally and Beaver Cleaver

After "Beaver," Dow was a guest in several episodic series including a memorable "Dr. Kildare," in which he played an unwed father. He also had roles in two soaps, "Never Too Young" and "General Hospital" (before it became famous). He is serious about acting and still does episodic television. He reunited with the surviving "Beaver" cast members (Hugh Beaumont, who played Ward, died in 1982) for a 1983 TV movie and for "Still the Beaver," a successful sitcom on the pay-cable Disney Channel. "I don't want just to walk on and walk off as some character from the 1950s," he insists.

Question: What do you watch today?

Dow: I'm not an authority on TV anymore. I don't sit down and watch a lot of TV. When I do sit down, I find that I'm not entertained. I'd rather do something else. Although I think "Family Ties" is terrific, the closest thing on TV today to "Beaver."

"Beaver" wasn't intended as a children's show. It was an adult show airing at nine o'clock. I think it was the purest of the true family entertainment series.

Question: How do you respond when people still recognize you as Wally Cleaver?

Dow: It never bothered me a whole lot, except when people would see me and say "Hey, Wally." I'm uncomfortable because that's not my name. It's difficult to deal with that kind of recognition. If somebody comes up to me and says to me, "Hey, I appreciate the show," that's different. Over half the time, people are rude—they're uncomfortable, so they don't know what to do, so they laugh and giggle. I don't interpret that as being laughed at, but still it's difficult to walk by a group of folks that laugh and point. It's not the kind of thing you become comfortable with.

I'm not a real, bubbly outgoing personality. I would like not to be associated with the character Wally. First of all, it has been more than twenty years since I did him, and in the second place, he's not taken seriously. He's kind of a milk-and-cookies character in a world where people want blood and guts. That's why I try to stay away from doing "Leave It to Beaver"-type things.

I do enjoy when people come to me and say "I enjoy your work on 'Beaver.'" For instance, Bud Cort told me Beaver was his favorite show

as a kid, and that Wally taught him how to act.

Question: At the show's height, you were receiving about a thousand letters a week. How did you feel?

Dow: My mother took care of all that. She read every letter and answered every letter. If they wanted a picture, I would sign it. But I'd be in school, I'd have to do homework, then try to memorize my lines. I didn't have time to do all that other stuff. But she didn't save those letters.

AN INTERVIEW WITH DWAYNE HICKMAN

Dwayne Hickman, now 51 years old, acted in "The Bob Cummings Show," before landing the title role in "The Many Loves of Dobie Gillis," (1959-63). On the show, he played the prototypical TV teenager of the early '60s. Later, he appeared in movies ranging from *Cat Ballou* to *Dr. Goldfoot and the Bikini Machine* and *Ski Party*. Since 1979, he has been a programming executive at CBS.

Question: You weren't a teenager when you played Dobie.

Hickman: I was older. The character was 17, but after the first episode, it was never mentioned how old I was.

Question: Did you dye your hair?

Hickman: Yes, but that never made any sense. The show's producers didn't want me to look like I did on the "Bob Cummings Show." Max Shulman thought that Dobie should be a blonde and I went along with it the first year. It was hard on my head to have it done because I had a crew cut. The second year I said I want to go to my natural brown color, which they allowed me to do.

Question: What happened to the

Thinker that you would talk to at the beginning of each show?

Hickman: I don't know. It was a big, life-size thing made of a kind of papery material. It wasn't metal or bronze. It's probably sitting in a warehouse somewhere. It probably should be in the Smithsonian if we only knew where it was.

Question: What about the rumors that you and Tuesday Weld (who played Thalia Menninger) would feud on the set?

Hickman: That was blown out by the press. There was a little friction; maybe I was a little more critical then. Looking back, maybe I was a little antsy. Then again, she was very young.

Question: What was your first impression of Warren Beatty, who

played your rival, Milton Armitage?

Hickman: Very sure of himself, very professional, confident, and smooth. Certainly had more confidence than I had. He always seemed assured of success even when he had none.

Question: What about your recording career? Didn't you make an LP called *I'm a Lover Not a Fighter*?

Hickman: My singing career was short-lived. That was not a great album. I don't think I'd ever do it again. Everybody was recording rock 'n' roll, that's why they approached me. Some did well with it, Ricky Nelson, for instance. Well, they were trying to find another Elvis Presley, no matter what it took.

Question: Why did you give up acting?

Hickman: I was never really interested in acting. I got into it by accident. My mother was an actress, and she got my brothers and I involved. I never really set out to be an actor. I've always stuck to playing an extension of myself, not that I was Dobie Gillis, but he was kind of an exaggerated version of things that I was already. I felt I was more of a personality than an actor. On the "Bob Cummings Show" I played Chuck MacDonald, a different type of character than Dobie, but they had much in common and that common element is me. The exact opposite of a Robert DeNiro, who never looks the same in every film.

Question: Who would you cast as Dobie Gillis today?

Hickman: I don't know. It's such a special role that I have no objectivity. I don't know if you could do this character today. He's such a '50s or '60s character, so innocent, so naive. Michael J. Fox could do it, and he'd be very good at it, but I'm not sure it works anymore.

Spies and Secret Agents

"THE MAN FROM U.N.C.L.E."

Time: 10 A.M. Scene: A tailor shop on Manhattan's East Side. Two men walk through the front door: the shorter one has blond bangs and a turtleneck; the taller of the two is more clean-cut and wears a well-cut suit. The man behind the counter eyes them perfunctorily and slams down the pants-pressing machine. The pair go into the changing room. Are they going to have a hem or two taken up? No, they draw the curtain, and one of them manipulates a hook on the wall. The wall sways, then opens. Suddenly they're facing a beautiful receptionist in a sparse, futuristic office. She pins triangular-shaped ID cards onto their jackets. Macy's was never like this. The two men casually stroll over to their craggy-faced know-it-all boss.

It's the beginning of another working day in the life of the Men from U.N.C.L.E. And how did *you* get to work this morning?

The spies you read about on the front pages were pretty grim people—Colonel Abel, the Rosenbergs, Francis Gary Powers—nothing romantic about them at all. Then James Bond came along. Bond meant box-office. And, since TV was not beyond swiping ideas from the movies, "The Man from U.N.C.L.E.," the first of the TV spy shows, was created. The men were small-screen Bonds: suave, cool, detached, and wise with women and weapons.

In fact, Ian Fleming was interested in producer Norman Felton's ("Dr. Kildare") concept about a TV super-spy and contributed the name "Solo." (It had been the name of a minor character, a Sicilian gangster, in *Goldfinger*.) But he was too ill to make any further contributions. That pilot, "Solo," was at first rejected.

Felton then enlisted the aid of producer-developer Sam Rolfe, who refined the concept into a super-intelligence agency—The United Network Command for Law Enforcement. U.N.C.L.E. was a combination CIA, Mossad, Secret Service, and Interpol.

For the lead character, still called Solo, they tapped Robert Vaughn, most recently seen in "The Lieutenant" series. David McCallum, a Scottish actor who had previously appeared in such films as, *Billy Budd* and *The Great Escape*, was cast as Solo's assistant, Illya Kuryakin. Illya was an afterthought. He wasn't in the pilot episode. He was supposed to appear in the second episode as a subsidiary character, but Rolfe saw something in McCallum and decided to expand his role.

Like the Bond films, "U.N.C.L.E." episodes were played tongue-in-cheek and were really more like spoofs—something that was probably lost on its youthful audiences. After receiving their instructions from Mr. Waverly, Solo and Kuryakin, armed with Walther P-38 pistols with shoulder stocks, scopes, silencers, and other additions (they cost about $1,100 each), would usually find an ordinary citizen who had become involved in that week's battle against the evil THRUSH (an acronymn that meant nothing). Every week, the two agents and their innocent citizen would get into trouble—tied up, hung out to dry, boiled alive—but in the end it would be the bad guys who would cry "UNCLE."

During its first year, "U.N.C.L.E." wasn't an immediate success. But NBC moved it to Monday nights, and in January, 1965, *Goldfinger* came out, which helped attract college kids to the show. Solo and Kuryakin

became teen idols. McCallum was short, blonde, and British, the latter being an especially desirable quality in Anglophiliac 1965. He wore a modified Beatle hairdo (he said he had been wearing his hair that way since 1956), and he usually eschewed wearing a tie in favor of a black turtleneck, which helped promote that piece of clothing as a staple of menswear.

And was he popular. When McCallum taped a segment of "Hullabaloo" (he also sang), it took four guards to free him from the audience as he left. He would be greeted at airports by signs saying such things as "Flush Thrush" and "All the Way With Illya K."

The PTA, however, didn't like the

The Man from U.N.C.L.E.— Agents Kuryakin (David McCallum, left) and Solo (Robert Vaughn, right) get orders from the boss (Leo G. Carroll).

show. In its national magazine, the group condemned "U.N.C.L.E." for "adding a mite to airways already polluted with extralegal violent action."

By 1968, however, spies and camp had glutted the tube, and the quality of "U.N.C.L.E." scripts deteriorated. In 1967, Felton debuted "The Girl from U.N.C.L.E.," with Stefanie Powers as Agent April Dancer, which was canceled after one season.

When "U.N.C.L.E." went off the air on January 15, 1968, it was replaced by another '60s classic: "Laugh-In." "U.N.C.L.E.," however, retained a huge following in reruns and still maintains a highly active fan club.

After "U.N.C.L.E.," Vaughn made a career out of being the "professional bad guy" in theatrical and TV films. In 1983, "The Return of the Man from U.N.C.L.E."—the 15 Years Later Affair—was aired, a tongue-in-cheek sequel. In the TV movie, Solo is asked: "How do you stay so young?" "Good makeup man," he replies. Both agents had retired: Solo had gone into computers; Illya into fashion. But even though they licked THRUSH once more, the joy had gone out of derring-do.

The world has become a more dangerous place since 1965, that's for sure. Acts of international terrorism have eclipsed the fantasy plots hatched by THRUSH. U.N.C.L.E.'s sophisticated devices have become ho-hum material in this post-Watergate age. And the elaborate precautions the agents needed to enter the secret U.N.C.L.E. headquarters are now used by half the office buildings in major American cities.

But maybe the Solo-Kuryakin team can be kept on retainer by the TV studios to teach a thing or two about wine, women, and the world to such macho pretenders as Lee Horsley, Tom Selleck, and Bruce Boxleitner.

McCallum on Illya

"I like Illya. I'd like to have him for a friend. But who knows if Illya has any friends? We're not doing a "Route 66" here with a couple of chums on the loose. We are totally individual. Napoleon Solo is obviously a swinger. But Illya is a quiet swinger. Nobody knows what Illya does when he goes home at night."

Vaughn on Solo

"I think the basic secret of Napoleon Solo's success is his detachment. He's enigmatic and mysterious. He isn't married. No one knows much about his personal life. Everyone secretly identifies with him because he leads such a dangerous and exciting life."

Some Memorable "U.N.C.L.E." Guest Spots

1. Sonny and Cher as a dress manufacturer's cutter and model become entangled in a spy plot that centers on a dress whose pattern contains a secret code!

I Spy—Scotty (Bill Cosby, left) and Kelly (Robert Culp, right) embark on another adventure.

2. Eddie Albert, before his "Green Acres" days, was Brother Love, the leader of a religious cult which masked a subversive group plotting to take over the world with a spectacular space achievement.

TV SPIES II: "U.N.C.L.E.'s" NIECES AND NEPHEWS

"MISSION: IMPOSSIBLE" (1966-73) concentrated on the technical aspects of espionage. In each episode, a group of secret agents, each an expert in a specialized field, would be presented with a problem—such as how to smuggle a political prisoner out of some foreign jail—which they would solve with their wits, gadgets, and guts. Most plots were tangled and confusing. If you looked away from the screen, you would miss something and then wonder just what was going on.

"MI" had one of TV's classic openings—right up there with the voice-overs from "Twilight Zone" and "Outer Limits." Leader Jim Phelps would enter an innocent-looking building and find a hidden package containing a tape. When he played the tape, this is what he'd hear: "Your mission, Jim, should you decide to accept it, is...As usual, should you or any member of your I.M. Force be captured or killed, the secretary will disavow any knowledge of your existence. This tape will self-destruct in five seconds." Five seconds later, indeed, the tape and recorder vanished in smoke and flame. Richard Nixon should have used such a tape.

FYI: Lalo Schifrin's memorable theme music is now played on the P.A. system in the Astrodome when an opposing team brings in a relief pitcher.

"THE AVENGERS" (1966-69) was the best-known British TV secret-agent series, famous for its black humor, stylized violence, and fantasy. It first aired in the U.K. in 1961, a year before the first Bond film, but it took the spy boom to make it internationally popular (it came to U.S. TV in 1966). Patrick MacNee played the debonair agent, John Steed, and his female companion was Mrs. Emma Peel (Diana Rigg), the widow of a test pilot. (She had replaced Honor Blackman, the Pussy Galore of *Goldfinger*, who was Steed's original British partner; before then, he actually had two male partners.) A satorially splendid pair, Steed wore three-piece suits and bowler hats; Mrs. Peel favored boots and leathers.

In March, 1968, Mrs. Peel found her lost husband, and Steed got a new partner, Tara King (Linda Thorson). They battled odd, warped geniuses, such as bizarre robots known as the Cybernauts, who planned to take over the world.

"SECRET AGENT" (1965-66) (originally known in the U.K. as "Dangerman") was another British import boosted by the spy boom. It began in England in 1960 as a half-hour show (Drake, the main character, then worked for NATO), but became a one-hour show in 1965. Patrick McGoohan played John Drake, a special security agent working for the British government. McGoohan insisted that Drake should

Get Smart— "Would you believe" that Maxwell Smart (Don Adams) had a phone in his shoe twenty years before cellular phones became popular?

never kill (he rarely carried a gun) or have immoral relationships. The show was also known for Johnny Rivers' hip rendering of its theme song, "Secret Agent Man" ("swinging on the Riviera one day, sleeping in a Bombay alley the next day").

"I SPY" (1965-68) was notable for featuring a black in a (noncomedic) lead role for the first time. Bill Cosby (Alexander Scott, or "Scotty") was teamed with Robert Culp (Kelly Robinson) as a pair of globe-trotting undercover agents, disguised as a tennis pro and his trainer. This casual pair had witty, clever dialogue (Kelly was a former Princeton law student who had played on two Davis Cup teams; Scotty was a Temple grad and Rhodes Scholar and was multilingual), and an obviously expensive production budget. Many shows were shot on exotic foreign locations.

"HONEY WEST" (1965-66), starring Anne Francis, was kind of an American version of *Modesty Blaise*, although it was actually a spinoff from "Burke's Law." Honey had inherited the family detective business from her late father, as well as her bumbling partner, John Bolt. She studied judo and karate and had an arsenal that included a lipstick case that became a radio transmitter. She also had a pet ocelot named Bruce.

"GET SMART" (1965-70) was a true '60s classic which spawned two expressions that have become part of the American vocabulary: "Sorry about that, chief" and "Would you believe." "Get Smart" was the classic spoof of spy shows, which is not surprising since it was co-created by Mel Brooks and Buck Henry. Don Adams was bumbling Agent 86, Maxwell Smart; Barbara Feldon (previously seen cooing on a tiger-skin rug in a hairdressing commercial) was sexy agent 99. They worked for C.O.N.T.R.O.L., the good guys, and they fought K.A.O.S., the bad guys. Max's weapons included a shoe-telephone that like a real-life pay phone rarely worked. Agents 86 and 99 got married in 1968 and had little twin secret agents in 1969. In 1980, Adams tried the comeback, TV-movie trip (*The Return of Maxwell Smart* and *The Nude Bomb*) but flopped.

Cool moments: Johnny Carson in a cameo role as a conductor on the Orient Express; the agents taking on a Nehru-suited fiend called the Groovy Guru.

"THE WILD WILD WEST" (1965-70) mated the Western and spy genres. President Grant's two favorite Secret Service agents, Jim West (Robert Conrad) and Artemus Gordon (Ross Martin), acted as if James Bond had lived in Tombstone, not London. West had gimmicks that included a derringer that shot a miniature grappling hook with a wire attached. The show also featured a gallery of truly bizarre villains.

SPY STUFF QUIZ

1. What was the name of the tailor shop which hid the U.N.C.L.E. headquarters?
2. Name five original members of the Impossible Missions Force.
3. What was the Cone of Silence?
4. Diminutive actor Michael Dunn played villains on two '60s spy shows. Name the characters and shows.
5. What was the name of the robot on "Get Smart"?

ANSWERS

1. DelFlorio's
2. Leader Daniel Briggs (Steven Hill);

Cinnamon Carter (Barbara Bain); Rollin Hand (Martin Landau); Barney Collier (Greg Morris); and Willie Armitage (Peter Lupus)

3. A plastic cone that was placed over the heads of two C.O.N.T.R.O.L. agents when they had to communciate top-secret stuff to each other. The problem was, however, that neither of them could hear the other.

4. Dr. Miguelito Loveless on "The Wild Wild West" and Mr. Big on "Get Smart"

5. Hymie

Super Duper Spy Quiz Bonus

What was the real name of Agent 99?
Answer: Susan Hilton

On the Road and on the Run

A decade before the running boom hit, several Americans knew what the joy of running was all about. The man on the run was a popular theme in mid-'60s TV: witness "The Fugitive," "Run for Your Life," "Run Buddy Run," "Route 66," "Branded," and "A Man Called Shenandoah."

"The Fugitive" (1963-67) was the frontrunner. Dr. Richard Kimble (David Janssen) had been accused, tried, convicted, and sentenced for murdering his wife, a crime he claimed he didn't commit. Kimble was being taken by Lieutenant Philip Gerard (Barry Morse) to prison to be executed. Suddenly, the train in which they were traveling was derailed, and Gerard was knocked unconscious. Kimble escaped and then ran for four seasons.

Every Tuesday night he was chased by Gerard while he himself went looking for the one-armed man who he swore killed his wife. Morse probably had one of the most frustrating jobs on '60s TV. Once, he was accosted in the streets by a distraught citizen who demanded: "Why don't you leave that nice man alone?"

In every episode, Kimble worked at an odd job (a custodian in a private boy's club, a self-service laundryman), often assuming a new identity. He always seemed to be on the verge of being captured by Gerard. But Kimble remained one step ahead of him, usually because he was aided by sympathetic townspeople.

The show's final episode on August 29, 1967 had one of the highest viewerships in TV history (the highest until the 1980 "Dallas" episode in

The Fugitive—Richard Kimble (David Janssen) rescues a woman (Barbara Rush) who has been temporarily blinded in a bus accident. Surprise! It's the wife of his nemesis, the dreaded Lieutenant Gerard.

which the identity of J.R. Ewing's would-be killer was revealed)—a 72 share.

In this episode, Kimble learned that the one-armed man had been captured in Los Angeles, and so he surrendered. But shortly thereafter, the one-armed man escaped. Kimble convinced Gerard to let him track the man down. Kimble tracked him to a deserted amusement park where a dramatic chase scene took place. Kimble and the one-armed man cornered each other on top of a tower. The one-armed man admitted the killing just as he was about to toss Kimble off the tower. But Gerard, who had pursued Kimble to the park, realized he had been wrong about Kimble. The detective then shot the one-armed man, who plunged to his death before he could be captured.

It's too bad this final scene didn't match the story Janssen had made up for pesky reporters who would always ask for details prior to the final broadcast: "Kimble, cleared of the murder, retires to a desert island to recuperate from his ordeal. At sunset he takes a swim. Just before plunging into the surf, he pauses, unscrews his wooden arm and tosses it in the sand. Fade out..."

"The Fugitive" was always a popular and well-written show, winning an Emmy for Outstanding Dramatic Series in 1965. The plot, some said, had similarities to the celebrated case of Dr. Sam Sheppard, who was accused of murdering his wife, not to mention Victor Hugo's classic *Les Miserables*.

The show's creator, Roy Huggins (who also created "77 Sunset Strip" and "Maverick"), was attracted to the rootless freedom of the old frontier where the fictional hero could roam freely without responsibility. Some said Kimble appealed to the housebound male who wished to be free of all responsibilities. ("Willed irresponsibility without a concomitant sense of guilt," said Huggins.) Still others claimed "The Fugitive" symbolized the loneliness we felt in an increasingly alienating society.

"The Fugitive" also had much international appeal. A top German magazine proposed to Janssen's agents that he wander Berlin in disguise as part of a "contest" in which readers would track down "Der Fluchtling" for prizes. In Spain, while attending a bullfight, "El Fugitivo" received *olés* louder than those for either the matador or the bull.

Little-known fact: William Conrad, who would play rotund detective "Cannon" in the '70s, was the off-camera narrator on "The Fugitive."

Huggins also created "Run for Your Life" (1965-68). Also on the run was Paul Bryan (Ben Gazzara), a successful, 35-year-old lawyer with an incurable disease. He closed down his law practice and started traveling around the world, hoping to cram a lifetime of adventure and excitement into what time he had left. He visited all sorts of exotic locations and met many interesting people. The show was on for three years, even though Bryan was supposed to be dead after two.

"The Fugitive" also spawned a short-lived comedy about a man on the run, "Run Buddy Run" (1966-67). Buddy was a timid accountant. His problem: While lolling in a Turkish bath, he accidentally overheard mobsters discussing a "hit." The thugs (led by Mr. D, played by Bruce Gordon—Frank Nitti on "The Untouchables") sensed that Buddy (Jack Sheldon) now knew the code phrase for the rub-out and had to be rubbed out himself. But it wasn't Mr. D that did in this show; humor was at a premium and "Run Buddy Run" only lasted half a season before being chased off the air.

A similar theme could be found on "Branded" which gave a Western twist to the Fugitive. (See page 94 for more on "Branded.")

As Kimble, battered suitcase in hand, stuck out his thumb to hitchhike, one of the cars which might have picked him up was a 1960 Corvette. In the front seat were its drivers, Tod Stiles (Martin Milner) and Buz Murdock (George Maharis), who cruised along that great American highway, Route 66. Tod and Buz got into a variety of romantic, threatening, and/or exhilarating situations.

"Route 66" also had one of TV's most famous theme songs, coolly composed by Nelson Riddle. Tod and Buz never encountered Kimble, but they did meet up with the likes of Alan Alda ("Soda Pop and Paper Flags," May 31, 1963) and Robert Redford ("First Class Mouliak," October 20, 1961). Tod and his new partner, Linc (Glenn Corbett) finally took the off-ramp in 1964.

The last '60s road show, "Then Came Bronson," came out two months after *Easy Rider* was released. "Bronson" featured a countercultural-type motorcyclist (Michael Parks) who traveled around the countryside trying to figure out the meaning of it all. "Bronson" is best known for having the least amount of dialogue in a one-hour show.

SEVEN ALIASES USED BY RICHARD KIMBLE

1. Jim Lincoln
2. Jim Fowler
3. Jim Russell
4. Jim Wallace
5. Jim Owen
6. Jim McGuire
7. Jim Corbin

TV Doctors

There have been TV doctors before and there have been TV doctors since— but during the '60s was when they operated the best. Duking it out were the yin and yang of the video M.D.'s: ABC's "Ben Casey" and NBC's "Dr. Kildare."

Ben Casey (Vincent Edwards) was a method-actor medic, a surly, aggressive neurosurgeon battling the medical establishment, while James Kildare (Richard Chamberlain) was a naive, wholesome intern. Both had mentors guiding their lives. Casey was checked by Dr. Zorba (Sam Jaffe), who looked like Ben-Gurion and acted as if he should have been running a pants-pressing store on Flatbush Avenue. Kildare was monitored by the stern Dr. Leonard Gillespie (Raymond Massey). Both young doctors had legions of female fans.

"Ben Casey," that "virtuoso of the scalpel and master of psychiatric insight," as *Variety* put it, made its debut in October, 1961. *The New York Times* reviewer immediately sued for malpractice: "There is a calculated element of shock in this new series that is extreme and unnecessary. Dr. Casey needs a quick tranquilizer."

Was he ever wrong. The show, a Bing Crosby production, became one of the most popular programs on ABC, then the poor-cousin third network desperately striving for respectability. "Kildare" led the ratings in 1961-62, but Casey vaulted ahead during the next season.

"Ben Casey" was created by writer-producer, James Moser, who had done the realistic '50s medical drama, "Medic" with Richard Boone. His new series, originally called "The Medicine Man," was bought on the strength of the concept, not the presence of Edwards. But it would be the 31-year-old, Brooklyn-born Vincento Eduardo Zoino—who previously had made twenty-two forgettable movies—who gave the show its strength.

"Am I going to die, doc?" the patient-of-the-week would ask Casey. Casey would respond in mumbling monosyllables, often with barely concealed hostility, as if to say, if one cure didn't work, well, there was always lobotomy. "It's not exactly for happy people, looking for diversions" said New York's *Herald Tribune*.

However, serious viewers were attracted to the show because of its lean, well-written scripts, often dealing with controversial subjects. Among the memorable episodes: Kim Stanley as a woman lawyer with a heroin habit; Sammy Davis, Jr. as a black, taunted as an Uncle Tom by a black Muslim; Jerry Lewis as an incompetent surgeon.

In one of the most controversial episodes, Shelley Winters played a hospital nurse who had an affair with an unmarried resident physician and became pregnant. When Casey learns the nurse has toxemia, which could threaten her life and unborn child, he urges a medical abortion. She refuses. The nurse also declines Casey's offer to arrange for an adoption. The episode had no real resolution; it ended with a fade-out of a nurse handing the newborn to its mother.

Casey's following was largely female. At New York's St. Vincent Hospital, nurses had their lights-out curfew extended from 10:30 to 11:00, so that they could watch him.

However, there were those who took the show less seriously. Comedians began making Ben Casey jokes. A hit record parody was released called "Ben Crazy." Casey gowns for youngsters were sold in dime stores.

"Ben Casey" finally checked out in 1966. Edwards never followed up his "Ben Casey" success. In 1970, he starred in the title role of "Matt Lincoln," a series about a hip psychiatrist, which flopped. During the '70s, he directed episodes of TV shows like "Fantasy Island" and "Battlestar Galactica." In the '80s, he appeared in such film bombs as *The Seduction* and *Deal of the Century*.

If Ben was too mean for your tastes, there was always "Dr. Kildare," which made its debut a month earlier, in September, 1961. This actually wasn't a new idea; "Dr. Kildare" had been a radio and movie staple during the 1940s. Lew Ayres, the original Kildare, once showed up as a guest patient in a "Ben Casey" episode—a supreme irony!

The show's producer, Norman Felton, gave Raymond Massey and Richard Chamberlain a copy of The *Book of Health*, a large medical encyclopedia by two doctors from the University of Texas. They pored over the book, acquiring much of the needed information. Chamberlain modeled Kildare on Dr. George Andros of Los Angeles County General Hospital, who was the show's technical consultant. Dr. Andros' advice: "Think sterile! Never touch anything with your hands except your tools and your patient. If your brow sweats, let the nurse mop it. If your nose itches, let the nurse scratch it."

James Franciscus was originally set to play Kildare but was committed to another show. (He later starred as the Kildare-like high-school teacher "Mr. Novak.") Instead, the role went to Chamberlain, a 27-year-old MGM contract actor, whose experience had been limited to bit roles. Chamberlain was so unknown that during the first year the series was shot, studio guards wouldn't let him through the gates without phoning the front office to ask about his identity.

Doctor Kildare (Richard Chamberlain).

Chamberlain became an instant heartthrob with teenage girls (Casey had appealed to slightly older women). His fan mail, an estimated 12,000 letters a week, exceeded that of any other MGM star, including Clark Gable. He also found himself endorsing unusual products such as the "Dr. Kildare pure chocolate candy bar," whose wrapper featured a picture of a grinning Dr. Kildare in his surgical whites. Boasted the manufacturer: "It's the first time in history that a photo of an actual person appears on candy!"

"Dr. Kildare" was soapier than "Casey," although it also tackled controversial issues such as euthanasia and unscrupulous funeral directors. The show went through some changes. By the third season, Kildare had been promoted to resident. In 1965, as it became more like a soap opera, "Kildare" was converted into a twice-a-week serial like "Peyton Place." The formula didn't work, and "Kildare," like "Casey," made his final house call in 1966.

Unlike Edwards, Chamberlain's career wasn't hampered by his Kildare role. He has gone on to become one of the industry's leading TV and movie actors.

The 1962-63 season saw a spate of other medical shows hoping to ride the success of Casey and Kildare: "The Nurses," "The Eleventh Hour," about psychiatrists, and "Don't Call Me Charlie," a forgettable comedy about a veterinarian. None of these shows became popular.

The doctor shows returned in 1969 with "Medical Center" and "Marcus Welby, M.D." Welby reversed the Kildare concept: the star was the mentor-figure, the kindly Dr. Welby (Robert Young) who had to contend with his younger charge, Dr. Steven Kiley (James Brolin), a hipper, more updated version of Kildare. "Medical Center" also paired a mentor-student team—Dr. Paul Lochner (James Daly) and Dr. Joe Gannon (Chad Everett). When it went off the air in 1976, "Medical Center" had become the longest-running medical show in TV history.

HOW THEY COMPARED: THE RATINGS BATTLE BETWEEN BEN CASEY AND DR. KILDARE

October 1961-April 1962: Kildare (9), Casey (18)

October 1962-April 1963: Casey (7), Kildare (11)

October 1963-April 1964: Kildare (19), Casey (out of top 25)

AN INTERVIEW WITH VINCE EDWARDS

Question: Do you ever think of bringing "Ben Casey" back?

Edwards: Every few years somebody revives the idea of doing "Casey." One of these days it will go forward. All the hit shows are medical shows — "M*A*S*H," "Trapper John," "St. Elsewhere."

I think we would do Casey now as a disillusioned idealist, fighting the business of medicine. When he first came out, he was fighting the bureaucracy. Then he learned all there is to learn. Now he's fighting some 30-year-old guy out of financial school who says "We gotta move those beds, we gotta make some money." Kind of be an interesting premise since medical costs have gone through the roof...it's the old greed syndrome.

Ben Casey (Vince Edwards) with guest star Shelley Winters.

Today doctors are more concerned with billing and getting their apartment units than with curing. Every doctor I know looks for investments—they all have extra money.

Question: Wasn't Casey making a good buck?

Edwards: Well, he was the idealist fighting the bureaucracy. His primary concern wasn't money; now he's back in private practice. Now he's a disillusioned idealist like most of the kids out of the '60s are today.

Question: Did you have a role model for Casey?

Edwards: Yes. Dr. Max Warner, who was head of neurosurgery at L.A. County General a staccato, no-nonsense dour kind of guy. I would say that part of his personality really got into the role. He's since gone into psychiatry...I knew there was something strange about him when he used to have a map on his wall with all the fires in L.A., and he put flags on it. He was an avid fire watcher. I knew he was not long for neurosurgery.

Question: What caused that reaction to the show?

Edwards: Look at the times, the superhero, a lot of anxiety, anguish, people disappointed with the system, the bureaucracy. Here's a guy, an antihero type, a no-nonsense non-stereotypical-looking doctor, who looked more like a truckdriver. Casey was a good role model for people who were frustrated. Here's a guy who wants to fight the system. You were coming out of the '50s and everything was pretty orderly. He was certainly different than the old "Dr. Kildare" types we had seen.

Question: How did you react to the fans' adulation?

Edwards: I was kind of surprised, but never got to see a lot of it. We would work twelve to fourteen hours a day, five to six days a week. I never left the soundstage. I'd hear about it, but I was too tired.

Question: You were played up a lot as being similar to Casey—gruff, difficult to get along with.

Edwards: There was a bit of me in Casey, but the writers took that ball, ran with it, and made it into a cliché. But people like that kind of stuff. They like to think Sly Stallone goes around in boxer shorts all day, punching guys out. They think he's really Rocky.

Question: What about your rivalry with Richard Chamberlain as Dr. Kildare?

Edwards: It was press-agent rivalry, but it was a healthy rivalry. When I played nightclubs, he came down and saw me a couple of times. He's a nice fellow. I'm happy for his career and the way it's been going.

Question: How about your career? Have you been hamstrung by the role?

Edwards: It's tough. Its a double-edged sword. Sometimes, I think I was turned down for roles because people thought of me only as Casey. I wanted the Sonny role in *The Godfather* very badly. I think I fired my agent over that one. But I'd do it again now for obvious reasons. The financial rewards are also gigantic, and I think we could say a lot. Very few good solid characters on TV. Over the last twenty years I could name for you on one hand the solid characters on TV—Casey was, Columbo, Eliot Ness, Kojak—can't think of too many more who are bigger than their show. Maybe Mr. T is an example of someone who is bigger than the show, a bigger-than-life character. He's one of the few real stars. TV doesn't look for personalities anymore.

TV Cops

In the '60s, TV cops plied Hawaiian beaches, cruised the freeways of L.A., and pounded the hot asphalt of Manhattan. They were young and blonde, middle-aged and crippled, icy cool and Nova hot. They sported tough, virile names like Joe Friday and Joe Mannix.

But no matter where they worked, what they looked like or what their names were, the cop—and his first cousin, the private eye—was always the Good Guy. None of this "Serpico" antihero stuff, because in the end, our cop always won. He was tough and fair, quite unlike the real world of the '60s, where many people's attitudes toward law enforcers had changed from "the policeman is your friend" to "off the pigs."

Except for a brief period in the mid-'60s when James Bond inspired a rash of law-enforcers relying on gimmicks and gadgets to be in favor, TV cops in the '60s relied on what all cops have always relied on—their guns, guts, fists, and wits. They were rarely as glamorous as Bond, but in their own ways were just as cool and efficient. They got the job done.

Let's start with the most efficient of them all—Eliot Ness. "The Untouchables" (1959-63), was based on the real-life exploits of Ness (Robert Stack) and his squad of incorruptable Treasury agents in Prohibition-era Chicago. Van Heflin and Van Johnson were producer Quinn Martin's original choices for Ness.

Dragnet— Dum-da-dum-dum: Jack Webb as Joe Friday wanting to know just the facts

Stack only got the role when the others were unavailable. The drama first appeared in 1958 as two one-hour shows on the "Desilu Playhouse"; the following year it became a regular series, produced by Quinn Martin ("The Fugitive").

Ness and his boys wore double-breasted suits and fedoras and spoke in staccato bursts as they shot their way into breweries and speakeasies, confronting such hoods as "Greasy Thumb" Jake Gusik, Al Capone, and the meanest meanie of 'em all, Frank Nitti.

Guns blazed, cars crashed, and bodies dropped. There were probably more dead bodies littering the streets of Chicago than on all other detective series combined. Not surprisingly, educators condemned the show as the epitome of TV violence. The show also caught flack from Italo-American groups who charged that it consistently used Italian-surnamed gangsters. The anti-defamation effort was successful (along the way, the show's sponsor found his product disappearing en route to sales points or never leaving warehouses), and after 1961, a veritable U.N. of baddies was used,

including a Russian-speaking thug named Joe Vodka!

Until the late '50s and through the early '60s, most TV cops had been cut from the traditional Hammett-Chandler seedy-side-of-town, gumshoe mold. But when Warner Brothers, looking to expand its TV properties beyond Westerns, wanted to create detective series, they revised the formula. They introduced the team/locale concept. The team: an experienced pair of handsome men, with a younger hanger-on and a sexy, often airheaded woman hanging around. The locale: glamorous and exotic. The plots: nothing special.

"77 Sunset Strip" (1958-64) was the first, using as its setting, Hollywood, or more specifically, the legendary Sunset Strip (a place, according to the show's theme song, where you'll meet the most exciting people, including the highbrow and the hipster, the starlet and the phony tipster). At No. 77 worked two private eyes, Stu Bailey (Efrem Zimbalist, Jr.) and Jeff Spencer (Roger Smith), who were former government agents. They were good-looking but rather unflamboyant. The glamour of Holywood was what was supposed to sell the show.

But what really sold "77 Sunset Strip" was the unexpected popularity of a minor character, Gerald Lloyd Kookson III (Edd Byrnes), a jive-talking parking-lot attendant better known as "Kookie." He originally played a menacing juvenile delinquent whose role wasn't supposed to be a recurring one, but exuberant reaction from teenage girls forced Warner to make him a regular. He became more than a regular: he became a bona fide celebrity, and even cut a hit record (a duet with Connie Stevens), "Kookie, Kookie, Lend Me Your Comb." In later seasons, he was booted upstairs to become a full-fledged private eye.

The Mod Squad—Cops go hip.

"77 Sunset Strip" spurred Warner to create other exotically located, albeit less-successful private-eye shows. "Bourbon Street Beat" (set in the French Quarter of New Orleans) and "Surfside Six" (a trio of detectives, including Troy Donahue, working out of a houseboat in Miami) bombed. "Hawaiian Eye," which featured opening shots of its stars Robert Conrad, Anthony Eisley, and Connie Stevens, on surfboards, was more successful. (Try and catch a 1962 episode "Total Eclipse" in which a very young Jack Nicholson plays a rage-crazed drunk.)

There was much cross-pollination between the three: Richard Long, after flopping on Bourbon Street, became a member of the team; "77 Sunset Strip's" Stu Bailey occasionally left the mainland to drop in on "Hawaiian Eye"; and Donahue showed up on all three shows.

While these four had glamour to sell, others specialized in emphasizing grit. Real-life police work was the specialty of "Naked City" ("There are 8 million stories," etc.) The series, based on a 1948 film, drew its power from being actually filmed on the streets of New York. "Naked City" was the forerunner of "N.Y.P.D.," an occasionally innovative series (using hand-held cameras and cinema verité techniques) that ran from 1967 to 1969.

But the king of realistic TV cops was Jack Webb's Sergeant Joe Friday of "Dragnet," a mainstay of '50s TV, which encored in 1967. "Dragnet" 1967 was basically "Dragnet" as it played in the '50s: Just the facts ma'am. It was full of unglamorous, plodding, meticulous police work torn from the actual files of the Los Angeles Police Department. Oh, there were some differences—Sergeant Friday had a new sidekick, Bill Gannon (Harry Morgan), the new show was in color, and Webb jazzed it up with doses of contemporary reality like drugs and hippies. (In the opening episode, for instance, Friday and Gannon took on an LSD user named "Blue Boy.") Webb was so square he was hip.

Realism was also the byword of "The FBI," which combined the talents of two old detective show hands—producer Quinn Martin and actor Efrem Zimbalist. Zimbalist as Agent Erskine was the archetypical FBI agent and the show had the blessing of FBI boss, J. Edgar Hoover, who allowed some background scenes to be filmed at FBI headquarters in Washington, D.C. It ran until 1974, by which time the FBI itself had lost much of its credibility.

As noted earlier, during the late '60s, cops had begun losing credibility with kids. So how do you get the young audience to dig again that the policeman is your friend? You want relevance? You want a show that would bring to life such hype as "The police don't understand the now generation, and the now generation doesn't dig the fuzz. The solution: Find some swinging young people who live the beat scene. And get them to work for the cops." Yep. This was ABC's ad campaign for "The Mod Squad," a 1968 cop show produced by Aaron Spelling and Danny Thomas. The show's name, by the way, was lifted from a "Dragnet" episode about a gang of young shoplifters.

The young swingers were Pete, from a wealthy, white family, who was busted for stealing a car; Julie, a poor white from a broken home, who had been busted for vagrancy; and Linc, a militant ghetto black busted during a race riot. They were given another chance by their boss, Captain Greer, who let them work undercover.

"The Mod Squad" lasted until 1973. They came back in 1979 in a TV movie, and ABC even dusted off the

77 Sunset Strip—A historic moment: Kookie (Ed Byrnes, right) turns over his comb (symbol of his "coolness") to his successor as parking-lot attendant, J.R. Hale (Robert Logan).

concept in 1983 with "The Renegades," a bomb about another group of hip undercover cops. In deference to affirmative action, this team had Oriental and Hispanic members.

The late '60s saw the birth of four more important series: "Mannix" (which rivaled "The Untouchables" for violence); "Hawaii Five-0" (which went on to become the longest-running detective show in TV history); "Ironside" (Raymond Burr as a crippled former chief of San Francisco detectives, which spawned several '70s shows featuring handicapped heroes such as overweight "Cannon" and blind "Longstreet"); and Jack Webb's "Adam 12." These carried the detective shows into the '70s—a decade where the genre had a stunning rebirth.

Car 54, Where Are You?— There's a hold-up in the Bronx and these two characters are out to stop it: Toody (Joe E. Ross, right) and Muldoon (Fred Gwynne). "Oooh! Ooooh!"

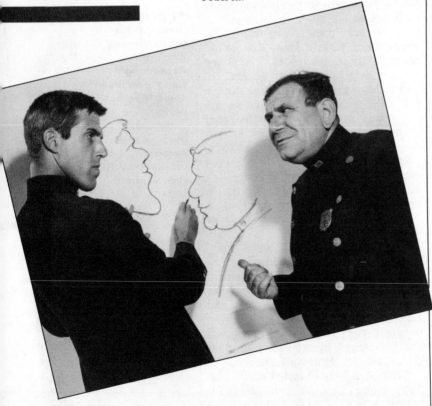

"CAR 54, WHERE ARE YOU?"

In the '60s you could even make fun of cops. One of TV's classic comedy shows was "Car 54, Where Are You?", which ran on NBC from 1961 to 1963. This show took place and was filmed in the South Bronx, now considered "Fort Apache," but then still a lower middle-class neighborhood.

The show was created by Nat Hiken (who created "Sgt. Bilko") and featured one of the former Bilko gang, Joe E. Ross, as the short, bumbling, dimwitted Officer Gunther Toody, who punctuated his gravelly voice with frequent excitable "ooh-oohs." His partner—talk about odd couples—was, the reserved, almost morose six-foot, seven-inch Officer Francis Muldoon, played by Fred Gwynne. Muldoon lived with his mother, Toody with his shrewish wife Lucille, and domestic nonsense often became embroiled with police work.

Also on hand were Paul Reed as Captain Block and Al Lewis as Leo Schnauzer. Charlotte Rae played Schnauzer's wife, Sylvia. Much of the humor took place in the locker room of the (fictional) 53rd precinct. Both Gwynne and Lewis later went on to "The Munsters"; Ross also got a facelift in his next series as a caveman in the silly and short-lived series "It's about Time."

The team clicked. In real life, Ross and Gwynne were also quite an odd couple. In an NBC press release from July, 1962, Ross explained how the pair got along: "We can always get along. Maybe that is why we get along—I never argue with Fred's theories about Aristotle, and he never argues with my statements about which night spot has the prettiest chorus girls.

"You know, Fred graduated from Harvard. I never finished high school. Fred has published three books. I can't honestly say I've read three. Fred started in Shakespeare at the Brattle Theater in Cambridge. I started in burlesque."

The show didn't do much for the morale of real cops. Cop cars unfortunately numbered 54 were jeered. One police force even eliminated its patrol car with the number 54.

The show's patrol cars were painted red and white to distinguish them from real

N.Y.P.D. cars that might have been cruising the Bronx at the same time the show was filming. Since the show was aired in black and white, the car looked like the genuine item.

The Westerns

During the '60s there were so many Westerns featuring characters with human-relations problems it's surprising that no one came up with the idea for a series called "Frontier Freudian," where all of them could be treated.

This genre—the so-called "Adult Western"—had already been established in the '50s with "Gunsmoke." For the first time, characters who had real human feelings and conflicts were presented in a Western setting. And now that good guys no longer necessarily wore white, Westerns didn't necessarily have to be shown only on Saturday mornings. "Gunsmoke" inspired a slew of adult Westerns in the late '50s. By 1959, thirty-two Western series were on TV; all of the top three and five of the top ten series were Westerns.

By 1963, most of the crop of '50s Westerns had been put out to pasture, including "Maverick," "Wanted Dead or Alive," "The Rifleman," "Bat Masterson," "Have Gun Will Travel," "The Lawman," "Cheyenne," "Tales of Wells Fargo," "The Life and Legend of Wyatt Earp," "Dick Powell's Zane Grey Theater," "Laramie," and "The Deputy."

The survivors included "Wagon Train" and "Rawhide," both of which lasted into the mid-'60s, and the most popular shows of 'em all— "Gunsmoke" (which survived until 1975) and "Bonanza" (which signed off in 1973). "Gunsmoke" had a head start (it had been a radio show for many years, before it debuted on TV in 1955), but it was "Bonanza" that was clearly *the* '60s Western.

"Bonanza," introduced by its twanging theme music and stentorian voice announcing "Bow-nan-za!," was set near Virginia City, Nevada during the Civil War, soon after the discovery of the Comstock Silver Lode. It told the story of a wealthy family of ranchers led by patriarch Ben Cartwright (Lorne Greene), a widower, father of three sons, and proprietor of the 1,000-mile square Ponderosa Ranch.

Like "Gunsmoke," "Bonanza" wasn't a traditional Western. It relied more on the relationships between the principals and stories of characters played by guest stars than it did on

The cast of Gunsmoke, the longest-running Western in the history of TV: James Arness (rear, left) as Marshal Matt Dillon, Milburn Stone (seated, left) as Doc Adams, Amanda Blake as Kitty Russell and Ken Curtis (top, right) as Festus Haggen.

shoot-em-ups. It was part soap opera, part horse opera, and it worked.

"My Three Sons" on a ranch instead of a ranch house, "Bonanza" wasn't. Each of Ben's three sons had been borne by a different wife, none of whom was still living. Adam (Pernell Roberts), the oldest, and the heir apparent, was the most introspective; Hoss (Dan Blocker), the middle son, was huge (six-four, 300 lbs.), gentle and dimwitted. Little Joe (Michael Landon) was the youngest, the most hotheaded, and the most inclined to become involved with a member of the opposite sex—a development that Papa Cartwright and the Brothers would immedialtely halt (now there's a case for "Frontier Freudian"!)

Making its debut on Saturdays in 1959, "Bonanza" started slowly, but after moving in 1961 to its familiar Sunday night slot, it became second only to "Gunsmoke" as the longest-running, successful Western in TV history. "Bonanza" was Number 1 from 1964-67, leaving "The Beverly Hillbillies," "Gomer Pyle," and "Bewitched" behind.

The show survived Roberts' exit in 1965 and Blocker's death in 1972, but it didn't survive a schedule switch to Tuesday nights; the show finally rode off for good in 1973.

"Bonanza" influenced the creation of two less-successful "family" Westerns. "The Big Valley" (1965-69), set in the Barkley ranch in California's San Joaquin Valley in the 1870s, had its "Ma Cartwright" in Victoria Barkley (Barbara Stanwyck), and it also had a bigger family: four sons and a daughter, which included Lee Majors and Linda Evans. Meanwhile, "The High Chaparral" (1967-71), also produced by David Dortort, "Bonanza's" producer, focused on the efforts of two families who were landowners in the heart of the Indian-dominated Arizona territory.

While most of the dozens of Westerns which aired during the '60s were uninspired, one that stood out was "The Virginian," which made its debut in 1962. It was the first 90-minute Western, and became one of the decade's most successful programs. James Drury played the title role, the mysterious antihero known only as "The Virginian," the foreman of the Shiloh Ranch in Medicine Bow, Wyoming, in the 1890s. Lee J. Cobb had a key role as Judge Garth, owner of the huge ranch. Its theme showed how the Western way of life was being undermined by progress from the East. In scope, it was not unlike a TV movie (five years before the TV-movie concept was created).

Westerns proved to be a suitable vehicle for one of the key themes of mid-'60s TV—the story of the introspective loner, modeled after the successful "Fugitive." Such series seemed to fit the national mood of introspection after JFK's assassination.

The most obvious "Fugitive" knockoff was "Branded," which featured Chuck Connors as a kind of a sagebrush Kimble. He played Jason McCord, an Army officer wrongfully court-martialed and then discharged, after being accused of cowardice at the Battle of Bitter Creek, where he was the only survivor. He roamed the West looking for the men who framed him. The problem was that he'd always run into someone who knew someone who was killed at Bitter Creek.

In the same vein was "A Man Called Shenandoah," starring Robert Horton as an amnesiac who roamed the West, and Rod Serling's "The Loner," a Western whose theme was just a tad too premature. It featured Lloyd Bridges as a disillusioned ex-

Union officer who wandered the frontier, looking for something to give meaning to his life. He would have been a great character in a score of late '60s to early '70s counterculture-type films.

In 1966, Westerns had a brief renaissance. Six new shows were introduced—"Iron Horse," "The Rounders," "Shane," "The Road West," "The Monroes," and "The Hero"—and six new flops were created. Two other late-'60s flops, however, were noteworthy only because of their controversial, offbeat themes. Though both "Custer" and "The Outcasts" were set in the Old West, both had a distinctive late-'60s feel about them.

"Custer" (1967) tried to humanize the legendary General Custer—a true '60s sensibility that no one is totally evil. But the public was in no mood just then for reverse mythmaking, and "Custer" was off the air by December, 1967.

Nineteen sixty-eight's violent, forgotten "Outcasts" featured an odd couple—Earl, a white aristocrat turned gunman (Don Murray) and Jemal (Otis Young), a freed black slave turned bounty hunter, who formed an uneasy alliance. (The theme was a knockoff of the Sidney Poitier-Tony Curtis film *The Defiant Ones*.) They hated each other and were bound together only by their common goal of making money by tracking down wanted criminals.

Said Earl to Jemal as they prepared to ambush a killer in the dark: "Well, you have a natural advantage. Don't you, boy?...Unless of course you smile." Too realistic, perhaps? You didn't hear Scotty and Kelly talk like that on "I Spy"; there was plenty of real-life racial tension in 1968, and the viewers didn't want to be reminded that it existed 100 years ago. It would take Archie Bunker three years

later to defang such bigotry.

By the '70s, the old-fashioned Western was in decline. Ironically, when "Gunsmoke" left the air in 1975, it was the only Western on the air. We seem to have lost our infatuation with the old Western. Now it's corporate shoot-em-outs in the Sun Belt ("Dynasty," "Knots Landing," and "Dallas") that have captured our imaginations.

PICKINGS FROM THE PONDEROSA

"We are anti-Momism. We have no brats who talk like Leonard Bernstein. We are against the phony West. Our men swear allegiance not to the silver, but to the land."—producer David Dortort.

"When you get right down to it, the strongest attachments are between men —fathers, brothers. It all helps to take a Western out of the 'yup' and 'nope' kind of thing."—Michael Landon.

BONANZA BITS

- By 1964, "Bonanza" was being aired in forty-nine countries, including Saudi Arabia, Cyprus and Thailand.
- The Ponderosa never existed; the show was filmed on Stage 16 of Paramount studios.
- "Bonanza" was the first Western to be televised in color. NBC's top management had decided it wanted a big color series (which would also sell color sets, manufactured by NBC's parent company, RCA).
- Hoss' real name was Eric. Hoss is Norwegian for "good luck." He was the son of Ben's second wife, Inger, who was of Scandinavian extraction.

TV Lawyers

My father, the lawyer, says he didn't watch those marvelous lawyer shows during the '60s. "They weren't real," said the man who preferred watching such shows as "Star Trek" and "The Twilight Zone." "They wrapped up things too easily and had too many mistakes in them."

That certainly was true of the king of lawyer shows, "Perry Mason," TV's most successful and well-remembered lawyer series, starring a dour Raymond Burr as the defense attorney who never lost a case. Orginally a series of novels by Erle Stanley Gardner, then a radio series, "Perry Mason" moved to the tube in 1957 and stayed until 1966.

Mason was also part sleuth who stitched together mysteries with the assistance of Paul Drake, his private investigator, and Della Street, his private secretary. Each episode had a certain sameness: A murder took place; D.A. Burger and his investigator, Lieutenant Tragg, would build what they thought was an airtight case against the innocent suspect; the suspect goes to Mason for help. Mason and Drake would then sift for clues. At the trial, the full range of courtroom histrionics were displayed, with witnesses cracking under Mason's relentless probing or else witnesses being produced at the last minute by a frantic Paul Drake, which changed the course of the case. D.A. Hamilton Burger, who lost every case that Mason won, was probably the most frustrated man on TV in the '60s.

As my father pointed out, most of the time, TV's portrayal of lawyers bore little resemblance to reality. But that didn't deter the public from making "Perry Mason" one of TV's most popular shows. It ended its long run on September 4, 1966 with an appropriate episode called "The Case of the Final Fade-Out." Mason defended a TV star accused of murdering his producer in order to gain ownership of his own series. (For this episode, Gardner played the judge.) Burr wasn't gone from the tube for too long. He reappeared in 1967 to battle evil again, this time as the paralyzed cop on "Ironside."

If Mason offered escape, the other great '60s lawyer show, "The Defenders" (CBS 1961-65), made you think.

"The Defenders" were a father (E.G. Marshall) and son (Robert Reed) lawyer team, Preston & Preston, involved in weekly courtroom dramas, which were more like morality plays. Each episode of this controversial and critically-acclaimed show dealt with ethical issues such as euthanasia, abortion, blacklisting, and civil disobedience. (An earlier one-season-only father-and-son attorney show, "Harrigan and Son" with Pat O'Brien and Roger Perry, had played it for laughs.)

It was worth staying home for on Saturday nights. Lawrence, the father, had twenty years of experience; Kenneth was a recent Ivy League law-school graduate, with a quick temper. But he got the best on-the-job training from his old man. Unlike Perry Mason, Preston & Preston occasionally lost a case.

The show was based on an original story by Reginald Rose (who also wrote the memorable courtroom drama *Twelve Angry Men*), and was first telecast as a two-part episode of "Studio One" in 1957, starring Ralph Bellamy and William Shatner as the father and son. The show was created by Rose and Herbert Brodkin, another "Golden Age" veteran.

The show's debut episode, "The Quality of Mercy," is typical of the high-quality drama. It asked the question: Should a doctor who destroys a Mongoloid baby at birth be found guilty of murder? It's a taut, well-argued one-hour drama, with both points of view presented. The elder Preston says he's opposed to the idea, but decides to take the case. Issues were never black-and-white. The doctor was not a killer; he was shown as a sensitive man, who acted as he did in what he thought were the interests of the baby's father. His humanity impresses the hard-boiled D.A. who begins the episode pressing for the death penalty. Instead of getting the chair, he gets off on a manslaughter charge.

Like other shows, it gave several well-known actors their earliest appearances: Gene Hackman (who played the baby's father in the debut episode); Jack Klugman (who played the D.A.). Martin Sheen, Jon Voight, James Farentino, and Dustin Hoffman all had their days in court.

Other legal eagles flew during the '60s, but none as successfully as "Perry Mason" and "The Defenders."

"The Law and Mr. Jones" (1960)—James Whitmore played crusading attorney Abraham Lincoln Jones, who was as moral and just as his first two names.

"Sam Benedict" (1962)—Edmond O'Brien played a lawyer based on the real-life adventures of flamboyant San Francisco attorney, Jake Ehrlich.

"Judd for the Defense" (1967)—Carl Betz left "The Donna Reed Show" to play a liberal, wealthy Texas attorney.

"The Trials of O'Brien" (1965)—Peter Falk got in practice for his future "Columbo" role, and, like the trenchcoat-wearing detective, New York trial lawyer Daniel O'Brien was sloppy in his personal life, sharp in business. He wasn't as upright as other TV lawyers had been. He was an inveterate gambler, hounded by bookies and the IRS, and he had a personal score to settle with his former wife.

Perry Mason—Super-attorney Mason (Raymond Burr) holds a newspaper with a headline as accurate as that memorable 1948 Chicago Tribune head-line which proclaimed, "Dewey Defeats Truman."

War Shows

Quick now. What was the most ludicrous idea in all of '60s television? a talking horse? a flying nun? "Gilligan's Island"? Nope. In a decade that brought TV ludicrousness to new heights, at the summit of silliness sits "Hogan's Heroes." Its premise: Life in a Nazi POW camp during World War II could be a blast. Stalag 13 was a Club Med with barbed wire. If life had imitated art back then, we probably would have lost the Big One. After all, our soldiers would probably have *wanted* to be captured—just so they could earn some R&R at these fun-loving Stalags.

The boys at Stalag 13 had a French chef, a steam room, a barber shop, and other amenities. Their days were spent pulling pranks and making mischief with their "stoopit" German commandants (Colonel Klink, Sergeant Schulz). This wasn't the antiwar satire that "M*A*S*H" provided; this was Sergeant Bilko in the Bunker. In fact, "Hogan's Heroes" owed much of its spirit to Phil Silver's Sergeant Ernie Bilko of "You'll Never Get Rich," the barracks-laffer of the '50s, which showed that a military environment was a good source for laughs.

One reason that "Hogan" could even conceivably be aired was because twenty years had elapsed since the end of World War II, making it a fit subject for humor. Who knows? Network execs may feel the same about Vietnam in a few years' time ("Ho's Heroes," anyone?)

Take Bilko out of the barracks and put him on the high seas and you got "McHale's Navy" (1962-66). McHale (Ernest Borgnine) was the Bilko figure, a scheming know-it-all who frequently clashed with his superior, Captain Binghamton (Joe Flynn) on a World War II P.T. boat. But who out there remembers "Broadside," created by the same man responsible for "McHale's Navy," about a group of World War II WAVES? It ran for one season; Kathleen Nolan was the chief wave, and Arnold Stang was the ship's cook.

The witty "F Troop" (1965-67), billed in its promos as a "comedy of arrows," was a satire of those heroic John Ford movies about life at an Old West military outpost. The men of F Troop were a bunch of incompetents, led by Captain Parmenter (Ken Berry), who had been promoted from private during the war when he accidentally led a charge in the wrong direction—toward the enemy.

Comic relief was provided by the numerous Indians, which set the cause of Native Americans back about 100 years. Still, "F Troop" had its cool guest stars like Wrongo Starr (a cavalry trooper with bad luck played by Henry Gibson) and Chief Bald Eagle (Don Rickles).

"Gomer Pyle, U.S.M.C." featured Mayberry's favorite service-station attendant who enlisted in the Marines in 1964. He showed the world that this hard-assed branch of the service could be a laff-riot (an idea that's almost as ludicrous as "Hogan's Heroes"). Nabors as Pyle contributed two memorable phrases to the '60s vocabulary: "Shazam!" (well, actually he swiped that from the old Captain Marvel radio show) and "Gowl-lee!," the latter said with mouth and jaw wide open.

After Nabors left the show in 1970, he survived rumors that he had married Rock Hudson, and today he lives in a mansion on Oahu (with a chandelier that once belonged to Napoleon!) and owns a macadamia-nut plantation on Maui. Even though this was the '60s, old Gomer never got shipped over to 'Nam. Now that would have been a "laff" riot.

Another khakied hick (Air Force division) was Will Stockdale (Sammy Jackson) in "No Time for Sergeants" (originally a movie starring Andy Griffith), which was ABC's 1964 competitor to "Gomer Pyle." But ol' Will was given his discharge after only a year and is presumably now back in the Ozarks.

So much for the laughs. Let's not forget that war—real war—is hell, and the war in question, World War II, was never portrayed better on the small screen than in "Combat." Its stark realism showing the boring, tense moments of fighting men (lots of slogging through mud) made it the "Dragnet" of war shows. "Combat" (1962-67) depicted the exploits of an American army platoon fighting its way across Europe after D-day. The cast was actually sent to boot camp for training before the actual production began, and real battle footage was used in the series. The platoon was led by crafty, tough platoon commanders Lieutenant Gil Hanley (Rick Jason) and Sergeant Chip Saunders (Vic Morrow). In the first year of the series, Shecky Greene played the platoon's resident comic and hustler (Private Braddock).

In the same season ABC also premiered "The Gallant Men," which met with less success than "Combat," lasting only one season. This show was set in Italy during WW II and told the story of the men of the 36th Infantry Division. Most of the time, however, the action was seen through the eyes of a news correspondent named Conley Wright (Robert McQueeny).

"Combat" was terminated in 1967. By then a real war could be seen every night on the 7 o'clock news, and it was a sight more violent and bloody than anything on "Combat"—except you couldn't tell who the Good Guys were anymore.

Other War/Military Shows

"THE LIEUTENANT" (1963-64) starred Gary Lockwood (one of the astronauts of *2001*) and Robert Vaughn (one of the men from U.N.C.L.E.). Lockwood was Lieutenant Bill Rice, an easygoing fledgling Marine officer; Vaughn was Captain Ray Rambridge, his superior, who wanted to make Lieutenant Rice more of a strict officer.

"TWELVE O'CLOCK HIGH," originally a 1949 movie starring Gregory Peck, became a Quinn Martin series from 1964-67. Robert Lansing played Brigadier General Frank Savage, who personally led his Air Force bombardier group on missions. Savage was killed off for the second season with

Hogan's Heroes—Oh those lovable Nazis! Hogan (Bob Crane) massages the neck of Colonel Klink (Werner Klemperer) as Sergeant Schultz (John Banner) watches.

(1965-66) was based on the movie of the same name. It starred Jack Warden as the skipper of the *Kiwi*, a leaky two-masted schooner.

Laughs

TV shows of the '60s were supposed to tread softly and sensitively. Slowly, very slowly, Americans learned that sacred cows could be slaughtered on television. "Saturday Night Live," "SCTV," "Fridays" and other modern-day "humor" shows get away with just about everything. But it wasn't so long ago that TV had taboos up to here.

"That Was the Week That Was" (a.k.a. "TW3," 1964-65), based on a similar English show, was the first TV attempt at mature political satire in prime time. The news of the week was satirized, especially world bigwigs, in revue form—using comedy sketches, blackouts, mock-news reports, and musical production numbers. But the American version lacked the bite and the popularity of its British counterpart. One reason was that it couldn't bridge the gap between sophisticated satire and broad comedy. Still, it was considered innovative for American TV at a time when sponsors often blue-penciled scripts for objectionable material.

"TW3's" news satire was often sharp and biting, definitely ahead of its time, but many people may have considered it too cerebral. Here's one typical scene: Two good friends, a Catholic and a Jew, are discussing the recent Vatican exoneration of the Jews in Christ's death. The Jew is relieved about that—but as he observes, "after 2,000 years, the Jew still can't join the Catholic's country club."

T he Smothers Brothers

Captain, later Colonel, Crowe (Paul Burke) assuming more of a prominent role.

"CONVOY" (1965) was a short-lived series about the problems of transporting troops and supplies across the Atlantic during World War II. John Gavin, who became Ambassador to Mexico under President Reagan, was featured.

"RAT PATROL" (1966-68) battled Rommel's Afrika Korps in North Africa during World War II. Unused footage from *The Battle of the Bulge* and *The Great Escape* was often used.

"GARRISON'S GORILLAS" (1967-68), inspired by *The Dirty Dozen*, featured a group of less-than-honorable commandos recruited from American prisons to use their skills against the Germans. They'd receive a presidential pardon if they succeeded.

"THE WACKIEST SHIP IN THE

The show was also a forum for the musical satire of Tom Lehrer, creator of such witty tunes as "National Brotherhood Week" and "The Vatican Rag."

The week's news would be summarized into a catchy song sung by the so-called "TW3 Girl," Nancy Ames. Among those in the cast were Henry Morgan, Phyllis Newman, Pat England, Buck Henry, Alan Alda, and Tom Bosley. The show is also notable for having brought David Frost, who had hosted the English version, to our shores.

When "TW3" went off the air in May, 1965, no show filled the void until the "Smothers Brothers Comedy Hour" in 1967. The Smothers attracted a large, predominantly youthful following who related to their anti-Johnson Administration, antiwar humor, presented at a time when the mood of the country had still not turned against the war.

Tom and Dick Smothers were a popular night-club and coffee-house attraction in the early '60s, who mixed folk ballads with comedy. Tom was the dumb brother (but in reality, the one who favored being controversial), while Dick was levelheaded and calm. Their first attempt at TV, a 1965 sit-com riding TV's fantasy trend (Tom played an angel who returned to Earth) bombed. But when they returned two years later... it was with a vengeance.

"The Smothers Brothers Comedy Hour," which made its debut on February 5, 1967, was topical, witty—and quite often in bad taste. CBS wanted a youthful-oriented variety program to go up against the seemingly unstoppable "Bonanza." And on the show's first night, the Brothers Smothers outgunned the Brothers Cartwright by an audience share of 36 to 26. CBS got more than they bargained for. Almost from the outset, the brothers and the network tangled over the hour's content.

Among the regulars was poker-faced Pat Paulsen, who ran for president in 1968 on a ticket whose slogan was "If nominated I will not run, and if elected I will not serve." CBS execs didn't get the joke, and they actually worried about the equal-time provision, so Paulsen had to be kept off the show until after the election.

After a particularly controversial episode on October 27, 1968, CBS asked that a tape of each upcoming segment be prescreened for network affiliates. On one occasion, Tom refused to deliver a tape until a day before air time, and CBS canceled that evening's show. It was finally aired three weeks later.

CBS and the brothers kept fighting, so finally the network, after first saying they would renew the show and then, despite the show's decent ratings, pulled the plug. The network wouldn't recant. In July, 1969, the "Smothers Brothers Comedy Hour" was replaced by "Hee-Haw." Counterculture pundits saw this as one more sign of America's inevitable drift to the right.

The Smothers Brothers with guest Pat Paulsen

SIX SEGMENTS CBS CUT FROM THE "SMOTHERS BROTHERS"

1. A skit on film censorship, featuring Tom and Elaine May

2. On the fall, 1967 premiere, Pete Seeger singing a stanza from the antiwar song, "Waist Deep in the Big Muddy." (He later was able to sing it in May, 1968.)

3. A 1968 Mother's Day message which concluded with the words "please talk peace"

4. Harry Belafonte singing "Lord,

Laugh-In—
Dan Rowan
(left) and Dick
Martin.

Don't Stop the Carnival" in front of a filmed montage of the 1968 Democratic Convention riots

5. An interview with Dr. Benjamin Spock, then convicted of aiding draft evaders
6. The word "mindblowing"

In a class by itself was "Rowan and Martin's Laugh-In" (1968-73)—a show as new as television, as old as the stage of a burlesque house. Building on the electronic lunacy pioneered by Ernie Kovacs, "Laugh-In" created a kind of video vaudeville—full of one-liners, sight gags, skits, blackouts, and celebrity cameos, edited into a frenetic pastiche—that was revolutionary for its time.

If you didn't like one gag, why then there would always be another one to tickle you, probably within the next forty seconds or so. And the gags kept coming even after the final credits had rolled and all you heard was the sound of one person clapping.

The show spawned several memorable words and phrases including "Sock it to me," "Here come de judge," "bippy," "Look that up in your Funk and Wagnalls," "walnuttos," and the "Fickle Finger of Fate Award." Two popular features were the cocktail party and the News of the Future. Memorable characters included Gladys, Tyrone Horneye, and Arte Johnson's German soldier ("Verr-rry interesting").

Hosted by a pair of veteran lounge comics, Dan Rowan and Dick Martin, its cast included Goldie Hawn, Judy Carne, Henry Gibson, Arte Johnson, Joanne Worley, Ruth Buzzi, and Gary Owens. Cameo appearances were frequent, including 1968 presidential candidate Richard Nixon, incredulously asking "Sock it to Me?" "Laugh-In" made the old Dinah-Jackie-Red-style variety show as dated as a whoopee cushion.

FOUR NAMES CONSIDERED FOR "LAUGH-IN"

1. Put On
2. The Wacky World of Now
3. On the Funny Side of Life
4. High Camp

AN INTERVIEW WITH GEORGE SCHLATTER (PRODUCER AND ONE OF THE CREATORS OF ROWAN & MARTIN'S "LAUGH-IN")

Schlatter: "Laugh-In" came in 1967 and had a great deal to do with Vietnam, strangely enough. Vietnam had created much of that anger, much of that student unrest, political upheaval. Into that kind of vacuum, that arena of hostility, came this brightly-colored, happy, little lump within which there were very barbed references to the Pentagon and the military-industrial complex, defense spending vs. health and education.

Vietnam was part of the environment that created the need for "Laugh-In". We came in and did jokes and humorous comment about very serious issues where no one thought you could do that. As a result, "All in the Family," "Maude," other relevant kinds of social satire followed.

Question: Why did "Laugh-In" succeed while an earlier satirical show like "TW3" didn't?

Schlatter: "Laugh-In" didn't have any anger; there was no political platform. We had a humorous overview with both sides. There was no guile, no malicious intent. We were not trying to change political views, but to comment humorously on all political

views.

It wasn't a mean show. We joked about everything. On "TW3" you had to read the evening paper to know what they were talking about. "Laugh-In" was entertainment. If you didn't understand political references, you did understand entertainment and liked the jokes. "Laugh-In" was a balance. When we'd get in trouble with the censor, when we'd lose a joke, it was because a joke was too biting or for legal reasons—then the show became too silly. But if we lost a joke because it was too bawdy or too sexy, the show became a little too political.

It was necessary to maintain balance between whimsy and bite, between broad visual humor and satire.

"Laugh-In" couldn't have been done earlier because the technical expertise didn't exist. Of course, the man who had more effect on me than anyone else was Ernie Kovacs. He had brought in use of TV as more than the means of transmission, the use of the electronic medium. Ernie's love of TV was transferred to me.

Use of electronic medium was born in the '60s. Modern editing techniques were a by-product of "Laugh-In." We did 500 physical splices in the first special, in addition to tape and film cuts. That created a need for the electronic editing that we now know. That probably had as much impact as the kind of energy, brevity, and compression of information that we did. Electronically we had a telling and more endurable effect. "Laugh-In" affected books, commercials, movies, Broadway. Everything went into snappier, kind of punch-line humor, but that's very gratifying.

We had tremendous difficulty in selling the concept, and the same problem exists today, unfortunately. The one disappointment about "Laugh-In" was that when it came out it was new and innovative and broke every existing mold and you thought, well, this will now generate a new surge of creativity and experimentation. It didn't.

All TV did was copy "'Laugh-In." The same thing happened with "Real People" [The '80s show which Schlatter produced]. Our media tends to get more like a cookie cutter than a true hotbed of innovation. You would think that if there was a breakthrough, it would generate more experimentation rather than less.

Question: One of the copies was "Turn-On," which you were also involved in creating.

Schlatter: On the basis of the first show, Bristol Myers bought in. They all said this was the most innovative use of the medium. Now a couple of guys got very uptight because it was brittle, wasn't plastic. It was the first time the Moog synthesizer was used. We also used shadowless light, multiple images, dioptic lenses, and a laugh track that was programmed into a computer. The host was a computer. This was 1969! In Denver it was canceled halfway through the show. A guy came on the air and said "The remainder of this show won't be seen."

I'm very proud of the show. All the technology introduced on "Turn-On" has now become commonplace. The show happened at a time when the country started turning to the right. Nixon was president. It was so disturbing to some people that in the settlement it was agreed that the show would be locked up and never shown.

Question: How did critics respond to "Laugh-In"?

Schlatter: Some critics responded violently. At first, the show wasn't that successful. The network bought it because it was cheap. It had a kamikaze time period. Lucille Ball and "Gunsmoke" were opposite it and they were the Number 1-and-2 ranked shows. Into that time period came this show that nobody had ever heard of—doing jokes, people painted at a cocktail party, people coming out of walls. It was the most fun anyone ever had. God! it was fun.

So much of the show was done improvisationally on stage. I would bring in a rack of costumes. Arte would put one on. Ruth would put one on, and then we would take a premise like you would in an acting class. Out of that came some marvelous things.

Despite all the improvisation, it was a very disciplined, scripted show. But within that discipline, anything that would happen went. One time we filmed Jack Benny tuning up his violin before he went on. We said cut and print. He said "I wasn't doing anything" and that showed up on the show.

Question: Did you have any favorite bits?

Schlatter: One of my favorite bits was this News of the Future—Dateline, the Vatican, 1988...With marriage in the church now an accepted practice, the Archbishop and his lovely bride, the former Sister Mary Catherine, both announced that this time it's for keeps—if only for the sake of the children. That lit up the switchboard like New Year's Eve.

Question: What do you recall about Goldie Hawn?

Schlatter: Goldie was one of the brightest, most intelligent members of the cast, but she did have kind of a minute attention span. She was very easily distracted. Any kind of rude noise or object that wasn't supposed to be there and flashed in front of Goldie, would divert her attention just long enough, and she would lose her place and say "Oh my God, I'm in trouble." Then she'd leave and say, "Can I do it again?" She'd come back and do it right and that would never go on the air. Anytime she blew it, that's what wound up on the show.

The first time I met her she was so flustered, she bit her nails, she wanted to answer my phone. I said "Lady, I don't know what I'm gonna do with you." She was so cute, but when people talked to her all they would see would be the side of her head. She was kind of camera shy. But there was no doubt she would be a superstar.

Question: The most famous moment was when candidate Richard Nixon did his cameo.

Schlatter: Getting Nixon to say "Sock it to me" was one of the most hysterical experiences of my life. He couldn't get the right emphasis. *Sock* it to me. No, that's too strong. Try it again with a smile. Sock it *to* me. No, no, just look at the camera, it's a question. Sock it to *me*?—He had to do six takes; it was funny.

It helped him because it showed Nixon to be involved in the mainstream in this hip, trendy show. We also wanted Hubert Humphrey to do it, and we chased his people all over the country, but he refused. Years later he said he should have done it.

Ironically, Nixon had more to do with the decline of satirical comedy than anyone else. When the politicians became funnier and more outrageous than the jokewriters that was the end of satire. We couldn't be funnier than a president saying "I'm not a crook" or someone like Tony Ulasewicz. Those were real people being truly outrageous.

SOUPY SALES

From the late '50s to the mid '60s, Soupy Sales wore a polka-dot bow tie and porkpie hat, danced "The Mouse," told bad puns, and more often than not had the remnants of a custard pie spattered on his face. By behaving this way on his live, at times, anarchic, "children's" TV show—whose hip zaniness presaged the humor of "Rowan & Martin's Laugh-In" and "Saturday Night Live" —he became a pop culture phenomenon whose viewers were estimated to be 65 percent adult.

During the ensuing years, Sales went hatless and traded in his bow tie for more conventional neckwear. But he barely changed his slapstick humor. Now there seems to be a revival of interest in Soupy's work, fueled perhaps by the trend to "silly" comics

as well as incipient nostalgia for the '60s among those who grew up then.

"But I don't want to be considered a blast from the past. I never went away," Sales asserts, over a fillet of sole lunch at New York's Friars Club. Indeed, while Sales never disappeared from the public eye (in addition to his frequent nightclub performances, he appears regularly on TV game shows), his profile has been considerably lowered since the mid '60s.

No, Soupy hasn't changed. But TV has. And those changes have left him distressed—to the point that it seems nothing would please him better than to throw several well-aimed pies in the faces of today's network executives. In fact, he's positively appalled at what's happened to both kids' shows and comedy on television.

"The only reason I'm doing nightclubs is that I don't have a creative outlet on TV anymore where I can write and do the things I want to do. I hope that will change," says the rubber-faced comedian at whom an estimated 20,000 custard pies have been hurled since they first hit him square in the kisser in Cleveland in 1950.

Soupy (that's his real name, by the way, changed legally from Milton Hines) grew up in Huntington, West Virginia, and graduated from college with a journalism degree. He then went into comedy, perfecting a shtick that took him from scriptwriting for a hometown radio station in the early '50s to hosting kids' shows in Cleveland, Detroit, Los Angeles, and New York.

TV comedy, he says, is becoming an endangered species. He speaks reverently of the days of live television.

"Even with a Bob Hope, everything is a laughtrack," he says of today's comedy shows. "Every joke gets a magnificent laugh. That's not comedy.

Soupy Sales, sans pie in the face. Pookie the lion watches.

Comedy is when you don't get a laugh with the first joke, you come back with a second and third joke."

Soupy also fondly recalls the days when kids' shows were hosted by people, not cartoon characters. "Who do you think your kid is going to listen to—me or Bugs Bunny?

"I didn't talk down to the kids. I wasn't like Captain Kangaroo or Mr. Rogers, and the kids appreciated it. They said, 'Hey, he's one of us.'

"People make such a thing about sex and violence on nighttime TV, but kids are more susceptible to sex and violence in the day when they come home from school than they are at night," continues Soupy at a mile-a-minute pace. "But those daytime soap operas—that's soft-core porn, no matter how you slice it. How do you expect kids to want to see someone get hit in the face with a pie when they can watch somebody making love?"

Soupy's show featured memorable characters such as White Fang, the world's meanest and largest dog, Black Tooth, the world's sweetest dog (both of which were seen by the audience only as giant black-and-white paws), Pookie, an adorable lion puppet, and secret agent Philo Kvetch (his painfully corny words of wisdom, "Show me a cow wearing rags, and I'll show you a bum steer."), dances ("The Mouse" and the "Soupy Shuffle"), and, of course, the show's climax—the pie in the face.

Besides reviving that vintage vaudeville gag, Sales is perhaps best remembered for the New Year's Day 1965 incident in which he asked his young listeners to sneak into their mommy and daddy's room and remove those "funny little scraps of green paper from daddy's pants" and send them to him at his TV station. When Soupy received enough money to take a small vacation, he was sus-pended by the station management. But that incident elevated him from kid-show host to cult hero. Articles in major magazines and dime stores full of Soupy merchandise followed.

But he never believed, as some critics have charged, that he had a subversive effect on his viewers, many of whom would become the college revolutionaries and yippies of the late '60s. "I don't see how," he claimed. " I never won. The dogs beat me. The guys at the door beat me. I always got a pie in the face."

Sci-Fi Shows

GOOOD EVENING!...BEAM ME UP TO...ANOTHER DIMENSION, A DIMENSION...OF MIND...WHERE THERE IS NOTHING WRONG WITH YOUR TV SET...WHOSE NIGHTMARE IS ABOUT TO BEGIN...

Television execs in the '60s had to deal with a problem that they didn't have to contend with in the '50s. How do you create sci-fi programming that could outdazzle the real thing—which was so easily available and so consistently amazing? What manner of show would capture viewers' imaginations more than John Glenn's flight or the moonwalk?

To show the world they had the Right Stuff, execs didn't come up with the Yuri Gagarin Variety Hour or NASA a-Go-Go. No, they needed programming that would be more meaningful than the stuff of Saturday morning TV and Buck Rogers serials. Indeed, old Captain Video and his video rangers might have been freaked by what TV had wrought with the outer-space drama. Up in space, the *Enterprise* flew on "Star Trek"; the Robinsons waited for a return transfer to Earth on "Lost in Space";

while another bunch of castaways coped with a bunch of oversized creatures on "Land of the Giants."

Space, of course, wasn't the only arena where the imagination was stretched. Way below the waves, an atomic sub battled bizarre creatures on "Voyage to the Bottom of the Sea." On "The Time Tunnel," a couple of characters in turtleneck sweaters would enter an Op Art cylinder and end up breaking bread with Abe Lincoln. Then, of course, there was the most fascinating dimension of all, inside one's mind—Rod Serling's "The Twilight Zone" and its little cousin, "The Outer Limits."

•"STAR TREK," which, of course, has gone on to be one of the all-time cult classics, had plots that were well-written pieces of sci-fi, often dealing with current social issues, disguised only by their outer-space trappings. The *Enterprise* mission included reconnaissance of previously unexplored worlds and transporting supplies to Earth colonies in space. ("Space, the final frontier. These are the voyages of the Starship *Enterprise*. Its five year mission: To explore new worlds; to seek out new life and new civilizations; to boldly go where no man has gone before.")

Captain James T. Kirk (William Shatner) ran the *Enterprise*, but the real fan favorite was First Officer, Mr. Spock (Leonard Nimoy), the half-Earthling, half-Vulcan with pointed ears and a completely logical mind, who was originally intended as a minor character. The emotionless Spock would often do battle with his overly-emotional shipmate, Dr. Bones McCoy, the chief medical officer (DeForest Kelley).

During its run, "Star Trek" wasn't enormously popular with the bulk of viewers—it was only Number 52 in its debut season (1966-67). It was can-

celed in 1969 because most of its fanatic viewers were teenagers, which meant that the advertisers wouldn't be attracted to the show. The show became even more popular after it was canceled, spawning three feature films in the late '70s and early '80s.

"Star Trek" was TV's first adult sci-fi series with continuing characters. Creator Gene Roddenberry insisted on scientific accuracy; every detail of the *Enterprise* was planned, and opinions of space experts, scientists, and doctors were consulted. Special effects—the phasers, beaming down, traveling through space—helped the show's popularity.

But, above all, was the show's message—optimism and good triumphed over evil—that differentiated it from the doom-and-gloom scenarios of many sci-fi projects of the '60s.

•"VOYAGE TO THE BOTTOM OF THE SEA" was based on a 1964 movie, which in turn had been based on Jules Verne's *Twenty Thousand Leagues Under the Sea*. The research submarine, Seaview, battled such dangers as outer spacemen, humanoid amphibians, ice creatures, dinosaurs, abominable snowmen, mad scientists, an army of marionettes, and a jellyfish-like monster—all of which had somehow managed to find themselves under the sea.

The show's creator, Irwin Allen, now known as "The Master of Disaster," because of his scare flicks such as *The Towering Inferno* and *The Poseidon Adventure*, was the master of TV sci-fi during the '60s. He plundered such classic works as *Twenty-Thousand Leagues Under the Sea* and *Robinson Crusoe* for his trips.

•"LOST IN SPACE" (the title for the pilot was "Space Family Robinson") was juvenile sci-fi. The Robinsons were an American family who split

Earth in 1997 for outer space since home was becoming too crowded. The plot: A foreign agent planned to blow up the Robinsons' ship while they lay frozen for their trip. Instead, he made it change course and was trapped on board himself. Two veterans of '50s shows, Guy Williams ("Zorro") and June Lockhart ("Lassie") starred. But a robot was its most popular character.

• "THE TWILIGHT ZONE" was undoubtedly one of the top TV shows of all time. Rod Serling was the show's creator, principal writer, and co-producer. An established TV playwright, Serling had battled with sponsors, so he decided to write a fantasy show instead of serious stuff. His 1957 pilot drama for a sci-fi series, "The Time Element," about a man who dreams about the Pearl Harbor attack and is assumed to be a crackpot, drew more fan mail than any other show that season and convinced CBS that there was a fantasy series to be had.

Still popular in reruns, the show has exerted a large influence on our popular culture. The term "Twilight Zone" has become a permanent part of the American vocabulary to describe a befogged person or an unexplainable situation. The eerie theme music shows up in comercials and comedy sketches. In 1983, a not-overwhelmingly successful movie, directed by five leading figures based on their favorite "TZ" episodes, was released.

Serling's introduction each week on "The Twilight Zone" might have been icy, but its equivalent on "The Outer Limits" was positively sub-zero.

"There is nothing wrong with your television set," said the authoritative voice as your TV set freaked out. "Do not attempt to adjust the picture. We are controlling transmission. We will control the horizontal, we will control the vertical. For the next hour, sit qui-etly and we will control all you see and hear. You are about to experience the awe and mystery that leads you from the inner mind...to the outer limits." Although the show also has its own cult, its blend of the macabre, supernatural and plain spooky never measured up to the "Twilight Zone."

• "THE ALFRED HITCHCOCK HOUR" was created and hosted by movie's master of suspense. It was a long-running suspense anthology with chilling music based on Gounod's "Funeral March of a Marionette." Hitchcock would greet viewers before the show ("Goood evening...") and later, to wrap up the evening's events, usually offering an unexpected or wry comment.

• "THE INVADERS" was a cult classic that should be revived. These alien invaders weren't friendly like ET; they resembled the ominous aliens of '50s sci-fi fright films like *Invasion of the Body Snatchers*. They walked, talked, ate, and slept among us. How could you tell who they were, then? By the way, they crooked their pinky.

Star Trek—Captain Kirk (William Shatner) and Spock (Leonard Nimoy). Beam 'em up!

WHEN MOVIES BECAME FILMS

'60S CINEMA

INTRODUCTION

On screen in the '60s, 007 kept the world safe for democracy; Bonnie and Clyde and the Easy Riders cruised America's highways; and Dustin Hoffman was advised to get into plastics. The hills were alive with the sound of music, but teens ran wild in the streets. Suave secret agents, dumb beach bunnies, bloodthirsty motorcyclists, and psycho cowboys paraded on screen in front of the first generation weaned on television.

Hollywood grew up in the '60s. Films reflected the changing American society, becoming sexier and more violent. Spurred on by competition from foreign filmmakers, American films began tackling more provocative subjects as well as borrowing new techniques such as quick cuts and multiple imagery. The production code and the Hollywood star-studio system both vanished.

Bonnie and Clyde—Faye Dunaway and Warren Beatty as chic outlaws of the '30s (1967)

110

By the '60s, nearly all the great movie stars of the past had either died or retired. Glamour faded, and ugly became "in." Audiences wanted stars to be "real," and, toward the end of decade we saw an outpouring of long hair, craggy faces, buck teeth, and five o'clock shadows. Many films stopped having happy endings, and it became increasingly more difficult to identify just who the Good Guys were.

This chapter will take a look at a key film of each year from 1960-69 (with two for 1967), as well as some of the individual genres that were distinctly part of '60s pop culture. You'll also find portraits of the top movie stars of the decade, as well as a list of thirty-two other memorable '60s films.

1960: Psycho

Psycho, based on Robert Bloch's novel, was Alfred Hitchcock's gift to the new decade—a film which anticipated the violence that would characterize many later '60s films. Many critics called the film violent, but the master of suspense and shock called it a black comedy. "Psycho is a film made with quite a sense of amusement—it's a fun picture. The process through which we take the audience is rather like taking them through the haunted house at the fairground." Of Hitchcock's '60s body of film, which includes The Birds, Marnie, Torn Curtain and Topaz, Psycho is the most enduring.

In 1960, the low-budget horror film was a Hollywood staple. Hitchcock, coming off the success of his classy 1959 spy thriller, North by Northwest, wanted to see what he could do with the genre. He personally financed Psycho, with the goal of making it as cheaply as possible (the total cost was $800,000; to date the film has made more than $20 million). He managed to do so, using members of his TV show production staff and hiring Anthony Perkins and Janet Leigh for relatively modest fees. The other star, Vera Miles, was under personal contract to Hitchcock.

The plot is merely melodramatic structure onto which Hitchcock manipulates the viewer's emotions. To summarize:

Marion Crane (Janet Leigh), a Phoenix secretary, is having an affair with the married Sam Loomis (John Gavin). After embezzling money from her office, Marion hightails it out of Phoenix, heading west to meet her lover in San Francisco. Because of a rainstorm, she stops for the night at the Bates Motel, a rickety building definitely not to be confused with a Holiday Inn. She chats politely but nervously with Norman Bates, the boy-next-door proprietor, and we learn about Norman's obsession with his elderly invalid mother, who lives in the Gothic house above the hotel.

This will be Marion's last night, as we well know. In one of cinema's most memorable scenes, she is stabbed fourteen times by a person who appears to be Norman's elderly mother. Norman comes in and stuffs Marion's body into the trunk of her car, which he ditches in quicksand.

After the murder, Marion's sister, Lila (Vera Miles), Sam, and private investigator Milton Arbogast (Martin Balsam), hired by her boss to recover the stolen money, come to the motel looking for Marion. They, too, chat with Norman, who tells them about his mother. While Arbogast is snooping around the mansion, he's killed by Mrs. Bates. When Arbogast doesn't return, the increasingly-suspicious Sam and Lila visit the local sheriff who tells them that Mrs. Bates has been dead for eight years.

Returning to the house, Sam keeps Norman occupied while Lila sneaks back to the house. Norman knocks Sam out while Lila flees to the cellar where she spies "Mrs. Bates" sitting in a chair. She touches "Mrs. Bates" and the chair turns around revealing a corpse. Soon after, Norman comes running into the basement clutching a knife and dressed as his mama. Sam stops him, and Norman is sent off to the police. At film's end a police psychiatrist explains that Norman, angered by the death of his mother, became a schizophrenic with a multiple personality and homicidal rages.

Whew!

Psycho is a film without a message—except, perhaps, to be wary of nervous motel clerks—and without any truly memorable performances. What gives the film its impact is just how easily Hitchcock succeeded in yo-yoing the audience's emotions. Other directors, like Brian DePalma, have tried to duplicate Hitchcock's ability to manipulate the audience, but none have succeeded as well. The film was true to Hitchcock's notion that suspense can be more frightening than what the suspense is actually about. Until *Psycho,* Hitchcock had avoided explicit violence; murder was never seen, always implied. The film isn't all that gory—there are only two murders—but it's the viewers expectations that create the feeling that something dreadful is on the verge of happening, especially since Hitchcock did the unprecedented by killing a film's central character within the first part of a film. The black-and-white footage and Bernard Herrmann's score heighten the mood.

Norman Bates broke all the standard Hollywood conventions regarding murderers. He was a little nervous, certainly, but never until the very end are we clued in as to just how un-

hinged he is. He was the boy next door with a homicidal streak, a prototype for a person that would become all too familiar in the years ahead; Lee Harvey Oswald, Charles Whitman, Arthur Bremer, Richard Speck were real-life cousins to Bates.

INSIDE THE SHOWER

P*sycho* was shot in black-and-white because Hitchcock felt the shower scene would be too gory for the audience. There are rumors, however, which claim that color footage from the film existed in Hitchcock's personal collection.

The shower scene took one week to shoot, with special scaffolding built for the scene (so Hitchcock could stand above and direct) and

J anet Leigh has plenty to scream about in Hitchcock's *Psycho* (1960).

more than seventy different setups for the segment, which only took forty-five seconds of film time. If you look closely, you'll observe that the knife never touches the victim's body. Hitchcock's fast cutting of the montage made it seem as if Janet Leigh had been stabbed repeatedly. We only see the blood (in reality, chocolate sauce) as it spatters on the wall and into the tub. It's a shocking scene, as we see the blood trickling into the drain. But in terms of violence, it was almost tame compared to the bloodbaths we'd see by the end of the decade in such films as *Bonnie and Clyde* and *The Wild Bunch.*

A double for Perkins was used during the shower scene. Perkins was in New York rehearsing for a play when that famous scene was filmed in Hollywood. Perkins would later say: "It is rather strange to go through life being identified with this sequence, knowing that it was my double. Actually, the first time I saw *Psycho* and that shower scene was at the studio. I found it scary...I was as frightened as anybody else."

Hitchcock didn't think it proper that Leigh be filmed nude, so he shot only her face and hands. A model was hired for other short glimpses of skin.

Hitchcock on the shower scene: "One man wrote to me after I had Janet Leigh murdered in a bathtub that his wife had been afraid to bathe or shower since seeing the film. He asked me for suggestions as to what he should do. I wrote back, 'Sir: Have you considered sending your wife to be dry-cleaned?'"

Janet Leigh says that every time *Psycho* is shown on TV she gets "piles of crank mail," with many letters threatening her with worse treatment than she received in the shower. "I didn't get scared by the shower scene, but these cranks could haunt me for the rest of my life."

The film was released while Hitchcock's weekly TV horror-anthology show was at the height of its popularity. *Psycho* was also one of those rare films whose ad campaign was built around the fame of the director rather than the stars. (Per Hitchcock tradition, the director appears in his own film. He's the man standing outside the real-estate office window at the beginning of the film.)

Psycho was shot on a set at which no visitors were allowed. Publicity stills were not released in advance; reviewers and theater owners weren't permitted to view the film until

opening day. Moreover, Hitchcock forced everyone to see the picture from beginning to end, a demand which he had written into the booking contract. The secrecy helped generate more publicity than Hitchcock dreamed of.

Today, the Bates home is a popular tourist attraction at Universal Studios. A 1983 film sequel, *Psycho II*, tried to rekindle our memories with mixed success. The improbable plot had Norman sprung from the loony bin after twenty years and returning to his beloved motel. But without the black-comedic touches of the master, Hitchcock, who had passed away in 1980, much of the impact was dissipated.

1961: Splendor in the Grass

Splendor in the Grass marked the film debut of a newcomer named Warren Beatty and the first film coupling of Beatty and Natalie Wood. It also marked the first collaboration of playwright William Inge and producer-director Elia Kazan. Although the film is set in the '20s, it captures the sexual repression of the early '60s, a time when good girls still didn't. If *Splendor* had been released later in the decade, when films reflected more liberated sexual attitudes, it would have been laughable. But in 1961 its attitude was on target.

Bud (Beatty) and Deanie (Wood) are high-school sweethearts in 1928 Kansas, hardly juvenile delinquents. Both have one parent who dominates the spouse and the child. Beatty is the son of a wealthy Babbitt-like oilman (Pat Hingle); she's the daughter of a lower middle-class grocer (Del Loomis) and a stern mother (Audrey Christie). Bud and Deanie always neck passionately—often by a waterfall—but the lovemaking is never consummated.

The lovers seek advice from their parents. Deanie asks her mother whether it's wrong for a girl to have sexual feelings. Her mother replies crisply "Good girls don't." Meanwhile, Bud's swaggering father keeps suggesting that he should find another girl—someone from the other side of the tracks, who does do it.

Bud and Deanie break off. Beatty begins dating the town "bad girl." Both Deanie and Bud suffer from the consequences of sexual repression. Bud collapses —from sexual frustration—during a basketball game; Deanie goes mad while soaking in the bathtub. She seeks help from a shrink in Wichita (a new concept way back then), and is committed to an institution, where she is cured. Bud, meanwhile, goes off to Yale and marries a low-life pizzeria waitress, whom he had impregnated.

The generation gap gets its comeuppance when Deanie's henpecked father finally stands up to his shrewish wife and tells Deanie where she can find Bud. At the end of the film, the couple have a moving reunion— the former lovers approach each other on a sunbaked, dusty road on Bud's ranch where they realize that Deanie's path has been the correct one. Patience and prudery win out again.

BEHIND THE SET

• *Splendor in the Grass* took its name from lines in a Wordsworth poem: "Though nothing can bring back the hour of splendor in the grass, glory in the flower..."

• It was shot in 1960, a full year before its release. Most of *Splendor in the Grass* was actually shot on Staten Island, then a rural area (the waterfall scenes were shot in upstate New York). It opened in October of 1961. No one under 16 was admitted without parents.

• It was advertised thus: "Most pictures end in a theatre. This picture ends late at night in your heart."

• Beatty, then 23, was likened to James Dean and Marlon Brando, but was still widely praised as one of the film discoveries of 1961. Many said Beatty, who had a traumatic adolescence, was playing himself as Bud. Beatty had made a Broadway splash in Inge's *A Loss of Roses,* a short-lived late-1959 play, which in turn had resulted from Beatty's discovery in a New Jersey playhouse by Inge and Joshua Logan. Within a few months of the play's closing, Inge had given Beatty the lead role in *Splendor.*

• *Splendor in the Grass* was the first play Inge (*Bus Stop* and *Picnic*) had written specifically for film. It was said to have been based on an incident in his youth.

• During filming, Natalie fell in love with Beatty, signaling the crumbling of her marriage to Robert Wagner. Fan mags of the era constantly showed the two co-stars together.

• Phyllis Diller made a brief appearance as a Texas Guinan-type speakeasy owner.

• Bosley Crowther called the film "One of the best films about children and parents we have ever seen."

Natalie Wood and promising newcomer Warren Beatty in *Splendor in the Grass* (1961)

1962: Lolita

The Girl of the Year in 1962 wore heart-shaped sunglasses, a bikini, and a seductive smile. Her name was Lolita—and in the summer of 1962 she was on a lot of people's minds.

"How did they ever make a movie out of *Lolita?*" That was the question raised in the ad campaign for Stanley Kubrick's 1962 film adapted from Vladimir Nabokov's provocative, satiric 1958 novel about the taboo subject of a middle-aged man's obsession for a 12-year-old girl.

They did make a movie—although those expecting the titillation of Nabokov's novel might have been disappointed. For instance, a *New Yorker* cartoon showed a group of people leaving a movie theater where *Lolita* was playing. "How could I enjoy it with that woman behind me going 'tisk, tisk, tisk' all the time," complained one movie-goer to his female companion.

The most obvious change was in the title character herself. The 12-year-old "nymphet," Lolita, was played by Sue Lyon, who was 14 years old but seemed older. Still, *Lolita* became one of the most popular films of 1962. It has been overshadowed by Kubrick's other two '60s masterpieces (*Dr. Strangelove* and *2001*), but it is still a fine film on many levels. Its keen satire captures the first tremors of the sexual revolutions of the early '60s, and its innuendo is superb. If the film had been made just a few years later, Lolita probably would have been shown as a young girl and the film would have been more faithful to the book. If the film was made today, Lolita would run around in a wet T-shirt (or less) and would make Brooke Shields in *Pretty Baby* seem as wholesome as Shirley Temple.

Here's the plot:

As the credits roll, we see a girl's leg thrust on the screen; we also see Humbert Humbert (James Mason) painting her toenails—one of the many ways Kubrick used suggestion to illustrate Nabokov's intent. The film then skips four years ahead with Humbert (James Mason) murdering the degenerate playwright Clare Quilty (Peter Sellers) following a drawn-out game of ping-pong in Quilty's decrepit mansion. The film then flashes back to Humbert's arrival in a New England town, where he takes a room in a boarding house run by Charlotte Haze (Shelley Winters), a widowed, oversexed frump.

The key reason Humbert decides to take up residence there is because of Charlotte's daughter. We first see Lolita sunning herself, in a bikini and heart-shaped glasses, in her mother's yard. Humbert is immediately entranced by the young girl ("I offer you a comfortable home, a sunny garden, a congenial atmosphere, and my cherry pie," Charlotte says). The girl treats Humbert with disdain, which increases Humbert's preoccupation. Humbert becomes so obsessed he even marries Charlotte just to be near her daughter. After the marriage, she discovers his diary in which he chronicles his obsession. Upset, she runs from the house and is fatally struck by an automobile. Humbert then becomes Lolita's guardian, taking her out of Camp Climax for Girls, where she had been sent by her jealous mother. They then embark on their life on the road together, shadowed always by the mysterious Quilty, who also has designs on Lolita. At the end, Lolita leaves Humbert, gets married and when we last see her, she has become a bored, young, middle-class housewife.

Kubrick's work on his previous films (*Paths of Glory, Spartacus, One-Eyed Jacks*) had marked the 33-year-old as one of Hollywood's most promising directors. *Lolita,* however, was the first film that he had total control over, a condition that would mark all his subsequent works.

While filming *Spartacus,* Kubrick bought the rights to the book for $150,000. But as *Lolita's* ad campaign implied, it seemed like an impossible task to make Nabokov's controversial book into a film. Kubrick and his partner, James Harris, convinced Nabokov to write the screenplay, which he did after some initial reluctance. (In 1974, Nabokov claimed that only twenty percent of the material in the film was his.) The first screenplay Nabokov and Kubrick wrote was submitted for approval to Hollywood's Production Code Board, which told producers how far they could go, morally speaking. They returned the script suggesting that the film not specify Lolita's age and not include any explicit love scenes between Lolita and Humbert.

That solved censorship problems, and Kubrick was then able to get financial backing. The film's underwriters were a group of Canadian bankers who said the film must be shot in London to keep the costs down. The film's final cost was $1.9 million.

Kubrick added his own satirical touches to the script; most notably enlarging Quilty's role from a minor character into a full-blown nemesis for Humbert. Kubrick also encouraged Sellers to improvise dialogue and to create a number of characters—which he would later do in *Strangelove.*

THE STORY OF SWEET SUE

To cast Lolita, Kubrick embarked on a year-long talent search, which included everybody from middle-aged women trying to look young to 9-year-olds trying to look sophisticated.

"After we saw Sue Lyon," said Kubrick at the time, "there wasn't even a close second for the part. She was the perfect nymphet."

Lyon ("Miss Smile of 1960"), who was raised in the suburbs of Los Angeles, had a few TV roles in "Dennis the Menace" and "The Loretta Young Show". She was 14 when shooting started on Lolita, 16 when the film came out. Said Lyon: "I never read the book—I don't think I could get through it. I made the movie instead." Her mother was more concerned: "The thing that worries me is that people may confuse my daughter with the slimy character she plays."

While filming in London, Kubrick kept Lyon carefully guarded from the public eye and the press. After the film was released we learned, according to one magazine article, that "She likes to Twist with boys from Hollywood High, and her favorite movie star is Paul Newman." She also observed: "I don't have anything against adults, now that I'm trying to enter their world myself. They do the best they can to understand teenagers."

She later appeared in Night of the Iguana in 1964 and returned to the public's eye in 1973 when she married convict Gary Adamson in prison (they were divorced not long after). Since then, she has appeared in some grade-Z flicks (Crash and End of the World), but little has been heard of the quondam nymphet, who's now about 40.

Here's what New York's Herald Tribune found out when one of its reporters interviewed patrons of a New York theater who had just seen Lolita:

Albert Scarkilli, 48, The Bronx: "I didn't see anything that justified excluding minors. The story is understandable; a middle-aged man goes overboard for a young girl. I would say she took him over. What man would take all that abuse, though?"

Linda Siatin, 19, Manhattan: "It wasn't for young people whose minds aren't developed. The acting was tremendous. But it was an unhealthy situation for people to have to think about."

Joan Farber, 20, Manhattan: "It left me feeling depressed coming out. People our age might be turned in the wrong direction seeing this kind of picture. But I was depressed anyway because I lost out on a job."

1963: HUD

Before HUD was the name of a cabinet department, it was the name of an ornery moden-day cowboy ("rhymes with stud") played by Paul Newman ("The man with the barbed-wire soul," said the ads) in a 1963 film that helped alter the classic Western. Like The Magnificent Seven three years earlier, Hud blurred the concepts of good and evil.

The film portrayed the death of the traditional ways of the West and the emergence of a new kind of modern frontier hero, a figure so bad he had no redeeming values—the type of person we'd come to love in the '70s in the person of J.R. Ewing on "Dallas."

As Judith Crist pointed out, other movie heels had something good to say for themselves, but not Hud. "We have not before encountered a man so immured from humanity...so completely uncaring, so alien—and yet so very much of our time and our society," Miss Crist wrote. He should've stuck around for the '70s and '80s. He would have been a "me generation" natural.

Hud takes place in modern-day Texas, where contemporary cowboys drive Cadillacs. Hud Bannon is a young, heavy-drinking, skirt-chasing rancher alienated from his father (Melvyn Douglas), an aging cattleman. Homer Bannon prefers the traditional principles of the West and doesn't like his son's opportunism, selfishness, and disregard for others. The conflict between the old and new West is told through the point of view of Lon, Hud's 16-year-old nephew (Brandon de Wilde). Lon idolizes Hud (even though Hud caused the death of the boy's father in a drunk-driving accident) but still has loyalty for his grandfather's ways. Meanwhile, Alma (Patricia Neal), the housekeeper, is attracted to Hud, but doesn't accept his advances.

The film's climactic moment comes when one of old man Bannon's cows is discovered to have died of hoof-and-mouth disease. Hud sees nothing wrong in telling his father to sell the herd before the government orders the animals killed. The old man naturally refuses Hud's scheme. Hud thinks his father is daft and tries to get him declared mentally incompetent. Their conflict heats up. "Why have you always despised me?" Hud asks his father. "Because you don't give a damn." Shortly after the cattle are finally slaughtered, the old man collapses and dies.

After a night of painting the town red, Hud returns to the ranch and tries to rape Alma, but Lon interrupts him. Alma leaves. Young Lon now sees the true character of his uncle and he, too, leaves the ranch. Hud watches him leave, shrugs his shoulders and opens a can of beer. Nothing fazes him. In his indifferent, amoral behavior, Hud was among the first of the '60s antiheroes.

Newman and director Martin Ritt became partners to work on the project. The two, along with screenwriters Irving Ravetch and

Harriet Frank, Jr., developed the character of Hud from a couple of lines in Larry McMurtry's novel *Horseman Pass By.*

Newman wanted a tough, uncompromising portrayal, an extension of his earlier role in *The Hustler,* and he achieved his goal; *Hud* contains one of his strongest performances to date. He received his third Academy Award nomination, but lost to Sidney Poitier for *Lillies of the Field.* From the cast, Oscars went to Douglas and Miss Neal. James Wong Howe's stunning cinematography of the West Texan landscape heightened the film's bleak atmosphere.

The film's use of the words "bitch" and "bastard" stirred considerable controversy. ("Everybody's got a right, including the picture business, to grow up," said Ritt.) The film did, however, receive code approval from the Catholic Legion of Decency.

P aul Newman and Patricia Neal in *Hud*

WHAT THE CRITICS HAD TO SAY ABOUT *HUD*

TIME: "A provocative picture with a shock for audiences who have been conditioned like laboratory mice to expect the customary "bad guy is really-good guy" reward in the last reel of a Western. Paul Newman is a cad to the end."

SATURDAY REVIEW: "There can be no two thoughts about Hud: He is purely and simply a bastard. And by the end of the film, for all his charm, he has succeeded in alienating everyone, including the audience."

BOSLEY CROWTHER: "Newman is tremendous—a potent, voracious man, restless with all his crude ambitions, arrogant with his contempt, and churned up inside with all the meanness and misgivings of himself."

Doctor Strangelove— Peter Sellers in the title role ponders the mineshaft gap (1964).

1964:
Dr. Strangelove or: How I Learned to Stop Worrying and Love the Bomb

In 1962, *Show,* Huntington Hartford's glossy, short-lived culture magazine, asked several leading film directors to imagine how they would make a film about the hydrogen bomb. The responses—from Bergman to Resnais to Truffaut—were all vague. The subject is too awesome to consider, most said; others could offer little more than the standard response about the mutations and mutilations that such a blast would cause.

They should have asked Stanley Kubrick who had established his reputation that year with *Lolita.* His idea, which would come to the screen two years later as *Dr. Strangelove or: How I Learned to Stop Worrying and Love the Bomb,* was daring and shocking.

Kubrick played the big boom for the big boff. *Strangelove* centers on a crazed USAF general who orders an atomic attack on the U.S.S.R. because he's convinced the Commies are fluoridating our water as part of a conspiracy to sap "our precious bodily fluids." As long as we're going down, we might as well go down laughing was his attitude—a risky proposition considering that the film was released only sixteen months after the Cuban missile crisis. Still, Kubrick believed (correctly as it turns out) that audiences would respond to such a treatment of nuclear war instead of to the moralizing of an *On the Beach*-type film. Despite a few indignant outcries ("The most shattering sick joke I've ever come across," fumed Bosley Crowther), most audiences showed they weren't offended by the black humor fashioned by Kubrick and his fellow screenwriters.

Strangelove is one of the few movies from the '60s that has improved with age, especially as the nuclear madness shows no sign of abating. At the time, though, it was daring stuff for some movie-goers. To mock the president of the United States as a weak-willed nebbish and the military as incompetent madmen (a theme taken up two years earlier in Joseph Heller's *Catch 22*) was still the type of stuff you might hear from comics like Lenny Bruce and Mort Sahl, not material you'd see in a movie. Within a few years, however, such irreverence would become a standard assumption of the antiwar movement.

For any era, it's a film classic.

Memorable performances in *Strangelove* abound: Sterling Hayden as General Jack D. Ripper, the cigar-chomping lunatic obsessed with his bodily fluids; George C. Scott as General Buck Turgidson, who offers a chilling parody of Pentagon-think, boasting that the U.S. will suffer only "acceptable casualties—10 to 20 million megadeaths—depending on the breaks." Best of all, Peter Sellers is featured in three roles—the nebbishy U.S. President Merkin Muffley (some people suggested that the bald-domed prexy was reminiscent of Adlai Stevenson; Sellers supposedly originally wanted to play him as a limp-wristed effete); Group Captain Mandrake, Ripper's prissy British aide-de-camp (who's actually the most rational character in the whole film); and as the sinister doctor himself, an ex-Nazi scientist whose mechanical arm insists on making the Nazi salute. Strangelove bore an uncanny (if premature) resemblance to Henry Kissinger, but both Sellers

and Kubrick denied that they knew Kissinger, who was then an obscure Harvard professor. It was rumored in the early days of the Nixon Administration that National Security Adviser Kissinger wasn't allowed to speak publicly for fear of the public associating him with Sellers' character.

Sellers was also supposed to play a fourth part—that of Major Kong, the Texan bombadier—but he broke his ankle and was replaced by Slim Pickens, best known for his roles as a sidekick in B Westerns. Pickens provides one of the film's most memorable scenes: At the end of the movie, Major Kong rides the plummeting A-bomb through the sky like a bucking bronco, waving his Stetson and shouting.

To research the film, Kubrick read seventy books on nuclear war, and subscribed to *Missiles and Rockets, the Bulletin of Atomic Scientists.* Not only did he produce and direct the film, he also helped write it along with Peter George and black-humor maven, Terry Southern. George had written the book on which *Strangelove* was based, *Two Hours to Doom,* a fictional account about how a nuclear war might start inadvertently. Kubrick bought the screen rights for $3,000 and began working on the book in his New York apartment with George, a former RAF lieutenant. He then decided to shoot it as a black comedy.

Some scenes were shot at an IBM office in London, where Computer 7090—the same data processor that calculated where Astronaut John Glenn would descend into the ocean after his orbit—was located. To lease that computer, the film company had to take out an insurance policy for $4 million; Sellers himself was insured for only $2 million.

Strangelove was shot at Shepperton Studios, London, to accommodate

The Sound of Music — Julie Andrews and Christopher Plummer as the von Trapps (1965).

Sellers. The key set was the war room, where the President and his generals gathered to discuss how to prevent Ripper's attack. The actors wore felt shoes so they wouldn't scuff the 13,000-square-foot jet-black laconite floor. (No one in the real Pentagon has ever acknowledged that a real war room exists.)

The climax of the film, as originally conceived, was to be a mad custard-pie melee, with the Russian ambassador de Sadesky and President Muffley sitting waist-deep in custard pies, making custard castles out of them and singing "For He's a Jolly Good Fellow," in reference to Dr. Strangelove. Kubrick had actually shot this sequence (the crew had ordered 2,000 pies a day while shooting) but then scrapped it.

The actual ending was the blackest of black humor. As exploding mushroom clouds, triggered by the Soviets' "Doomsday Device," fill the screen, the film departs with the strains of "We'll meet again/don't know where, don't know when, some sunny day." Again, Crowther: "It is malefic and sick."

Columbia canceled the premiere of *Strangelove* in London in December, 1963, because of JFK's death. It premiered simultaneously on January 29, 1964, in New York, London, and Toronto.

Later that year, the film *Fail Safe* was released, which, unlike *Strangelove,* played the subject of a nuclear attack straight, without humor.

STRANGELOVE'S MOST MEMORABLE MOMENT

Muffley on the hot line to the Soviet Premier Dimitri Kisoff: "Hello!...

Hello! Dimitri...Yes, this is Merkin. How are you?... Oh fine, Just fine. Look, Dimitri, you know we've always talked about the possibility of something going wrong with the Bomb?...The Bomb? The HYDROGEN BOMB!...That's right. Well, I'll tell you what happened. One of our base commanders..."

1965: The Sound of Music

It is Julie Andrews of the soaring voice and thrice-scrubbed innocence who makes me, even in guarded moments, catch my breath."—Kenneth Tynan.

"Everything comes out right, the Nazis aren't *really* Nazis, and it's happy-ending time."—Ernest Lehman, *Sound of Music* screenwriter.

The Sound of Music shone through all the madness and horror of the '60s; a beacon of sunshine from—where?—another world? another decade? The film proved the color of corn wasn't green, but gold. What was its appeal? It stressed a great many of the right values that were becoming in increasingly short supply —love, duty, parental love, patriotism—as well as the sunny presence of Julie Andrews.

Yes, it was corny, but it was also well staged and well crafted by two consummate professionals. It was directed by Robert Wise, who eliminated some of the cloying sweetness of Rogers and Hammerstein's musical, and written by the respected Ernest Lehman (who had written *West Side Story* and whose next project would be *Who's Afraid of Virginia Woolf?*) The film was shot on location in Salzburg, Austria, which undoubtedly enhanced its appeal, but, as Lehman said, "No one goes to the movies just for the Alps." Until the late '70s, *The Sound of Music* was the top box-office attraction of all time (in the '60s, it had surpassed *Gone with the Wind*). Almost single-handedly, it revived the fortunes of 20th Century-Fox, which had been decimated by the cost overruns of *Cleopatra.*

To summarize the plot: Maria (Miss Andrews), who can't hack it in the nunnery (she's always running away to groove on the nearby landscape), splits to the outside world, where she gets a job as governess for the seven children of the crabby widower, Captain Von Trapp (Christopher Plummer). She sings in the hills outside Salzburg and teaches the family how to be happy — until the Nazis invade their peaceful little world.

This is the movie musical that made Julie Andrews the star after *Mary Poppins* had introduced her to the movies the previous year. She had starred in the Broadway version of *My Fair Lady,* and was miffed when Audrey Hepburn got the lead in the movie version (its producers wanted a "name" to play Eliza Doolittle). *The Sound of Music* gave Andrews her chance for revenge. She was worried at first about the wisdom of taking the part. "After all," she said, "what can you do with nuns, seven children, and Austria?"

Plenty, obviously. The film was nominated for Ten Academy Awards and won an Oscar for best picture, although Miss Andrews lost out for best actress to Julie Christie (who won it for *Darling*).

The Sound of Music film had its first public preview in the winter of 1965 in Minneapolis because "we wanted a totally fresh audience," said Fox chief, Richard Zanuck. Even

though it was a miserable night, a capacity crowd came. At intermission, the entire audience stood and applauded for five minutes.

After the film went into general release, the critics unleashed all their fury. Said *Playboy* (why would they want to review it in the first place?): "Rarely has such a mountain of molasses avalanched over such a wide, wide, screen...pure Trapp-clap throughout." Pauline Kael in *McCall's* said: "Whom could it offend...only those of us who, despite the fact that we may respond and are aware of how self-indulgent and cheap and ready-made are the responses we are made to feel...The best of all possible worlds, that's what the SOM pretends we live in...it's the sugarcoated lie that people seem to want to eat." Judith Crist labeled it as "square and solid sugar" and urged that "Calorie counters, diabetics and grown-ups from 8 to 80 had best beware." Other critics called it the "sound of marshmallows" or the "sound of money."

Never had a public proved the critics so wrong. In most cities where it played, within the first week after opening, seats sold out for three consecutive months. In Atlanta, Syracuse, Colorado Springs, Cedar Rapids, and Orlando, attendance at *The Sound of Music* in eighteen months exceeded the towns' total populations. In Salt Lake City, attendance during the same period exceeded its population by three times. In Moorhead, Minnesota, it ran more than a year in the town's lone movie theater, causing a demonstration by students of Moorhead College, who picketed under the banner of POOIE (People's Organization of Intelligent Educatees) and brandished signs saying "49 weeks of schmaltz is enough; we want something new" and "Don't get caught in the von Trapp."

In 1965 and 1966, the film was shown in 3,200 theaters around the world— almost one-tenth of the worlds total of 35,000. It broke box-office records in Thailand but wasn't that boffo in Germany. Ironically, in the city of Salzburg, Austria, the *Sound of Music* proved not to be a popular attraction. One Welsh woman went to see it every day for a year. One Manhattan surgeon only saw it nine times—whenever he was depressed. "It's my psychiatrist's couch and an undrugged high at the same time," he said. With a philosophy like that, who needs Valium?

WHAT *THE SOUND OF MUSIC* WAS CALLED IN FOREIGN MARKETS

Germany—*My Song, My Dream*
Hong Kong—*Fairy Music Blow*
Egypt—*Love and Tenderness*
Portugal—*Music in the Heart*

Italy—*All Together with Passion*
Thailand—*Charms of the Heaven
   Sound*
Spain—*Smiles and Tears*
Argentina—*The Rebellious Novice*

SIXTIES SISTERS

As a result of *The Sound of Music's* success, nuns became a popular subject for films again. In 1966, MGM cast Debbie Reynolds as *The Singing Nun;* also in 1966, Columbia put Rosalind Russell and Hayley Mills in *The Trouble with Angels* and its sequel, *Where Angels Go, Trouble Follows.* By '67, swinging sisters had trickled down to TV, when Mary Poppins was crossed with Maria to create "The Flying Nun."

1966: Blow-Up

Blow-Up was Italian director Michelangelo Antonioni's ("the Goya of the go-go generation," as one writer called him) first English-language film (his previous works included *Red Desert* and *L'Avventura*). The movie helped make the so-called "art film" more accessible to the masses.

Taken at face value, *Blow-Up* is essentially a murder mystery with Hitchcockian overtones. Its appeal also derives from its setting—"Swinging London," at that moment the world epicenter of popular culture. And some great scenes of Swinging London are shown: miles of miniskirts, a pot party, the Yardbirds playing in a rock club and smashing their instruments a la The Who. (MGM's press release about the film said: "The story is set against the world of fashion, dolly girls, pop groups, beat clubs, models, parties, and above all, the "in" photographers

who more than anyone have promoted the city's new image.")

But, of course, an Antonioni film has to be more or else it wouldn't be an Antonioni film. And in *Blow-Up,* Antonioni's going full tilt, using Swinging London as the focus to peel away the tinsel and examine the emptiness beneath. Before filming *Blow-Up,* Antonioni admitted that he was fascinated by photographers. He called them "The new aristocracy of pop culture," adding that "in London, their status is extreme."

Blow-Up centers around Thomas (David Hemmings), a brash, self-centered photographer. He roams around London in a sports car, usually looking bored—a Mod version of Marcello Mastroianni in *La Dolce Vita*—shooting whatever catches his fancy, whether derelicts or high-fashion models. It makes no difference to him. One day, he sees a couple embracing in the park and shoots the scene with his camera. He's spotted, but refuses to turn over the film to the woman (Vanessa Redgrave). Later, she tracks him down to the studio, demanding his roll of film in exchange for her body. They have a brief, impersonal, hence typically '60s, sexual encounter.

Her quest is made clearer when Thomas develops the roll. Sly devil that he is, he had substituted another roll. When he blows up the image, he spots what appears to be a gun in the bushes. Has he recorded an act of passion or an act of murder? That gets to the film's key question: What is real, or does truth only exists in one's mind?

Blow Up—
David Hemmings as Antonioni's Mod man with a camera (1966)

Thomas decides to solve the mystery, which as most critics pointed out, seemed out of character for a man whose only loyalty had been to himself. He goes to the park, finds the body, but, when he returns to his flat, he finds it has been ransacked. When he returns to the park, the body is gone.

The film's final sequence is the most bizarre. Thomas stumbles onto a tennis court where a group of mimes are pretending to play. He watches them with a glazed expression, then his eyes dart back and forth as if he were following an invisible ball. Finally, we actually hear the sound of a ball being hit—although no ball appears on the screen.

Like Kubrick's *2001, Blow-Up* means what you want it to mean. Reality is what you make it, man. Antonioni had said this project "will definitely be ambiguous." He was right.

Prior to its debut, *Blow-Up* was already generating controversy, largely because of the scene in which Thomas tumbles around the floor of his studio with a bunch of half-clad teenyboppers. The Catholic Church gave *Blow-Up* a C rating for "condemned," and the MPAA denied the film its seal of approval. For a while, MGM itself was reluctant to associate its name with the film, but eventually took its chances. Smart move. *Blow-Up* was subsequently named Best Film of 1966 by the National Society of Film Critics.

Said Antonioni: "I hate my films and I do not wish to talk about them."

DAVID HEMMINGS, FOR REAL?

David Hemmings, then 25, briefly became the Mod man of the moment, although he was never really part of the Mod scene. Since 1966, he has appeared in dozens of plays, TV, and theatrical films, from *Camelot* and *Barbarella* to *The Love Machine, Airwolf,* and *Dr. Jekyll and Mr. Hyde.* Hemmings may have had long hair and Mod clothing, but he spoke like a true member of the establishment in a 1966 interview the week before *Blow-up* was released.

Hemmings said: "This Mod scene in London all started with the photographers. They created an image, first with the singing groups, then with the clothes and the models. It was something the young people could react to. Then came the sexual promiscuity. But it doesn't lead to anything. Just noise and rebellion. There's nothing really creative. Take the singing groups—their stage performances are so unprofessional. Their guitars are out of tune. They don't know what they're doing so they do the same thing over and over. Its awful.

"What bugs me about my generation is the lethargy. They don't *do* anything. They just sit around waiting for something to happen. They have so much money and they're too young to remember what people had to go through to get that for them. So they're just against everything and passive. If you ask me, I think they are all waiting for another war."

CRITICS CHOICE

BOSLEY CROWTHER: "The sharpest piece of cinema of the year, the most artful use of color, movement, and design to suggest and unfold a realization of alienation and emptiness."

VARIETY: "As a commentary on a sordid, confused side of humanity in this modern age, it's a bust...goes far beyond the limits of good taste."

1967: The Graduate

A perceptive letter to the *New York Times* from a Stony Brook University student who had just seen *The Graduate* caught the mood of the young viewers who flocked to see the film, the surprise hit of 1967-68: "I identified with Ben," the student wrote. "I thought of him as a spiritual brother. He was confused about the future and about his place in the world, as I am. It's a film one digs, rather than understands intellectually."

Precisely. The film's protagonist, Benjamin Braddock, as played by Dustin Hoffman, *was* an odd antihero. He wasn't a long-haired radical. He rarely raised his voice. The ever-escalating Vietnam war was never mentioned in the movie. But Hoffman had a sense of personal morality, which may be the film's most potent message. He *communicated*—in the same way that James Dean had communicated to the young of a previous generation in *Rebel Without a Cause*.

Benjamin Braddock is the all-American college boy (captain of the debate club, editor of the school paper, track star). After graduation from an Eastern university, he returns to his parents' luxurious home in Beverly Hills. He seems dazed and confused, turned off to the materialistic and hypocritical values of his parents. ("I want my life to be ...different," is the best way he can describe his angst.)

After lounging around for several weeks without direction, he allows himself to be seduced by Mrs. Robinson (Anne Bancroft), the neurotic wife of his father's partner. They conduct an unpassionate, nervous affair in a hotel room. He reluctantly agrees to date the Robinsons' daughter, Elaine (Katharine Ross), and falls in love with her, pursuing her through a series of tragicomic events until the film's memorable climax. After driving all night from Berkeley to Santa

Barbara, Ben crashes Elaine's wedding ceremony, where he literally snatches the bride from her husband-to-be. The final scene shows the couple, she still in her gown, sitting in the rear seat of a city bus smiling awkwardly at each other.

The young couple's fate was the subject of much speculation. Has it been a Pyrrhic victory for Ben? Would they end up like their parents? There are those who say that Hoffman's 1979 film *Kramer vs. Kramer* should have been called "The Post-Graduate," since his role as Ted Kramer seemed a reasonable approximation of where Benjamin Braddock might have ended up twelve years later —like other members of his generation, the new sensitive male, divorced, torn between his career and his role as father.

BEHIND THE SET

The Graduate was based on Charles Webb's 1963 novel of the same title. Webb, who claimed never to have seen the movie, wrote the book in 1960 when he was 61. When it was published in 1963, it met with mixed reviews and had a hardcover sale of 5,000 copies. Director Mike Nichols and producer Lawrence Turman had bought the rights in 1964. Nichols, who had successfully switched his career from comedy to cinema, had scored with his film adaptation of the stage play *Who's Afraid of Virginia Woolf?* in 1965.

Nichols and Turman were having problems with the film version of *The Graduate* and were delaying production until they found the right young man to fit the concept of the story's title character. Originally they were looking for a blond surfer-type ("a walking surfboard" is how the cast call described the role) to play Benja-

min. One of those who had tested for the Benjamin role was Christopher Connelly of "Peyton Place." (Nichols also wanted Jeanne Moreau and, some say, Doris Day for the Mrs. Robinson role.) But they changed their minds when they saw Hoffman in an off-Broadway play called *Eh?* where he played a Cockney plumber. Hoffman, then 30, was a decade older than the protagonist. Nichols offered Hoffman $17,000 for the role. Until that time, Hoffman had never earned more than $3,000 a year since he began working as a New York stage actor in 1958. The homely, five-foot, six-inch Hoffman was an unlikely choice for the role. *Life* called him a "swarthy Pinocchio;" the New York *Daily News* said he "resembled both Sonny *and* Cher."

In his screen-test, he did the love scenes with Katharine Ross. Her first impression, she told *Life,* was "he looks about three feet tall, so dead serious, so humorless, so unkempt. This is going to be a disaster because he seemed so desperate."

"I'd never asked a girl in acting class to do a love scene before. No girl asked me, either," Hoffman told an interviewer. He was so nervous that he reached out and grabbed Miss Ross' rear end.

The bedroom scene with Miss Bancroft was also difficult. Hoffman said it was not because he was in bed with her, but because the crew was watching. To overcome his nervousness and shyness, he pretended that he was another man trying to bed Bancroft while all the crew members gawked at him. Nichols said Hoffman's nervousness indicated that he "understood the sufferings of Braddock." In fact, the character was not unlike Hoffman—shy, intelligent, trying to be moral.

The film opened on December 21, 1967, to largely superlative reviews.

After the film was out, Hoffman was still collecting $55 a week unemployment, because he had blown the $17,000 salary waiting for his next part. That would soon come along as the crippled street hustler, Ratso Rizzo, in *Midnight Cowboy.*

The Graduate was a huge financial success, surpassing the previous domestic box-office champ, *Mary Poppins. The Graduate* was one of the first films to click with the so-called youth market—the vast majority of young people who were no longer content with beach party and motorcycle films as examples of their generation. One of the film's many strong points was using Simon and Garfunkel tunes on its soundtrack, which may have initially helped draw young audiences. It was one of the first uses of the New Rock in a non-performance movie setting, and also helped cement Simon and Garfunkel's status as musical spokesmen for the "Baby-Boom" generation. One song from the movie, "Mrs. Robinson," became one of the biggest records of 1968 and also contained one of Paul Simon's best phrases, which summed up the drift away from tradition: "Where have you gone, Joe DiMaggio?"

The Graduate won five Golden Globes from the Hollywood Foreign Press Association and was nominated for best picture. Only Nichols won for best director. Hoffman lost the best actor to Rod Steiger (*In the Heat of the Night*). Katharine Hepburn (*Guess Who's Coming to Dinner*) beat out Miss Bancroft for best actress. Miss Ross lost to Estelle Parsons of *Bonnie and Clyde* for best supporting actress.

The film remains a popular attraction today—although modern career-minded students may think that anyone who wouldn't want to work for a corporation or live in a split-level house might be a bit weird.

Not everyone dug *The Graduate,* of course. The National Catholic Office for Motion Pictures gave it an A-4 rating for Catholics ("morally objectionable for adults, with reservations"). In January, 1968, the New York City Transit Authority bowed to pressure from a Queens City Councilman (John Santucci) and removed an advertising poster from subway platforms showing Miss Bancroft and Hoffman in bed together.

1967: Bonnie and Clyde

I f Bonnie and Clyde were here today, they'd be hip. Their values have been assimilated in much of our culture—not robbing banks and killing people, of course, but their style, their sexuality, their bravado, their delicacy, their cultivated arrogance, their narcissistic insecurity, their curious ambition, have relevance to the way we live now."— Screenwriters David Newman and Robert Benton.

As the generation gap widened in the late '60s, the old heroes—the athlete, the astronaut, the cowboy— no longer satisfied American youth. New heroes were needed to embody the hopes and aspirations of the new generation. So whom did they choose? Rock stars who burned their guitars, third-world revolutionaries, acid gurus, and perhaps the strangest of all—Bonnie Parker and Clyde Barrow—a couple of low-life, bush-league gangsters of the '30s, transformed by Hollywood into chic outlaws.

Go figure that one. *Bonnie and Clyde,* released in August, 1967, turned out to be one of the biggest box-office surprises of the decade, as well as one of the most controversial.

Eighteen years later, critics are still arguing about the film's attractiveness to the under-30s. Was it the violence? Did they identify with the protagonists' anti-establishment outlook? Was it Arthur Penn's direction? Or was it the strong performances of Warren Beatty and Faye Dunaway?

BEHIND THE SET

The idea for *Bonnie and Clyde* began in 1964 when its writers, David Newman and Robert Benton, were working as art director and editor, respectively, of *Esquire* magazine. They wanted to collaborate on a screenplay— something neither of them had ever previously done. Their inspirations: the New Wave cinema of French filmmakers Francois Truffaut and Jean-Luc Godard, a perception that American mores were changing, and fascination with a book about gangster John Dillinger. They also wanted no one but Truffaut to be the film's director. Some friends gave them working capital; another friend at the French Film Office in New York liked their idea and forwarded it to Truffaut, who would later spend time with the writers, offering constructive criticism. But he would not commit himself.

They looked fruitlessly for a director for eighteen months. Even Arthur Penn—who would later say yes— rejected their work. During this time, they kept themselves busy by latching onto the high-camp boom by writing *It's a Bird, It's a Plane, It's Superman* for Broadway.

At the same time, Beatty, still considered a young rebel, was looking to get an in with the Hollywood establishment. He read the scenario and was impressed, but he said he would only become involved if he owned the film. Benton and Newman sold Beatty an option for $10,000 against a final payment of $75,000. Beatty decided he also would produce and star in the film. Warner Brothers really didn't think the film would click, so they humored him when he demanded a rising percentage scale against possible grosses.

Beatty's interest and persistence also finally won over Penn. Penn brought to the film his sense that the alienation of the young during the '30s was comparable to that of the youth of the '60s. He believed the allegory would be strengthened by emphasizing an era unfamiliar to the younger generation.

The screenplay took much historical license, changing names, adding characters and deleting others. Bonnie Parker's story had been done already, in a 1958 low-budget thriller starring Dorothy Provine, which was more accurate historically but had little cinematic impact. The real-life Bonnie Parker was a dumpy, cigar-smoking woman; in Penn's film, she was transformed into a stylish belle. Penn also played up Barrow's alleged impotence as a key ingredient of the film's plot. A key character, dimwitted gang member C.W. Moss (Michael J. Pollard) was actually a composite of several gang members.

Beatty had originally wanted his sister, Shirley MacLaine, to play Bonnie, but Penn won out and tabbed Dunaway, whose previous films had included *The Happening* and *Hurry Sundown,* for the role. Dunaway was told to lose weight for the part, so she went on a near-starvation diet and shed thirty pounds. To achieve a lean, tense look, she wore weights of sand around her wrists, ankles and waist.

Penn filmed *Bonnie and Clyde* in a kind of documentary style that accurately captured the atmosphere of the

Midwest and Southwest during the Depression. He also incorporated techniques from the French New Wave cinema. A soundtrack of banjo music at times gave the film a comedic touch. Bonnie and Clyde are essentially played as hayseed Robin Hoods; a couple of goofy kids robbing banks for kicks. As the film progresses, the violence also intensifies, which makes the comic aspects seem even more macabre.

The most violent moment, and one of the most talked-about film sequences of the decade, occurs at the end of the film when the pair, lured into an ambush, are killed in a powerful hail of a posse's gunfire. In an extended scene, shot by four cameras, each at different speeds, we see the couple's bodies jerk and twist as they are riddled with bullets. A piece of Clyde's head flies off, not dissimilar to what happened to JFK, an effect which Penn consciously strove to emulate. This overkill or "ballet of blood" had the effect of creating sympathy for the pair.

The film made its debut in August, 1967, as the leading American entry and opening-night feature at a Montreal film festival, held in conjunction with Expo '67. It grossed $20 million that year and captured two Oscars (it was nominated for ten), including best actress.

After a riot-torn, demonstration-marred summer and fall, Bonnie and Clyde hit a nerve with contemporary youth. The young couple were seen as folk heroes who also went up against the establishment—and were killed for their behavior in an act far more bloody than any crime they had committed. Perhaps Americans had become so inured to violence that the fact that the real-life Barrow gang killed eighteen people didn't register anymore. For a time violence was chic; it was during the same period when the ultra-liberal *New York Review of Books* printed a recipe for a Molotov cocktail on its pages. After *Bonnie and Clyde,* blood spattered on the screen in buckets, but few films, save for Sam Peckinpah's *The Wild Bunch,* succeeded as well in combining violence with artistry.

One by-product of *Bonnie and Clyde* was that it created nostalgia for the '30s. The "Bonnie and Clyde" look was a fashion sensation of early 1968. (New York Knicks basketball superstar Walt "Clyde" Frazier got his nickname by emulating Clyde Barrow's dress—as well as from his ability to steal the ball from opponents.) The film's theme song, Flatt and Scruggs' "Foggy Mountain Breakdown," became a Number 1 song in England and a smash here, as did Georgie Fame's "The Ballad of Bonnie and Clyde," which was actually banned on several radio stations because the recording contained a simulation of gunfire. Meanwhile, Bonnie Parker's sister released an LP: *The Truth about Bonnie and Clyde as told by Billie Jean Parker.*

WHAT THE CRITICS HAD TO SAY ABOUT *BONNIE AND CLYDE*

Bosley Crowther hated it: "Another indulgence of a restless and reckless taste and an embarrassing addition to the excess of violence on the screen." He also argued with historical accuracy of the film.

Time: "A strange and purposelessness mingling of fact and claptrap that teeters uneasily on the brink of burlesque." A few weeks later, the magazine reversed its opinion and called the film "The Sleeper of the Decade."

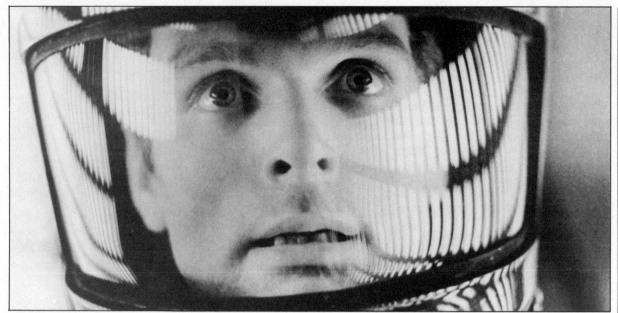

2001: A Space Odyssey— Astronaut Keir Dullea on his way to Jupiter (1968)

1968: 2001: A Space Odyssey

WHAT DOES IT ALL MEAN?

You're free to speculate as you wish about the philosophical and allegorical meaning of the film," said Stanley Kubrick in a 1968 interview, speaking about his *2001: A Space Odyssey,* which became the cult movie of the year, and some say, the decade.

Indeed, that was one of the more popular parlor games of the late '60s— especially if you were under the influence. Just what did Kubrick mean by the Dawn of Man sequence? Just what did that psychedelic light show—better than anything the Fillmore East ever showed—mean? What did the Monolith mean? Is technology greater than man? Is man greater than technology?

What, indeed?

Kubrick made a film that was the first largely nonverbal commercial success. Almost a half-hour elapses before the first man appears, much less the first words uttered. Its dialogue is minimal; what dialogue there is is crisp, efficient, and boring. Its techniques borrowed heavily from the underground cinema, grafting it to the wide-screen wonder of Cinerama. The 200 or so special effects, supervised by Douglas Trumbull, who did the same thing for *Close Encounters,* were state-of-the-art, simulating the feelings of hurtling through outer space.

The actual plot seems like little more than standard sci-fi: Astronauts go to a far planet to probe whether intelligent life exists beyond Earth. But underneath this simple plot, Kubrick is probing some heavy metaphysical things, which are communicated visually, not verbally.

The principal human characters, Dave Bowman and Frank Poole (played by Keir Dullea and Gary Lockwood), the Jupiter mission astronauts, are dullards. The true star of the film is HAL (the acronym being the letters before IBM), a computer so advanced that it is more human than any other character in the film. He has an engaging personality and speaks in well-modulated tones (his voice was supplied by Douglas Rain, a veteran Canadian Shakespearean actor).

HAL is Big Brother taken to the extreme, regulating every aspect of the astronaut's flight and planning to strategically outmaneuver them when he senses they may not be competent enough to be part of the mission. In one of the most chilling scenes, the two astronauts enter what they think is a soundproof pod to discuss how to deal with the intransigent HAL. But HAL is one step ahead: he has the ability to read lips and he's able to thwart their plans. For some viewers, HAL's disconnection elicited a more sympathetic response than the death of a human being might.

The film is composed of four segments:

1. The Dawn of Man takes place four million years ago as ape-men (who are actually actors in ape costumes, except for two baby chimpanzees) try to survive on the desert. But it's not until they contact an ominous monolith do they learn how to turn stones and bones into weapons, allowing them to survive.

2. We're on the moon in the year 2001. American scientists have discovered a monolith buried there, which is broadcasting signals to Jupiter. The transition of four million years to this scene is one of the most effective and beautiful in the film. From the "Dawn of Man," an ape tosses up a bone, and, as it whirls in midair, the film cuts to a bone-shaped spacecraft spinning slowly in space. It's an orbiting American space station. As it revolves around the Earth, the accompanying music is the "Blue Danube Waltz." During this section, we also get to see Kubrick's amusing pop-culture touches, the familiar product brand-names extending their influence to outer space: Pan Am, Bell (picturephone), Hilton, How-ard Johnson's Earthlight Room, plus floating stewardesses and zero-gravity toilets.

3. The third section is the journey of the Jupiter spaceship with the two astronauts, along with three astronauts in artificial hibernation, and HAL.

4. The last segment is Jupiter and Beyond—the famed psychedelic "trip" sequence in which the one surviving astronaut, Bowman, learns the meaning of life. After experiencing twenty minutes of colorful effects, he enters a room filled with period furniture. He goes through middle age, old age, and death and is then transformed into a fetus-like "starchild" floating in space.

There's no explanation. As Kubrick said, you can make up your own. In the context of the times, when nothing made sense, it was the young who reacted most favorably. *2001* was the name of the disco featured in *Saturday Night Fever;* its stirring theme music, Strauss' "Thus Spake Zaruthustra," came to be used to open Elvis Presley's Las Vegas stage shows and in dozens of TV commercials. Today's audiences may be more concerned with the fate of the Ewoks and E.T., but without *2001,* those films may not have been possible.

BEHIND THE SET

The film was shrouded in secrecy after Kubrick announced he was planning to make a sci-fi follow-up to *Dr. Strangelove,* inspired by a short story *The Sentinel,* by the well-known British sci-fi writer, Arthur Clarke. When MGM announced the project on February 22, 1965, it was originally titled "Journey Beyond the Stars." The film, Kubrick's first in color, took three years to make and cost $10 million.

Kubrick and Clarke wrote a 130-page prose treatment and consulted with dozens of scientific authorities and agencies. The treatment was reworked and rewritten into a screenplay and then reworked again.

As with *Strangelove,* Kubrick supervised every aspect of production, from the construction of an enormous spinning centrifuge to simulate the spaceship's interior, to the extraordinary man-ape costumes, to the music.

Kubrick received ample help from NASA. Astronaut Deke Slayton was hired as a permanent production consultant. NASA also put Kubrick in touch with forty companies and institutes involved in the study of and preliminary preparations for interplanetary space travel. MGM ordered from the British company Vickers Armstrong Ltd. a huge centrifugal machine, thirty-eight feet in diameter, revolving at a speed of three mph. Inside this contraption a condition similar to weightlessness could be produced.

After a New York preview at which many people walked out, Kubrick trimmed nineteen minutes from the film. Many critics reacted negatively to the film at first—especially the more traditional writers, accustomed to more linear presentations. But because of the trippiness of the final quarter of the film, *2001* found a receptive audience with teens and college students. Walk into any movie house in the spring of 1968 and chances are you'd see dozens of youngsters sprawled on the floor during the final segment. No wonder *Rat,* the underground newspaper, said: *"2001* is the head flick of all time...note the people fighting at intermission to get those 50-cent chocolate bars or the spaced-out few who contemplate the curtain for long minutes after the movie ends."

1969: Easy Rider

Easy Rider today may seem like a cross between a Cheech and Chong movie and a travelogue, but in 1969 this tale of two motorcycle-riding hippie-types searching for America and getting blown away for their efforts, was about as hip as you could get.

Here was '60s paranoia personified! It was them vs. us. The enemy was everywhere—whether they were the shotgun-totin' rednecks who offed Captain America and Billy in the film, the cops in Chicago who cracked open demonstrators' heads the previous summer, or the front four of the H. Frank Carey football team who chased me around the locker room snapping towels. There was no doubt about it: THEY would stop at nothing—even murder—to get us.

Young audiences, especially if their allegiance was to the counterculture, related. I knew which side I was on...and hey, man, *Easy Rider* put the stamp of approval on being a persecuted victim of Pig Amerika. For two years after I saw the film, if I went into a restaurant and didn't get served immediately, I assumed I was getting the same *Easy Rider* treatment—callous disregard because of the length of hair and dress—that greeted Captain America and Billy as they traveled across the Southwest.

Woodstock, which happened a month after *Easy Rider's* release was, in a way, a sort of show of support for the martyred heroes of the film. See, look how many of us there are. They won't get us.

At the time, I certainly didn't question the movie's premises. Nor did it bother me, as it did some adult critics, that the heroes used profits from a

Easy Rider—
Jack Nicholson
as a small-town
lawyer who
checks in with
Captain Ameri-
ca and Billy —
but doesn't
check out
(1969)

cocaine deal to finance their trip. Nor did it bother me much that the characters were never developed as human beings.

The film's narrative tells the story of two hippie-like characters, Wyatt (a.k.a. Captain America, played by Peter Fonda) and Billy (Dennis Hopper), who travel on motorcycles from California through the South-west and South heading for the Mardi Gras. The film offers a Cook's tour of the counterculture: a commune, dope smoking, an acid trip sequence, and one of the best rock soundtracks, including everything from Jimi Hendrix and the Electric Prunes to Bob Dylan and the Byrds.

Not surprisingly, Easy Rider has dated easily. Drugs and long hair have become such an accepted part of our day-to-day culture that one tends to forget when they had outlaw status. The film was out-of-date when I saw it again in revival in 1972; by then, even those rednecks probably had shoulder-length hair and were digging Marshall Tucker or the Allman Brothers. In fact, when the film is shown in the '80s, modern-day younger audiences laugh hysterically.

And why not? Fonda was a Hollywood hippie with his neat, razor-cut hair, Carnaby Street shirt, and leather pants. Hopper was the hippie as derelict—fringed jacket, stringy hair, walrus moustache, cowboy hat, puka shells around his neck. Every other word out of his mouth was "man." He stumbled around in a cannabis haze most of the time.

They *are* comical. But *Easy Rider* was noteworthy and Hollywood-wise for another reason: It showed the studio moguls that "the youth movie," once thought to be geared only for cretins at drive-ins, was now a valid (i.e., profitable) genre. In ER's wake came the slew of "hip" youth movies of the early '70s such as *RPM* and *The Strawberry Statement.* None were as successful as *Easy Rider.*

The film was also noteworthy because it marked the first substantial role for Jack Nicholson who previously had been featured in several AIP flicks. In *Easy Rider,* he actually saves the film. *New York Times* critic, Vincent Canby, likened Nicholson's entry into the movie as a "real-life character set into a cartoon." He plays George Hanson, an alcoholic civil liberties lawyer who befriends the duo when they share a cell with him in the jail of his small Southern town. The boys are in there for creating a public nuisance; Jack's cooped up because he's sleeping another one off. He uses his small-town connections to spring them from jail and then joins them on the road, wearing a seersucker jacket and his high school football helmet.

When Nicholson smokes a joint for the first time, it's one of those quintessential '60s experiences that everyone remembers ("You hold it deep in your lungs, George," Captain America coaches). As the trio sits around a campfire, passing a joint, Hanson relates his elaborate theory about how the Venusians are taking over; it's reminiscent of every dopey, dope-induced conversation you ever had or care to recall.

Hanson's murder by rednecks changes the film's mood from paranoia to violence and also presages the deaths of Wyatt and Billy. It's probably the film's most powerful moment. From then on, the film degenerates into what we once called a bummer—the Mardi Gras is a nightmare; the acid trip holds nothing but terror—until it finally culminates in the pair's murder.

ON THE SET

When it opened on July 14, 1969, most critics saw *Easy Rider* as just another in the line of AIP motorcycle films, such as Fonda's *The Wild Angels*—even though the film had been the American entry at the Cannes Film Festival. Columbia took great pains to dispel that image, creating an ad campaign with the Kerouacian notion that "A man went looking for America and couldn't find it anywhere. "

Fonda was on tour promoting another film when he conceived an image of two young men experiencing, as he saw it, "the ultimate freedom," a trip across the United States on motorcycles.

Originally, AIP was going to produce the movie. But AIP chief Sam

Arkoff wanted the right to replace Hopper as director. No dice, said Fonda and Hopper. They then successfully pitched the project to Bob Rafelson and Bert Schneider (creators of the Monkees) at Columbia, who delivered the financing. Fonda and Hopper, respectively, produced and directed the film and collaborated with Terry Southern on the screenplay. It was made on a budget of about $375,000.

It was said that 90 percent of the film was ad-libbed. Even amateur players, the townspeople who stopped to watch the movie being shot as the company moved across country, ended up being cast. Rather than attempt to teach them dialogue, Hopper told them what had gone before in the story and let them ad-lib.

The crew set out from Hollywood without a schedule or time limit, with a basic story outline, but without a script. The company would drive until they spotted a place they liked, then shoot a scene.

They claimed not to have encountered any problems along the way, but before they left Hollywood, Fonda had some trouble with the one set that was built for the film, a hippie commune with a hay-lined barn. Fonda developed an allergy to the hay and, not wishing to delay production, ignored the coughing. The coughing persisted and settled in his lungs. Several weeks later, he couldn't hold out any longer, and went to a clinic in New Mexico. He was hospitalized for a week with bronchial pneumonia. Doctors said another day or two without treatment would have been fatal.

Ironically, the role of Hanson was supposed to go to Rip Torn, but he had too many disagreements with Fonda and Hopper. Bruce Dern was also said to be up for the part, but he wasn't offered enough money.

Nicholson said he patterned Hanson's drawl from listening to Lyndon Johnson. Nicholson told *Time* in 1970 that during the campfire scene: "I smoked about 155 joints. Keeping it all in mind stoned, and playing the scene straight and then becoming stoned—it was fantastic."

CRITICS CHOICE

Look: "Go. Think about it. Squirm!"

Rex Reed: "A bold, courageous statement of life seldom matched in motion pictures! I couldn't shake what I'd seen, even after I left the theatre."

Richard Schickel, *Life:* "A lyric, tragic song of the road! An historic movie!"

Bruce Bahrenburg, *Newark News:* "Middle-brow tripe being given life at the box-office by middle-aged praise."

MEMORABLE DIALOGUE

George to Billy and Wyatt: "What you represent to them is freedom...It's real hard to be free when you're bought and sold in the marketplace. But don't ever tell anybody they ain't free 'cause they're gonna get real busy killin' and maimin' to prove they're free."

Captain America: "We blew it."

"They look like a bunch of refugees from a gorilla love-in."—Comment by a redneck in a cafe where Billy, Wyatt, and George are refused service.

EASY RIDER TRIVIA

1. Who played the executive that the two sell dope to?
2. One of the prostitutes the boys visit in the New Orleans brothel is better known today as a choreographer and also had one of the big-

gest hit records of 1982. Who is she?

James Bond Galore

JFK dug him... Pussy Galore karate-chopped him... The Reds wanted him dead. He was Commander James Bond, Agent 007, with a license to kill for Her Majesty's Secret Service. When 007 was on the case, the Free World was a safer place.

Bond was born in the '50s in Ian Fleming's novels and is still around today, but the '60s was the true Golden Age of Bond. That was when a fairly obscure Scottish actor named Sean Connery brought Fleming's character to the screen. As the ads for *Dr. No* proclaimed: "Sean Connery Is James Bond." Accept no substitutes.

Connery transformed Bond into a person who would epitomize the '60s male hero—cool under pressure, assured with women, equally familiar with weaponry and wine, emotionless, noncommittal, cynical tongue planted firmly in cheek. So what if he wore a hairpiece?

And let's make one thing perfectly clear. When we're talking Bond, we're really only talking about the Big Four films from 1962 to 1966: *Dr. No, From Russia with Love, Goldfinger,* and *Thunderball.* Later for *You Only Live Twice* and *Diamonds are Forever* with a tired Connery, *On Her Majes-*

ty's Secret Service with someone called George Lazenby, and anything with Roger Moore (although he was nifty as Simon Templar, the Saint, a semi-Bond TV knockoff).

For such a man, you didn't have just ordinary films. You needed films like the Big Bad Four—full of sex, fantasy, violence, evil, and gadgetry.

What villains! Bond battled the sinister, hook-handed Dr. No (who wore a Mao jacket in 1962, fashion buffs take note), the slimy Goldfinger (whose goal was nothing less than the looting of Fort Knox) and Oddjob, his Oriental hatchet-man (or more properly hat-man—his bowler had a razor-sharp steel brim), and the wily Rosa Klebb (*From Russia with Love*), who concealed a poisoned dagger in the toe of her shoe.

What women!—more fantasy women than a newsstand full of *Playboys:* the athletic, Amazon Honeychile Ryder (Ursula Andress) emerging from the surf in *Dr. No,* a dagger strapped to the belt of her wet bikini, revealing more than most audiences were used to in 1962; Pussy Galore (Honor Blackman, late of "The Avengers"), whose name was enough to provoke blushing in the audience, never mind her tight-fitting ensemble; Jill Masterson (Shirley Eaton), who got a free, final gold-plating job across her curvaceous body for ratting on Auric Goldfinger; *Thunderball's* Domino Vitale (Claudine Auger), who also made her entrance in a bikini—on the back of a turtle. She later had Bond suck a sea-urchin's poisonous sting from her foot, and fetishism never seemed so exotic. In the same movie Domino and 007 make love underwater; her bikini top floats to the top.

What gimmicks! Bond's Aston-Martin DB-V shot oil slicks, jettisoned unwanted human cargo with its ejector seat, and outraced its rivals with

The name is Bond...James Bond. Agent 007 cozies up to Honeychile Ryder (Ursula Andress) in *Dr. No,* the first of several movies adapted from Ian Fleming's novels (1962).

its chariot scythe, smoke screen, and by confusing its foes with a rotating license plate.

What escapes! Scorpions, laser beams, locked steam rooms, and spine-stretching machines were all used to try and eliminate Bond. He survived them all.

Fleming, for his part, saw the Bond novels and films in sync with the times, telling one interviewer: "We live in a violent era...In our last war, thirty million people were killed. As for sex, seduction has to a marked extent replaced courtship." Bond's creator, however, wasn't around to benefit from the boom. Fleming died in August, 1964, during the filming of *Goldfinger.*

The first two films (*Dr. No* and *From Russia with Love*) were more like spy thrillers (*From Russia with Love* is considered by Bond aficionados to be the best pure Bond), while the last three Connery films involved increasingly more amazing agents of destruction.

At first, *Dr. No* was not that successful in the States. Cracked one exhibitor: "I can't sell this Limey detective to our people in the South." Paperback book sales of Fleming's novels increased, however, with the success of *Dr. No.*

From Russia with Love was a bigger box-office success than *Dr. No* and received an unexpected boost of popularity when John F. Kennedy said he was an avid fan of the Bond novels, rating *From Russia with Love* as being one of his top ten favorite books.

Goldfinger came out in December, 1964. In the winter-spring of 1965, Shirley Bassey's hit version of "Goldfinger" was on the charts and, as Bond grew popular, American audiences were treated to a revived double bill of *From Russia* and *Dr. No.*

Thunderball was the most lucrative Bond film. Its arrival in the theaters coincided with a rush of Bond merchandising around Christmas, 1965 — aftershave (said the ad copy: "007 gives any man the license to kill...women"), suits, socks, attache cases, games, and toys. During opening week, *Thunderball* played round-the-clock at the refurbished Paramount Theater in Manhattan.

By 1967, Connery was getting tired of Bond (he had always sought other roles in between the 007 films), and his 1967 film, *You Only Live Twice,* shows it. In 1969, George Lazenby, whose experience had largely been in British TV commercials, became the first non-Connery Bond when he appeared in *On Her Majesty's Secret Service.* Connery came back in 1971 in *Diamonds are Forever* and 1983's *Never Say Never Again.* In the '70s, Roger Moore played Bond in such films as *Live and Let Die* and *Octopussy.*

Yes, more than twenty years later, someone who calls himself "Bond" is still on the case. One wonders whether even 007 can really handle the complexities of the modern world anymore. But 007 stopped Goldfinger from robbing Fort Knox; who's to say he couldn't as easily have sprung the hostages from Teheran? Unfortunately, no one asked him.

How did Fleming's books get to the screen? Since the mid-'50s, Fleming had actively pursued deals to make his character into a film; at one point Fleming originally wanted Alfred Hitchcock to direct the films. But the closest he got was a 1954 CBS version of *Casino Royale* with Barry Nelson as Bond.

In 1961, Harry Saltzman, a Canadian producer working in England, and Albert "Cubby" Broccoli, an American producer, bought the options on all the Bond novels except *Casino Royale,* which Fleming had previously sold. A six-picture deal with United Artists was secured.

Who would be cast as the hero? Patrick McGoohan, Richard Johnson, and Roger Moore were considered. But Broccoli had liked what he saw of Connery in the 1959 Disney film, *Darby O'Gill and the Little People.* Connery, a Scottish actor, was not like Bond—he was disheveled and disorganized. When Fleming met Connery for the first time, his reaction was "I was looking for Commander James Bond, not an overgrown stunt man." He refused to test for the role. "You either take me as I am or not at all," Connery demanded. He was taken and then molded by Director Terence Young, who had much of Bond's sense of style himself, into the Bond persona by being instructed about the proper fashions, foods, and wines. It was Connery who decided to play the role tongue in cheek.

CONNERY ON BOND

"Portraying Bond is just as serious as playing Macbeth.

"He has no mother. He has no father. He doesn't come from anywhere, and he hadn't been anywhere before he became 007. He was born—kerplump—33 years old. So I had to breathe life into an idol. I saw him as a complete sensualist, his senses highly tuned and awake to everything. He liked his wine, his food, his women. He's quite amoral. I particularly liked him because he thrived on conflict. But more than that, I think I gave him a sense of humor."

HE SAID IT DEPT.

"In a world where the enemy is hardboiled, tough-minded, and disillusioned, we have been taught that we must be tough-minded, hardboiled, and disillusioned, too. To succeed against the Communists, one had to be capable of behavior as repulsive as anything they manage. Our principal teacher, of course, was the late Ian Fleming," said John Kenneth Galbraith to scholars in 1967 at the University of London's Institute of American Studies.

SECRET SPECIAL 007 QUIZ

1. Who was M and who played him?
2. Who was Q?
3. Who played Miss Moneypenny?
4. What did SPECTRE stand for?
5. How did Oddjob die?
6. Who was *Thunderball's* villain?
7. Who was Red Grant?
8. What is James Bond's favorite cocktail?
9. Connery appeared in other films than Bond during the '60s. Can you name four of them?

ANSWERS

1. The head of Her Majesty's Secret Service, played by Bernard Lee
2. HMSS' weapons and security expert. Desmond Llewellyn played him.
3. Lois Maxwell
4. Special Executor for Counter-Intelligence, Terrorism, Revenge, and Extortion
5. He was electrocuted at Fort Knox.
6. Emilio Largo
7. A villain in *From Russia with Love*
8. Vodka martini, shaken, not stirred
9. *Woman of Straw, The Hill, Marnie* (directed by Hitchcock), and *A Fine Madness*

Fun in the Sun—
The Beach Movies

I t's all good clean fun. No hearts are broken, and virginity prevails," said William Asher, who directed several of the beach films for American International.

Despite such virtues, most critics considered the beach movies to be the cinematic equivalent of "Gilligan's Island." For the wrong reasons, they're right. These corny, entertaining, and unpretentious films certainly

didn't do anybody any harm; the plots never pretended to take themselves seriously. Both featured an ensemble cast of morons adrift in a self-contained world of sand, sea, and palm trees.

The gang on the beach films was just as unconnected with reality as the castaways—as were the plots. Or make that "plot" because each film had basically the same plot, offering a variation on the question: Can an aging teen idol from South Philadelphia get some action from a buxom, yet virginal ex-Mousketeer on the sands of Southern California? Not that the teens who filled drive-ins every summer between 1963 and 1966 to watch these films identified with Frankie Avalon's angst. As they snuggled in the front seats of their Mustangs (watch out for the gear shift!), these teens would be advancing the sexual revolution a lot more quickly than the characters on the screen.

But these films have dated well. They've fashioned their own pop mythology, which has increased, rather than diminished, their appeal.

What we have here is a version of American youth that might have been or never was—clean-cut, smiling, perpetually on summer vacation, not worried about war, the economy, or revolution. These kids were the offspring of Andy Hardy, not the leather-jacketed hoods who knifed their way through the films of the '50s or even the tennis-shoe wearing, beatnik-agitating Easterners. They were the last gasp of wholesomeness before American youth plunged into the abyss of the late '60s.

These films were the sun-surf-and-music versions of *Pillow Talk;* Frankie Avalon and Annette Funicello were the Pepsi Generation's Rock and Doris. And yes, in nearly every film, Frankie would try to get the modest Dee Dee (Miss Funicello, grown up

Annette Funicello and Frankie Avalon cozy up in *Beach Blanket Bingo* (1965).

and well-developed from her Mouse-keteer days) in the sack or at least prone on the blanket. And Miss Funicello, ever the virgin—although by 1965, she was expecting a baby in real life—would resist Frankie's advances ("I'm not afraid of you, Frankie...I'm afraid of myself").

She loved playing the role as guardian of chastity. If boys and girls happened to be sleeping in a large room, she placed a sheet in the middle separating the two. She wouldn't wear a bikini, preferring a more modest one- or two-piece bathing suit.

But a hint of sex was in the air. "What happens when 10,000 kids meet on 5,000 beach blankets?" asked the blurb for *Beach Party*. Unfortunately, not much, except for a lot of overcrowded beach blankets. *Beach Party* and its sequels and imitators promised more than they delivered ("Bikini Beach... Where Bare As You Dare Is the Rule!"). We saw lots of bikini-clad flesh, but no sex, except perhaps an occasional closed-mouthed kiss. Sweating, passionate bodies were caused by hours of frugging and twisting on the hot sand to the beat of the Hondells and the shaven-headed Pyramids.

Intruding on this Malibu Nirvana were an assortment of oddball adults—but never parents. They included an anthroplogist investigating the sex habits of Southern California teenagers (Bob Cummings), inept cyclist Eric Von Zipper (Harvey Lembeck), Big Drag (Don Rickles), a witch doctor (silent-screen comic Buster Keaton), and a PR man (Paul Lynde) hawking an aspiring singer named Sugar Kane (Linda Evans of "Dynasty"). If these were what adults were supposed to be like, then why not remain kids forever?

Not all adults connected with the beach movies were incompetent loons, however. Two adults, Sam Arkoff and James Nicholson, were particularly shrewd examples of the species. Nicholson and Arkoff were, respectively, the producer and president of American International Pictures, and had a knack of mining youth, until the '50s a neglected film audience. During the '50s they lured teens to the drive-ins by promoting Gothic and horror films (*I Was a Teenage Werewolf,* and Roger Corman's *House of Usher*), spear-and-sandal spectaculars (*Goliath and the Barbarians*) and juvenile delinquency potboilers (*Dragstrip Riot*).

By the turn of the decade, parent groups were becoming outraged at the JD films, believing them responsible for all teen ailments from acne to zip guns. Rock 'n' roll was tainted by the payola scandals, and Elvis had returned from the army chastened and shorn. Two films, 1959's *Gidget* and 1960's *Where the Boys Are*, had been the first to show happy youngsters romping on the beach. AIP thought it was safer to seek a more clean scene, so they shifted their focus from juvenile delinquency to juvenile decency.

Beach Party was probably conceived as a one-shot attempt by AIP to imitate the success of *Where the Boys Are* as well as to exploit the burgeoning West Coast "surf music" sound. It was originally going to be shot during vacation time at Palm Springs, but because a rival company was filming *Palm Springs Weekend* with Troy Donahue, the AIP brass decided to move the proceedings to the beach.

Beach Party was so successful that during the next three years it spawned a series of other movies starring the regular gang—*Muscle Beach Party, Bikini Beach, Beach Blanket Bingo, Pajama Party,* and *How to Stuff a Wild Bikini.* Each took about four months to film. Other less sucessful efforts at repeating the formula took the beach gang to the auto-track (*Fireball 500*) and ski lodge (*Ski Party*), or mingled the comedy with horror films (*The Ghost in the Invisible Bikini*) or spy thriller cum Gothic (*Dr. Goldfoot and the Bikini Machine*, with Vincent Price).

Rival companies got into the beach-movie scene, but most of these efforts, while starring better-known rock acts (Sonny and Cher, the Four Seasons, the Righteous Brothers), made the AIP films seem like high art. AIP and its rivals kept cranking out the films until 1966.

But even beach party kids grow up—as do their audiences. By 1966, Arkoff and Nicholson's sensitive antennae sniffed that kids were changing. They smelled just what it was that the kids wanted. So they lugged their camera crews off the sand and sent them out onto the freeways chasing motorcyclists and running wild in the streets, tracking down acidheads and young revolutionaries. It was time for more youth exploitation films. Just a different kind of youth.

SOME COOL BEACH MOVIES MOMENTS

GIRLS ON THE BEACH—Would-be swingers con innocent sorority sisters into thinking they're personal friends of the Beatles. They arrange to have the Fab Four come to Balboa to play a benefit concert for the sorority. The moptops don't make the scene but the birds save the day by transforming themselves into the female Beatles (they look like the Go-Gos) and singing "I Wanna Marry a Beatle." Notable also because it's the only beach movie in which the Beach Boys actually appear.

SWINGIN' SUMMER—One of Raquel Welch's earliest roles. She plays a bespectacled bookworm who is transformed into a beateous beach bunny.

BEACH BALL—Edd Byrnes took the freeway from "77 Sunset Strip" down to the beach to play the manager of a rock band (The Wigglers) who have been dispossessed of their instruments by a mean adult. This movie also contains the answer to one of the all-time great trivia questions, namely, did the Supremes ever sing a song about surfing? The answer is yes as you'll see at the end of this film when the three bewigged Motown warblers lip-sync a forgettable number called "Surfer Boy."

BIKINI BEACH—This is an incisive social comment on the cultural impact of the British Invasion. Frankie Avalon has a dual role here. One of his identities is Potato Bug, an English singer, who wears a redheaded Beatle wig and round, wire-rimmed glasses. He looks like a dippy John Denver, but the girls stand on the beach screaming at him. The guys, including Avalon as he normally appears, stand there disgustedly, fingers in their ears.

GO STEP ON A CRAB! DEPT.

The *New York Times* in its witty little blurbs on the TV page summed up the beach movies thusly. Typical adult squares!

Beach Blanket Bingo—"picnic for pinheads."

Bikini Beach—"ghastly."

Pajama Party—"amiable and idiotic."

Muscle Beach Party—"For morons, and if you don't believe it, dig it."

Beach Party—"a nitwit special."

Born to Be Wild—Motorcycle Movies

Their credo is violence...their God is hate...The most terrifying film of our time."—The lobby card for *The Wild Angels,* 1966.

"The picture you are about to see will shock you, perhaps anger you!... although the events and characters are fictitious, the story is a reflection of our times...." —Introduction to *The Wild Angels,* 1966.

"What've you got?" sneered Marlon Brando, as a "fearsome" rebel motorcyclist in the 1954 film, *The Wild One,* when asked what he was rebelling

Peter Fonda as a leader of motorcycle outlaws in *The Wild Angels* (1966)

against. That was the most coherent expression of his alienation his character could muster in the film that was considered a shocker for its time. But only twelve years later, the wild one would seem the mild one; a guy like Marlon would be stomped to death by a new gang of cyclists who expressed *their* alienation by wearing Nazi regalia, smoking pot, fighting, and raping.

Such model citizens made their screen debut in AIP's 1966 film, *The Wild Angels,* which became the prototype for a film genre that flourished in the late '60s, a period in which our tolerance to violence was becoming increasingly higher. In that post-JFK assassination, early-Vietnam era, you had to shock just to distinguish your product from what was happening on the front page. The motorcycle film fit the bill. Its protagonists weren't loony cartoon cyclists like Eric Von Zipper, but more like two-wheeled Luftwaffe.

AIP wanted Roger Corman, one of the most acclaimed B movie directors, to make a "contemporary" project to replace its Beach Party films, whose audiences were growing less enamored of Frankie and Annette. Corman had made a name for himself with his low-budget, but well-received, adaptations of Edgar Allan Poe stories, starring Vincent Price, such as *The Pit and the Pendulum.* Impressed in Corman's consciousness was a photo in *Life* magazine of a funeral of a Hell's Angel, the outlaw biker gang that had been receiving much press coverage because of their unconventional escapades. Corman and his assistant, Peter Bogdanovich, together with screenwriter Charles Griffith, decided to create a film around the subject.

To research the film, Griffith got a Hell's Angels friend to allow him and Corman to hang out with the gang at a joint called the Gunk Shop in Venice, California. Corman cast many real Hell's Angels in the film and also insisted that every actor cast as an Angel be able to ride his own bike. Because of this edict, George Chakiris—who originally had the lead and had requested a stuntman—was booted off the film and replaced by former supporting actor, Peter Fonda (who until then had appeared in wholesome roles in *Tammy and the Doctors* and *Lillith*). Bruce Dern was elevated to the second banana spot. Nancy Sinatra as Fonda's lover, "Monkey," had a chance to make her boots walk all over you in this one.

The movie, shot cinema-verité style, was originally called "All the Fallen Angels." It was about "Heavenly Blues" (the name comes from a popular psychedelic type of morning-glory seeds), the leader of a motorcycle gang patterned after the Hell's Angels. A member, "Loser" (Dern), has his bike swiped by a rival Mexican gang, so they go after it. Loser is shot by cops and then rescued by the gang from the hospital (but not before the gang rapes a nurse there). Unfortunately, he croaks because of insufficient medical attention.

Now comes the part which gives *The Wild Angels* its cult status: the funeral scene. Loser's funeral becomes a party; the minister is bound and gagged as the gang has an orgy in the chapel. Loser's corpse is propped up in a position of honor; he's wrapped in a Nazi flag, a joint in his mouth. His old lady is gang-raped by his friends. At the cemetery, violence erupts; they're chased by locals. The cops are brought in to clean up the mess. Blues stays by Loser's gravesite saying to himself, as the pigs near: "There's nowhere to go!" Such existential angst epitomized the frustration of the time and also foreshadowed Fonda's classic line "We blew it" at the end of *Easy Rider.*

The Wild Angels was first shown at the Venice International Film Festival because Corman had a large following in Europe. Europeans liked the film, but American critics were less enthusiastic. Bosley Crowther called it "a brutal little picture." and *Newsweek* described it as an "ugly piece of trash." Reviews aside, *The Wild Angels* became the most profitable AIP movie to date and kicked off a spate of similar films, each one promising more lurid thrills than its predecessor.

Nineteen sixty-seven saw more cycle films: *Rebel Rousers, Hell's Angels on Wheels* (featuring Jack Nicholson as "Poet," a frustrated gas-station attendant who joins a gang), *Wild Rebels, Born Losers* (the first film appearance of the character Billy Jack, played by Tom Laughlin, who would go on to become a cult hero in the early '70s), and *Devil's Angels* (starring John Cassavetes; its ads proclaimed, "Violence is their God!...and they hunt in a pack like rabid dogs").

The films' audiences weren't in the cities; they could be found at drive-ins in the Midwest and South. Many critics pointed out the similarity to Westerns as being one reason why they were so popular in these particular locales.

By the early '70s, the motorcycle film ran out of gas. Violence had lost its ability to shock. Instead, it became stylized in films such as *The Wild Bunch, Straw Dogs* and *A Clockwork Orange.* Most people found it increasingly difficult to identify with the Hell's Angels. Books like Tom Wolfe's *The Electric Kool-Aid Acid Test* tended to paint the Angels in a somewhat positive light—they took LSD and became cool, so they must be OK. But the Angels lost whatever credibility they had—especially with the counterculture—after Altamont and because right-wingers referred to them as misguided "patriots."

CHUTZPAH DEPARTMENT

The Hell's Angels filed a $4 million lawsuit against AIP, saying the film presented them in a "false and derogatory manner." When the film was released, Fonda was on trial in Los Angeles for marijuana possession—a false charge as it turned out, but it proved to be a wonderful tie-in for the film's youthful audience. AIP even marketed posters of Fonda on his cycle taking a toke.

OTHER CYCLE FILMS

Somewhere a cycle film fest will run, that must include the following:

• HELL'S BELLES (1969)—This bike flick stole its plot from the 1950 Western classic, Winchester '73, substituting motorcycles for guns.

• THE GLORY STOMPERS (1968)—Dennis Hopper heads a gang who kidnap Chris Noel, planning to sell her into white slavery for $100.

• RUN ANGEL RUN (1969)—A desperate biker sells information to a magazine for $10,000 and is hunted by his former associates.

• ANGELS FROM HELL (1969)—A first! Tom Stern plays a psychotic Vietnam vet who returns home to build an army of outlaw bikers.

• HELL'S ANGELS '69 (1969)—Starring real-life Angel boss, Sonny Barger. His gang become dupes of two wealthy brothers who use them to divert attention from a robbery of Caesar's Palace.

No noose is good noose, says Clint Eastwood in *The Good, the Bad and the Ugly,* one of the most successful Sergio Leone spaghetti westerns (1968).

Guns and Garlic— The Spaghetti Westerns

I am showing the Old West as it really was. Cinema takes violence from life. Not the other way around. Americans treat Westerns with too much rhetoric."—Sergio Leone, best-known director of the "Spaghetti Western."

"He makes no friends...a few enemies...a few dollars...and none of them last. He has no name...he's known only by his reputation...he is perhaps the most dangerous man who ever lived...."—United Artists publicity blurb describing Clint Eastwood's "Man with No Name" character in *A*

Fistful of Dollars.

The Spaghetti Western blazed across the screen during the late '60s in a hail of blood, guts, and gunfire, which made it seem as if the screen was drenched with about three-dozen cans of Hunt's tomato paste. These gory, poorly-dubbed Italian-made imitations of American Westerns were quite unlike any Westerns we had known. Who were the good guys? Who were the bad guys? Who could tell?

In the early '60s, European producers began developing an infatuation with the American Western. Between 1963 and 1965, 130 Westerns were produced in Europe by Italians, with various Spanish, French, and West German companies. In 1964, twenty-four of the 144 Italian-made movies were Westerns.

The master of the genre was Sergio Leone, a short, squat, bespectacled self-described disciple of John Ford. Leone, who at one time used the pseudonym "Bob Robertson" as his screen name, created a formula that clicked in both Italy and the United States. Leone wasn't the first to make Spaghetti Westerns, but he was the most successful. Unlike many of the other Italian Westerns, Leone's stressed period detail and authenticity.

Leone's first Western was *A Fistful of Dollars,* which was released in 1964 in Italy and came to the United States three years later. Talk about international cinema—*Fistful* was shot in Spain by an Italian director with a multinational cast, and based on a Japanese film (Akira Kurosawa's 1961 Samurai film, *Yojimbo*).

Fistful was the film that made Clint Eastwood—then known for his role as Rowdy Yates on TV's "Rawhide"—an international superstar. Leone, who had wanted to make Westerns for years (his biggest film until then was 1959's spear-and-sandal *Colossus of Rhodes*), had seen a screening of "Rawhide" in Rome and felt that Eastwood would be the appropriate star for his film.

In March, 1964, Eastwood was taking a hiatus from his TV show when his agent approached him with the script (then called "Magnificent Stranger"), which the actor found "wild, slightly satirical, and enigmatic." The budget was said to be about $200,000; Eastwood received $15,000. There seemed to be little risk; he'd be offered an expenses-paid trip to Europe with his wife, and he assumed the film would never play the U.S. because it was too weird for American tastes.

Eastwood, wearing a poncho and sombrero, plays the cynical, cheroot-chomping "Man with No Name," who rides into the Mexican border town of San Miguel after being pardoned from prison. He gets caught in the crossfire between two rival, equally corrupt families, whom he plays off against each other for his own interests. Through his beady, steely eyes, he looks out at a world that's dangerous and disintegrating. Then, having meted out his brutal justice, he leaves town as mysteriously as he arrived. As for violence—the massacres, beatings, shootings—said Eastwood: "'*Psycho* was fifty times more violent."

In 1967, *Fistful* was imported here after achieving much success in Italy (it grossed $5 million), then it was shown in the rest of Europe. Later that year, the sequel appeared, *For a Few Dollars More,* in which Eastwood (now getting paid $50,000 plus a percentage) and Lee Van Cleef play two cynical gunmen who form an uneasy alliance to search for an outlaw.

The third and most expensive in the cycle, *The Good, the Bad, and the Ugly* (1968), featured Eastwood, Van Cleef, and Eli Wallach in a gory display of battles, shootouts, and killings, but with an ironic, comedic undercurrent. The trio of unlikely partners search for a Confederate government treasure chest during the Civil War. The violence of our heroes paled in comparison to the havoc wrought by the war. Some observers interpreted its plot as a comment that the violence in Vietnam was more severe and serious than the violence committed by urban youth.

By 1968, the Spaghetti Western began fading. There were too many of them and too many looked the same. But Leone had one last bang. He came to America in 1969 to shoot *Once Upon a Time in the West,* which featured a different, but star-studded cast (Henry Fonda, Charles Bronson, Jason Robards, and Claudia Cardinale).

It got so you couldn't tell the imitators from the originals. A 100-percent, purely American film, the moderately successful *Hang 'Em High* (in which Eastwood gave a preview of the "Dirty Harry"-style character he would play in the '70s—the vigilante who singlehandedly wipes out evil) was criticized by *Variety* as "a poor imitation of a poor, Italian-made imitation of an American Western."

The success of the Spaghetti Western is easy to explain. Eastwood personified a true '60s type: the laconic antihero, estranged from authority, whose creed was don't trust anybody except yourself, and whose motto was action, not words. He was James Bond—without the authority of Her Majesty's Secret Service to back him up. With his films, Leone captured the drift of America to a more violent and disjointed country. As Andrew Sarris noted: "The America of Sergio Leone is an America of rape and pillage, an America moving toward that nihilistic nowhere with which Europe has been so familiar."

Movie-Star Portraits

JULIE CHRISTIE—The highest-flying bird of the British cinema invasion. The Indian-born beauty made a splash in *Billy Liar* and then won an Academy Award as the amoral London swinger in *Darling.* Christie won more hearts as Lara in *Dr. Zhivago,* the '60s version of *Gone with the Wind.* Delicate, but dangerous.

DORIS DAY—A box-office fave keeping the flame of the '50s burning through the first half of the new decade. America's favorite virgin cheered for chastity as the walls of the sexual revolution were tumbling down. She ran around with Rock Hudson in frothy comedies like *Lover Come Back, Pillow Talk,* and *Send Me No Flowers.* For a change of pace she starred with Cary Grant in *A Touch of Mink* and with James Garner in *Move Over Darling* (Day's role was originally set for Marilyn Monroe). Favorite Day rumor to live down: that she was romantically linked to L.A. Dodger speedster Maury Wills.

STEVE MCQUEEN—Nobody messed with the craggy-faced, perpetually-squinting star of *The Great Escape, Bullitt,* and *The Thomas Crown Affair.* The *New York Times* described him best: "McQueen embodies his special kind of aware, existential cool—less taut and hardshell than Bogart, less lost and adrift than Mastroianni, a little of both." The '60s man at his macho best.

PAUL NEWMAN—The twinkly-eyed last great star. Newman made his mark in the '60s for his portrayal of three antihero individuals fighting the system: *The Hustler, Hud,* and *Cool Hand Luke.* Raindrops kept falling on his head, however. He was often nominated for, but never won, an Academy Award.

SIDNEY POITIER—The leading black actor of the '60s who proved that ability had more to do with achieving success than color. He projected an intense dignity which dismayed black militants. They call me *Mister* Tibbs. Shaft, he wasn't. He could do no wrong, whether romancing Katharine Houghton in *Guess Who's Coming to Dinner,* disciplining a bunch of British school brats in *To Sir with Love,* or assisting distressed nuns in *Lilies of the Field.* For the latter, he became the first black actor to receive an Academy Award.

ELIZABETH TAYLOR AND RICHARD BURTON—*The* Hollywood fun couple of the '60s, getting more ink than Jack and Jackie, Lyndon and Lady Bird, Sonny and Cher, and Bonnie and Clyde combined. Every month, mags like *Modern Screen* and *Photoplay* would tantalize readers with the latest tale of woe, deception, or heartbreak in the Liz and Dick and (sometimes) Eddie saga. They met in *Cleopatra* and were sin-sational muttering dirty words and playing head games in *Who's Afraid of Virgina Woolf?,* which

compensated for their string of lack-luster films during the rest of the decade like *The V.I.P.s., Dr. Faustus, The Sandpiper, Night of the Iguana,* and *The Comedians.*

An A to Z of Memorable Films from the '60s

A HARD DAY'S NIGHT (1964)—Richard Lester makes the Fab Four into cinematic stars as well, with his flashily-edited look at an imaginary day in the Beatles' life.

ALFIE (1966)—Michael Caine as a Cockney swinger ponders one of the key questions of the '60s: What's it all about?

BARBARELLA (1968)—Jane Fonda as campy space-age sex symbol, based on the popular French comic strip. The film from which Duran Duran got its name.

Elizabeth Taylor and Richard Burton

BOB AND CAROL AND TED AND ALICE (1969)—An artifact of the swinging '60s poised on the cusp of the Me Decade: Natalie Wood, Robert Culp, Dyan Cannon, and Elliott Gould get into wife-swapping, pot-smoking, and sensitivity training.

BREAKFAST AT TIFFANY'S (1961)—Blake Edwards' look at Truman Capote's amoral, sophisticated Holly Golightly (Audrey Hepburn). "She's a phony, all right," says Holly's agent, "but a real phony!"

BUTCH CASSIDY AND THE SUNDANCE KID (1969)—Paul Newman and Robert Redford try the buddy system for the first time, playing fading Western outlaws.

CAT BALLOU (1965)—Spoof of Westerns with Jane Fonda as schoolmarm-turned-outlaw, and Lee Marvin in an Oscar-winning dual role as a drunken gunman and desperado with a tin nose.

COOL HAND LUKE (1967)—What we've got here, besides a failure to communicate, is the sound of Paul Newman a-workin' on the chain gang. Another Newman hero who won't let the system get him down.

ELMER GANTRY (1960)—Burt Lancaster won an Oscar as a con-man evangelist of the '20s who made us wonder if he was really as bad as all that.

EXODUS (1960)—Who says Paul Newman isn't Jewish?

GOODBYE, COLUMBUS (1969)—Ali MacGraw's film debut as a Jewish American Princess in love with nebbishy Richard Benjamin, based on Philip Roth's novel. The memorable wedding scene features twin cantors and enough chopped liver to fill a Brooklyn landfill.

THE GREEN BERETS (1968)—The Duke as a Green Beret colonel defends the American way and convinces typically smarmy U.S. journalist (David Janssen) of the rightness of our presence in Vietnam. In another era and another war it would have worked. Wayne co-directed.

THE HUSTLER (1961)—Paul Newman's gritty dress rehearsal for the heel in Hud, as small-time pool shark Fast Eddie Felson taking on billiards kingpin Minnesota Fats (Jackie Gleason). The film made Newman a superstar.

LA DOLCE VITA (1960)—Cynical journalist Marcello Mastroianni sours on the "good life" but is powerless to change himself. Federico Fellini's preview of the moral decay to come.

THE LONGEST DAY (1962)—Darryl Zanuck's epic about the D-day invasion not only starred John Wayne, Robert Mitchum, and Henry Fonda, but cast Paul Anka, Fabian, and Tommy Sands as three U.S. Rangers. The last of the great WW II spectaculars.

THE MAGNIFICENT SEVEN (1960)—Based on Kurosawa's *Seven Samurai,* and the prime inspiration for Leone's Spaghetti Westerns. A gang of seven professional gunmen is hired to rid a terrorized Mexican village of bandits. For the first time in a Western, good guys don't wear white.

THE MANCHURIAN CANDIDATE (1962)—John Frankenheimer's taut, powerful drama of brainwashing and assassination. Some critics compared Frankenheimer's camera angles to Orson Welles' in *Citizen Kane*.

MIDNIGHT COWBOY (1969)—Dustin Hoffman's follow-up to *The Graduate*. Jon Voight plays a would-be Texas stud who comes to Manhattan looking for women. Instead, he meets a crippled street hustler, Ratso Rizzo (Hoffman), and a strange friendship begins. Rated X (although it's awfully tame by today's standards), the movie still won the Best Picture Oscar for 1969.

THE MISFITS (1961) — Weak plot, but notable for being the last film of both Clark Gable and Marilyn Monroe. Arthur Miller wrote the screenplay for his then-wife; John Huston directed. Gable plays a macho cowboy-type guy named Gay.

THE ODD COUPLE (1968) — Felix and Oscar on film, with Jack Lemmon and Walter Matthau playing the mismatched roommates.

THE PAWNBROKER (1965) — Rod Steiger's harrowing portrayal of a former concentration camp inmate who now owns a Harlem hock shop. The scene in which a black prostitute bares her breast to Steiger tested the limits of the Hollywood production code.

THE PLANET OF THE APES (1968) — Rod Serling adapted Pierre Boulle's sci-fi tale of the future about an Earth where apes rule, and humans serve. Unlike 2001, all apes here were humans in simian costumes. Beware of its sequels.

THE PRODUCERS (1968) — Zero Mostel and Gene Wilder produce the world's worst musical, Springtime for Hitler, in the film that many aficionados consider as Mel Brooks' finest hour. Check out Dick Shawn as a crazed hippie named "LSD."

ROSEMARY'S BABY (1968) — Roman Polanski's look at some strange goings-on at New York's Dakota apartments. The Devil made her do it.

TRUE GRIT (1969) — John Wayne wins a long-overdue Oscar for his portrayal of over-the-hill lawman Rooster Cogburn.

VALLEY OF THE DOLLS (1967) — Trasho supremo based on Jacqueline Susann's potboiler about three girls rising to the top in show biz. Patty Duke, Sharon Tate, Barbara Parkins, and pills, pills, pills.

THE VICTORS (1963) — Carl Foreman's powerful, ahead-of-its-time antiwar film. Most memorable scene: An American deserter is executed by firing squad while the soundtrack plays Sinatra crooning "Have Yourself a Merry Little Christmas."

WHATEVER HAPPENED TO BABY JANE? (1962) — Old movie queens don't die, they end up in Grand Guignol epics of Hollywood decadence like this. Bette Davis and Joan Crawford star as sisters in this film, a Sunset Boulevard meets House of Usher. Sauteed rats, anyone?

WHO'S AFRAID OF VIRGINIA WOOLF? (1965) — Mike Nichols' version of the Edward Albee play in which Liz and Dick, now married, play a frumpy middle-aged couple who inflict an evening of alcohol, coarse language, and ego-battering games on a younger couple (Sandy Dennis and George Segal). The new American maturity in film begins here.

THE WILD BUNCH (1968) — Sam Peckinpah's ballet of blood in which bandit boss, William Holden, leads his gang on one final raid. Violence a go-go.

WILD IN THE STREETS (1968) — Max Frost (Christopher Jones) becomes America's first hippie president and imprisons all adults. "Fourteen or fight!" Yippies borrowed the concept of putting LSD in the water system from the movie to freak out Chicago's Mayor Daley at the 1968 Democratic convention.

Z (1969) — Costa-Gavras' message film depicting a junta's assassination of a Greek liberal was required viewing for all college students in 1969.

The Grooviest

F A D S   A N D   F A S H I O N S

INTRODUCTION

The '60s was a decade in which everything new was old again—usually in a matter of months. Fashions changed at a pace never quite previously seen. Hair crept down to the shoulder, skirts crept up the leg and everyone wanted to be young. For brief moments, the brightest stars in the pop culture firmament were named Twiggy, Snoopy, Chubby and Jackie.

This chapter will look at not only the revolution in men's and women's fashions and hairstyles, but at other fads and fashions including toys for kids (skateboards, Barbie Dolls) and toys for bigger kids (the pill, the Mustang), as well as recreational activities ranging from twisting to turning on, tuning in, and dropping out.

1961: Hugh Hefner and bunny Bonnie J. Halpin, a hostess at the Chicago Playboy club (1961)

The Twist

What a year 1961 has been so far. We blew it at the Bay of Pigs; the Berlin Wall went up; and Babe Ruth's home-run record was broken by Roger Maris. Now what's this we're seeing? Adults staying out all hours and dancing the Twist at seedy night clubs. Parents buying 79-cent albums by groups called "Tubby Chess and his Peppermint Stick Twisters" and having chip 'n' dip Twist parties in their rec rooms. Middle-aged would-be swingers throwing out their sacroiliacs trying to show off just how hip they can be. What kind of decade is this going to be?

No, 1961 is too difficult a year to comprehend. Let's go back to a simpler time, like 1959, when a dancer was a dancer and you could be darn sure old Ike would never wear a d.a. haircut.

Nineteen fifty-nine was the year when the Twist was first danced—by kids. If you had twirled your radio dial to one of those low-wattage, rhythm-and-blues stations, you would have heard a new dance tune, the B side of a record by Hank Ballard, a pioneering R&B artist known for his risqué songs in the '50s such as "Work with Me Annie" and "Annie Had a Baby."

"The Twist" received little airplay outside the R&B stations, but it didn't escape the notice of Dick Clark, who noticed some kids dancing the new step on his teen tastemaking program, "American Bandstand." The dance partners didn't touch, but each person gyrated like they were vigorously wiping their backs with a towel or stubbing out a cigarette with their feet. In fact, their feet hardly moved.

It was as simple as that. For white

America, it was a radical, explicitly sexy dance, no doubt about it, even though it wasn't that different from what black kids had been dancing to for years. But Clark, whose fingers were on the pulse of teen America like no one else, sensed something. He realized "The Twist," indeed, met the criteria of any good "American Bandstand" song—it had a good beat, and you could dance to it. Through "Bandstand" it could be beamed to the teens of America. But first he needed a singer.

Danny and the Juniors ("At the Hop," "Rock & Roll Is Here to Stay") were originally supposed to cut the record, but they weren't available, so a replacement was found. He was a 20-year-old former chicken plucker named Ernest Evans, rechristened Chubby Checker by Clark's ex-wife Barbara who said that the young man looked a little bit like Fats Domino.

Checker had already made four unsucccessful records; on one of them, "The Class," he imitated the Chipmunks, the Coasters, Fats Domino, and Elvis Presley. A studio band from "Bandstand" cut the instrumentals, and Checker shortly thereafter recorded the vocal tracks. Note-for-note, the disc was almost a duplicate of Ballard's record; even Checker's vocals, down to the last "eee-yow!" resembled Ballard's.

Spurred by Checker's performance on "Bandstand," sales of the Cameo-Parkway disc zoomed, and soon the record rose to Number 1 in 1960.

While he had aped the vocals, Checker is credited for popularizing the dance steps. Still, no one expected the dance to take off as well as it did. Certainly not Checker who followed up the Twist with three other less successful dance records, "The Hucklebuck," "The Pony," and "The Mess Around."

The Twist was written off as another juvenile dance fad. Then, the totally unexpected happened. In late 1961, adults began Twisting. Elvis Presley hadn't inspired this kind of reaction among adults. Prior to 1961, most American adults wouldn't even listen, much less dance to, rock 'n' roll. Their attitude was summed up by Frank Sinatra: "R&R was the marching music of every sideburned delinquent on the face of the earth." But perhaps because of the aura of youthfulness projected by the Kennedys, the Twist caught on, first with the Jet Set, then with Mr. and Mrs. America.

One of the bridges between the adult and teen worlds was Ahmet Ertegun, the president of Atlantic Records, who was well connected with both arenas. One night, he took some society friends to the Peppermint Lounge—a seedy tavern off Times Square where patrons wore leather jackets, ducktail haircuts, and beehive hairdos—to see the house band, Joey Dee and the Starlighters.

The swells dug the Twist; by October 1961, gossip columnist Cholly Knickerbocker (Igor Cassini) took note of the tony Twisters there and spread the word. After word leaked, the Pep became front-page material. The club's original patrons were left cooling their Cuban heels on the pavement outside, next to their motorcycles, while they watched the likes of Judy Garland, Billy Rose, Tennessee Williams, the Duke and Duchess of Bedford, and Norman Mailer being admitted to the smoky, noisy dive.

The adult boom gave new life to the Twist. The dance and Chubby Checker became big business. Checker was shrewdly marketed with a line of Twist products. New York stores offered women "twister outfits," from hats to shoes. A hairdresser advertised a Twist hairdo that bounced and rotated to the dance's rhythms. There were Twist shirts,

A twist on the Twist: Suzy Brooks, 13, of Council Bluffs, Iowa, does the twist with a checkerboard stacked with checkers. The object of this game: to keep the body rotating and the head still. Suzy succeeded as a "Checker" twister.

Chubby Checker

cufflinks, wallets, pajamas, candy, and Thom McAnn's "Twister" shoes.

Everybody began cutting Twist records. There was "Dear Lady Twist," "Twist Twist Senora," "Soul Twist," "Slow Twistin'," "Twistin' Postman," and "Bristol Twistin' Annie." Checker's original Twist record became a Number 1 hit again in 1962. Hollywood turned out three eminently forgettable movies: *Hey Let's Twist, Twist Around the Clock,* and *Don't Knock the Twist.*

By 1963, new dances—the Hully-Gully, Mashed Potato, Frug, Watusi—all variations on the Twist, soon emerged, leaving the original item as dated as the Lindy Hop. But the Twist had made its impact on changing dance styles. Not until almost fifteen years later would it be socially "in" for couples to dance together.

And what of the Twistmaster, Checker? He had a few minor dance hits—the Fly, the Limbo (How low can you go?). The arrival of the Beatles doomed Checker. ("I feel no rivalry toward them. I wish them all the luck in the world," he said. "They may be able to stop the Twist, but can they stop me? That's the question. Ain't nobody gonna stop me.") He made a decent living on the rock-revival circuit, all the while trying to peddle himself as a solid, contemporary singer. But people wouldn't buy an image change from him at all—slimmed-down or otherwise.

The Peppermint Lounge closed ("without a twist or a shout," said one New York daily) in December, 1965, when its liquor license was revoked. It reopened later as a seedy go-go club living on memories, before finally closing in 1969. But a New Wave dance club with the same name on the same spot opened in 1980, with many of the young patrons wearing pompadours and fishnet stockings and looking as if they had stepped out of 1961.

Of course, the Twist never died. Even now, in a garish catering hall somewhere in the heart of suburbia, a band—let's call them Lenny Mel and the Mel-tones, five middle-aged men with bad hairpieces—will still get a rise out of the guests by proclaiming "around and around and up and down we go." And some middle-aged would-be swinger will still throw out his sacroiliac trying to show off just how hip he is.

SOME EXAMPLES OF TWIST MADNESS

• At New York's Metropolitan Museum of Art in November, 1961, the fashion industry's $100-a-plate Party of the Year featured Joey Dee, who played for $150 an hour. Museum director James J. Rorimer groused: "I did not invite them. I wasn't aware of this." At the same time, Mrs. Rorimer was over in a corner, learning to Twist. The party raised $70,000 for a new wing for the museum.

• Society gossip columnist Elsa Maxwell revealed that Princess Olga of Yugoslavia had agreed with her at the Polish Ball that the Twist shouldn't be danced in public places, only at private parties.

• At the White House dinner dance honoring Lee Radziwill, Lester Lanin's orchestra played the Twist. Oleg Cassini and Mrs. Philip Geyelin danced it. (It was later reported that Washington teens stopped dancing the Twist after this event.)

• Two hundred and fifty prominent New Yorkers Twisted at a benefit concert at the posh Four Seasons restaurant. They included Huntington Hartford, Porfirio Rubirosa, and Henry Ford's daughter, Charlotte. Chubby Checker was the guest of honor.

• New York's Safety Council said that

in one week in October, 1961, forty-nine out of fifty-four reported cases of back trouble were due to too much Twisting.

• In Syracuse, New York, the widow of an auto salesman who died of a heart attack after Twisting at a company party sued for workmen's compensation under the state law and won.

Discotheques

By the mid-'60s, people may have stopped Twisting, but they didn't stop dancing. Instead of dumps like the Peppermint Lounge, where sharkskinned combos provided the beat, the action moved to disco-theques and later multi-media clubs. The emergence of discotheques showed the increasing acceptance of rock music among those over 25. Discotheques (record library, literally started in Paris in the '50s, then spread to London. Here, jet-setters Frugged and Jerked to recorded music spun by a disc jockey, who manipulated the dancers' moods by the loudness and the kind of discs he spun.

In the beginning, they were called "a highbrow version of a juke joint plus a disc jockey." By 1964, there were more than fifty discotheques in Paris, and the trend had been imported to America. The earliest New York discos (such as Le Club, which opened New Year's Eve, 1962) were really private clubs (with "members" paying a stiff admission fee), catering to the

Who's that behind those Foster Grants? It's yet another fun couple of the '60s — discotheque doyenne Sybil Burton, Richard Burton's former wife, with her new husband, Jordan Christopher. It's December 1965 and they're arriving in Los Angeles for Christopher's Hollywood screen test.

Killer Joe Piro was the king of the mid-'60s discotheques: a dance master who became a favorite of society matrons who wanted to learn to Frug and Jerk. His revue, when they appeared on the Ed Sullivan Show, included go-go girl Goldie Hawn (to Piro's immediate right).

same class of clientele as the tonier Paris clubs.

Then, in May, 1965, came Arthur, the New York discotheque owned by Sybil Burton, who had just been dumped by husband Dick for Liz Taylor. Arthur was to the '60s what Studio 54 was to the '70s, the place for the glitterati to dance as well as to be seen. It was the first and most successful discotheque, the club on which the other clubs of the '60s were patterned. Its disc jockey also developed the concept of seamlessly mixing records with each other, keeping the dancers constantly moving.

To enter Arthur on E. 54th St. was to be thrust into the red-hot center of Pop Society. You'd walk past the photos hanging on the wall of some famous Arthurs—Chester A., the president, the King, and Gelien (the real

name of Tab Hunter)—and observe the dance floor, described by one writer as the "nation's newest orgone box, with built-in stereophonic torture chamber," with dancers resembling "clothes in an agitated washer." Isn't that Tennessee Williams Frugging? Nureyev doing the Dog?

Discotheques like Arthur were adult playgrounds, since the teens who formed the vanguard of the rock audience weren't old enough to drink. But many places had little liquor consumption, while some didn't serve any at all.

Director Mike Nichols suggested the name Arthur, after a remark by Beatle George Harrison made in *A Hard Day's Night* to a question asking what he called his hairstyle. Sybil patterned her bistro after the Ad Lib, London's innest club. On hand to Frug

and Jerk opening night: Tennessee Williams, Rudolf Nureyev, and Huntington Hartford.

Silver-haired Sybil, then 36, cemented her celebrity status by marrying one of the musicians who played at Arthur, Jordan Christopher, leader of the Wild Ones, who also happened to be eleven years her junior. (She had admired Jordan's "arrogance and elegance" when his band played the Pep. "To pull a Sybil" became an expression meaning to marry a younger man. Arthur lasted until 1969, but the glam crowd had long since boogied off elsewhere.

After 1966, the hippest night on the town wouldn't be had at the discotheque, but at the local multimedia or "total environment" club, which borrowed from the light show/ freak out/acid test then gaining popularity on the West Coast. The idea here was that you could have the psychedelic experience without swallowing a coated sugar cube. As the handbill to one club proclaimed: "Cheaper than analysis! Safer than LSD! Blast your hang-ups away!"

Stumble into any of these joints, and you'd be assaulted by a nonstop montage of flashing lights, stroboscopic lights, black lights, multicolored and ameba-shaped lights, movies, slides, TV, and loud music. One New York club had twenty-one movie screens that showed twenty-one different movies simultaneously. Andy Warhol opened one of the first, *The Exploding Plastic Inevitable.* No wonder *Life* advised its readers: "You better wear earplugs, dark glasses, and shin guards."

The most popular was Manhattan's Cheetah, which also featured an on-premises boutique, where you could change into Mod threads before going out and Boogalooing. The inside of each dressing booth was decorated with a photograph of a leering member of the opposite sex. Later came the Electric Circus, billed as the "Ultimate Legal Entertainment Experience." Talk about groovy, dig this: Nobody was forced to wear shoes (it cost 50 cents unless you came barefoot), no alcohol was served, you could have your face or body painted, and you could consult an astrologer.

By the end of the '60s, clubgoers decided they preferred illegal experiences, especially those you could smoke. Rock concerts—where audiences swayed and nodded rather than danced to a pulverizing beat—had taken over. The discotheques and multimedia clubs fell dark.

Dance clubs remained underground until around 1974 when they re-emerged as discos, beginning the biggest mass dance phenomenon since the Twist.

THOSE GIRLS IN THE CAGES

A common attraction at most mid-'60s discotheques were the go-go girls. They danced in cages, wearing fishnet stockings and false eyelashes, and gyrating wildly. *Newsweek* estimated in March, 1967 that there were 8,000 go-go girls in the country; housewives, divorcees, and students were among those bumping and grinding. In many clubs, go-go girls replaced chorus girls and strippers. "We can't find girls to strip on amateur nights," moaned the owner of a Houston strip joint. "They've all gone to work in the go-go parlors and they're not interested in stripping anymore."

Intoned *Newsweek* sagely: "Many are from loveless homes, and many are in search of attention. Most retire after two years because they develop ailments like strained necks, dislocat-

ed ribs, and eyestrain" (from squinting into the spotlight). The go-going rate was $2.50 an hour to $200 per week.

"If my father knew, he'd have a heart attack," said a 21-year-old topless dancer at Chicago's Rat Fink Club.

"The life of a discotheque dancer is very very lonely," said another. "You have no trust in others. You don't know whether the boy you meet likes you because of the way you dance or because he wants to go to bed with you. It bars you from finding a husband."

The Look: Women's Fashions

"IF YOU'RE OVER 19, YOU'VE HAD IT" —*Women's Wear Daily.*

"Where can I buy clothes?"—An indignant middle-aged woman while shopping in a Detroit store. "Everything is styled for mini-girls."

Nowhere during the '60s was the tyranny of the young more evident than with fashion. For the first time, the fashion lead came from the young, not those in the mainstream. As Marylin Bender's *The Beautiful People,* a definitive study of the fashion revolution of the '60s, noted: "Fashion stopped being clothes and became a value, a tool, a way of life, a kind of symbolism. It had become human packaging. To be a 'NOW' person, you must have a total 'look.' "

In the early '60s, fashion took its lead from Jacqueline Kennedy, a combination of high-fashion model, movie star, and royal queen. Prior to the '60s, fashion influence had been exerted by movie stars and costume designers, but by the '60s, the Hollywood star system was fading and there were few actresses American women could emulate.

Jackie was clothes-conscious. She spent $50,000 on clothes in the first sixteen months after the election. Following her lead, women bared their arms to the shoulder and wore brightly-colored costumes that were clearly Paris-inspired. Because of her, women began wearing pillbox hats and "swollen" bouffant hairdos (although by the end of '61, she had switched to a simpler coiffure). When she wore stacked-heel walking shoes on TV during the famous White House tour, stores everywhere were swamped with requests for this new style. The proliferation of shocking-pink fashions was directly traceable to Jackie's preference.

The Jackie look disappeared during her period of mourning. But her influence was just as powerful when she re-emerged. In the fall of 1966, when Jackie shortened her skirt three inches above the knee, she made any woman who didn't emulate her seem downright reactionary.

THE GARMENT OF THE DECADE: THE MINISKIRT

Consider the knee, a knobby, ugly protrusion which, with the creation of the miniskirt in the mid-'60s, became yet another demarcation line along the generation gap. If a woman bared her knee (or more), then she was instantly identified as Mod, free, swinging. If she chose to cover it, she was assumed to be square, dull, and conservative. For women, skirt length was as provocative a statement as hair length was for men. You could blame the Beatles for inspiring men to lengthen their locks, but who were the agent

provocateurs who caused women to shorten their skirts?

Observers divided the blame between two designers, Mary Quant and André Courreges. Quant assumed a conciliatory posture about who should be considered the miniskirt's creator by saying: "Tuned-in designers around the world have the same ideas at the same time."

Quant, whose fashions became synonymous with the "Swinging London" of the mid-'60s, first cut her skirts short in the '50s as a fashion protest on behalf of the emerging British youth culture. Her Chelsea boutique, Bazaar, designed especially for a young clientele, since the stuffy British fashion establishment wouldn't cater to them, was more like a "youth club" than a store.

It was here that the new fashion of the Mods found its locus. Eventually Quant's designs mushroomed into a worldwide, million-dollar-a-year operation. By the late '60s, Quant had become enough of an easily-recognized celebrity (she had a lucrative tie-in deal with J.C. Penney to market her works) that she did an endorsement for AT&T. "Mary Quant, what do you like best about the States?" Replied Mary: "The Algonquin Hotel, corned beef on rye, and your telephone system."

Quant also supplied the philosophy behind the fashion revolution. When a journalist asked her what was the point of fashion, she replied, "Sex." Her fashion philosophy emphasized youth, which she later amended to mean an outlook, not a chronological age. For her efforts on behalf of promoting Swinging London, Quant received the OBE in 1966. At the Buckingham Palace ceremony, Quant wore one of her own creations, showing seven inches of thigh.

However, it was Courreges, a Basque working in Paris, who made the short skirt respectable. The

Jackie Kennedy, wearing a characteristic pillbox hat, set fashion styles for women in the early '60s.

Mary Quant, creator of the miniskirt, displays her Order of the British Empire after having received it from Queen Elizabeth on November 15, 1966.

No fuss, no muss—it's the paper dress.

March, 1964 issue of *Vogue* was the first to show his new short skirts. Courreges also created the prototypical mid-'60s look—the short skirt or square-cut white dress and flat white boots (to be adopted later as "go-go" boots). The woman who wore the Courreges look served notice that she had cut her ties with her past.

The miniskirt hit these shores in 1964. It was a big hit with the Jet Set, but shocked the fashion establishment. Coco Chanel, for one, groused: "Fashion cannot come up from the street. It can only go down in the street." Pundits explained the new skirts' popularity in economic terms (skirts raise with the stock market—in the boom '20s they went six, then nine inches off the ground and lowered after the crash, so it was natural for them to rise in the affluent '60s).

Others attempted sociological explanations. Said fashion photographer Irving Dean: "It's spitting in the eye, protesting against bourgeois values and generations past against the establishment." Others saw the skirts as perfect for the freedom of the new dances—as well as the freedom of the new morality. On city streets, heads were turning whenever a miniskirted girl strutted by.

One of the first spinoffs of the miniskirt was the minidress (1965), featuring Pop Art, Op Art, stripes, checks, waves, and Mondrian-type patterns (divided geometrically by intersecting bands and brightened by contrasting blocks of color).

The mini's march was inexorable. By the end of the '60s, women who should have known better were exposing their knees. But by then, the original mini had been replaced by the micro, which climbed five, six, then seven inches, until it was almost thigh-high.

The fashion establishment, never too keen on the idea, fought back.

Instead of the mini or the maxi (which was as long as the micro was short), they proposed a compromise: the midi (middle of the calf), or they avoided the knee-jerk controversy altogether with the pantsuit. By the early '70s, the furor had subsided. Knees entered conversations only as they related to the athletic performances of Joe Namath and Mickey Mantle. In the '80s, the miniskirt made a small comeback among girls too young to remember the original. But by then, no one was looking anymore.

According to British model Gai Wright, here's how to sit while wearing a miniskirt. "Put your knees together and bend them, step back on your right toe, sit on the edge of the seat with knees together and feet apart. Your skirt will hang properly and not overly embarrass your escort."

She added, "When I wear a miniskirt in London, nothing happens. In America, women cluck their tongues, tell me to go home and get dressed, tug on my skirt to make it longer. The men? They ask for a date."

MAXI-QUOTES ABOUT THE MINISKIRT

Nearly everyone had something to say about the miniskirt.

"I have been looking at girls since I was six, and I know what they are like. Ankles are nearly always neat and good-looking, but knees are always not."—Dwight D. Eisenhower.

"It enables young ladies to run faster and because of it, they may have to."—New York City Mayor John V. Lindsay.

"It is better for men to discover than for women to reveal."—Gina Lollobrigida.

"This skirt is the right outfit to wear not only for dances and the

Op Art meets the minidress.

The long and the short of it: On Oscar night, 1967, British actresses Julie Christie and Wendy Hiller provided a contrast in dress length. Miss Christie presents the Best Actor Award to Miss Hiller who accepts it for Paul Scofield. He won the award for his performance in *A Man for All Seasons.*

beach, but for taking part in a strike or peace march or demonstrating against American bombings in Vietnam."—*Noi Donne,* a Communist-oriented Italian fashion magazine.

"A vestment of harlots."—Daphne Triggs of St. Hilda's College, Britain, speaking at an Oxford Union Hall debate about skirt length.

"I hate the miniskirt. Everyone thinks I'm responsible. I think two or three inches above the knee is all right, but now it's more than ten!"—Jean Shrimpton, model.

THE PAPER DRESS

In the years before recycling became something to think about, paper dresses were the ultimate '60s consumer item—wear 'em a few times and throw 'em out. "I wore the news today, oh boy."

Originally, these easily-disposable garments were introduced in the spring of 1966 by Scott Paper Company, at $1.25 each, as a premium to promote its new "Color Explosion" in toilet paper, towels, and napkins. It was made of a flexible, triple-ply, fire-resistant paper reinforced with rayon scrim—and you could get it in an Op Art version, if you so desired.

A year later, the fad was still raging. In those pre-ecology days, a vice-president of Kimberly Clark could say quite seriously that because of paper dresses "people no longer have a guilt complex about throwing

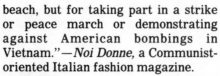

'60s Supermodel Jean Shrimpton

things away." *Business Week* said that by the spring of 1967, sales of the disposable garments ranged from $50 million to $100 million.

Some people thought the dress looked like a paper bag, but it caught on. Scott sold 500,000 dresses in eight months. They decided to call a halt to them "because we didn't want to turn into dress manufacturers." Other manufacturers and designers began creating their own versions. The Joseph Magnin Department Store created its own paper dress boutique called "The News Stand."

Mars Manufacturing Corporation of Asheville, North Carolina, became the nation's leading producer of paper dresses, selling 80,000 per week. Their line included not only the basic item ($1.75) but a spiffy bell-bottomed jumpsuit ($4) and an evening gown ($5). Another manufacturer, Sterling Paper Products, offered a $7.50 zebra-print pantsuit, a $15 bridal gown, and an $8 maternity dress. Sterling was also planning to develop paper resort wear so that vacationers could buy paper clothes at the hotel when they arrived, and throw 'em away when they left. No more luggage—no packing—but many angry bellhops. Formfit Rogers had a $3 ensemble including a bikini, which could be worn only two or three times. The wildest line was created by Hallmark, the greeting-card company—they sold a complete party kit: a flower-printed shirt together with matching cups, plates, place mats, napkins, matches, and even invitations.

The secret was a paper called Kimberly Stevens' Kaycel, a blend of 93 percent cellulose and seven percent cotton. Because the demand for Kaycel was so great, the company had to ration it. Other companies then used DuPont's Reemay and Kendall's Webril.

Seen wearing the paper dress were the Duchess of Windsor, Joan Kennedy, and Lee Radziwill, who wore a gold paper mini with a gold-sequined collar.

Miss Body Chemistry of 1967 plunged into a heated pool in Baltimore to demonstrate a paper bathing suit for the press, and the top—guaranteed to neither melt nor shrink—just fell off and floated away.

THE ELECTRIC DRESS

In 1967, Diana Dews, then 23, designed the electric dress for a boutique called Paraphernalia. By using pliable plastic lamps sewn into the clothes in segments and connected to a rechargeable battery pack worn on the hip, like Batman, she produced minidresses with throbbing hearts and pulsating belly stars, dresses that literally switched on and off. She also designed electric pants with flashing vertical side seams and horizontal bands that marched up and down the legs in luminous sequence.

"They're hyperdelic transsensory experiences," said the designer, who marketed her product for $125 to $225.

Miss Dew was also planning to design a dress that spelled out words and one that was wired to play music. "My clothes are designed to turn people on. Get rid of their inhibitions. Like taking LSD—with none of the hang-ups," said Miss Dews.

The Blues Magoos rock group had the coolest Dews creation of all: A motorcycle jacket, which cost Dews $700 to construct, that had two vertical rows of six large circular lamps in front and a triangle of three on the back. Each sleeve carried another lamp, cut like a military hash mark. Most of the remaining unelectrified space on the jacket was laced with

braids of vinyl piping in dazzling primary colors.

"My things are experiences. Part of the environment. They can be more than just something to wear. They can be entertainment, like art or theater—a new way to enjoy yourself," said Miss Dews, who demonstrated her creation on "The Tonight Show," among other places.

PANTSUITS

For women who wanted to avoid the skirt-length controversy, pants provided a suitable alternative.

Back in the mid-'60s, however, the garments weren't for all occasions. Girls in my high school didn't win the right to wear pants to school—except on the Halloween-like "Dress Down Day"—until 1968. Many restaurants banned women who wore them. Actress Susannah York made the papers when she was barred from New York's fashionable Colony restaurant because she was wearing pants. (She later came back wearing a dress.)

By the fall of 1966, women's pantsuits were being increasingly adopted by the fashionable set. Jackie K. ordered a beige-and-white wool suit from Valentino; Babe Paley ordered one in black velvet.

After that, there was no turning back.

THE GRANNY DRESS

"The muumuu has gone Mod," declared *Time* in October, 1965, about this garment which covered the wearer from neck to ankle, with Victorian furbelows and bows. But this garment wasn't for the Little Old Lady from Pasadena. Real grannies wouldn't wear one. No, these were strictly the province of teenage girls.

It began with a few California surfers who could sew. Girls imported bright, flowery muumuus from Hawaii to wear after surfing (they had originally been used by missionaries to cover the exposed breasts of native women). They trimmed the excess material, accentuated the bodice for a trim fit, slit the skirt for free movement, and finished it off with yards of ruffles and fluorishes. From the street, the style spread to the store, where the dresses sold for $10 to $15.

"They are a good change from Capris and a top for parties," said one 20-year-old. "They make you feel so dressed up," said a 14-year-old. In March, 1966, three teenage daughters of a Cornell University researcher were suspended by their high school principal when they wore the dresses to class.

THE MAXISKIRT

The Maxi was not a threat but a rather drastic alternative to the mini, which had climbed to eight inches above the knee. Coco Chanel, who always hated the mini (she called it "the most absurd weapon woman has ever employed to seduce men"), spurred two Paris designers, Daniel Hechter and Jacques Delahaye, to design a skirt that reached down to the ankle. It was to be worn with boots and winter coats for a new look for evening, according to Henri Bendel president, Geraldine Stutz. Said British designer Ossie Clarke: "This summer will be one last fling to show your legs. Next year the idea will be to wrap 'em up warm."

The Maxi didn't catch on as its proponents hoped it would. By 1970, the minis and maxis ceased hostilities with the creation of the midi, which went to the mid-calf.

THE TOPLESS BATHING SUIT

Nineteen sixty-four was the year the bottom fell out of the top, as Art Buchwald observed about the advent of the topless bathing suit. The garment was created by Rudi Gernreich, a respected, award-winning couturier, who said it was supposed to illustrate a fashion trend that he believed would materialize in "five or ten years." When back-view photos were shown in national publications, all hell broke loose. The shock was worldwide. "The American way of life is on the side of everything that gives the possibility of trampling on morals and interests of society for the sake of ego," *Izvestia* said. Mme. de Gaulle said she would boycott any store that sold the suit.

In reality, the suit was a put-on. During an interview with *Women's Wear Daily,* Gernreich was asked about future trends in sportswear. Because women on the Riviera were sunning only in their bikini bottoms, he predicted that in a few years women would be wearing topless bathing suits. The prediction was published as fact and Gernreich was deluged with orders for the nonexistent garment. So he decided to design such a suit.

In June, 1964, Gernreich showed buyers and press a pair of knitted trunks that were held up by a pair of stringy straps. *Look* then published a photograph of it on a model, taken from the back.

The press clamored for more. *Women's Wear Daily* ran a photo of a favorite Gernreich model, Peggy Moffitt, as a front view, reproducing it to the smallest size. *TV Networks* a week later reproduced the same photo.

Gernreich was dismayed that he had received orders for the suit. He

Do you know anyone who didn't own at least one pair of bell bottoms?

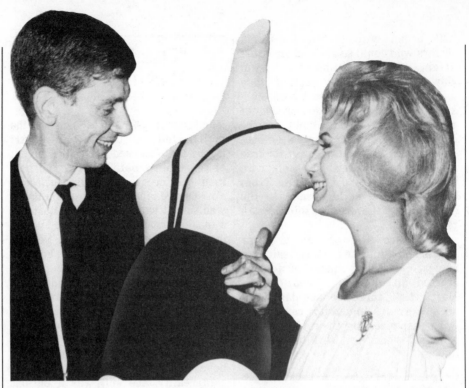

Toni Lee Shelley, a model, was arrested when she wore a topless bathing suit on a Chicago beach in 1964. Her attorney, Alan Berg, holds a dummy wearing a topless suit that he used in her defense. However, she lost the case.

had only shown it as a prophecy and was worried that his rival, Emilio Pucci, would show it first. "Fashion was at an awful standstill," Gernreich would later say. "It was timely to get it out of the rut."

And the orders came. First from Hess Brothers in Allentown, Pennsylvania, and then from the more trendy stores like Magnin's in San Francisco, Neiman-Marcus in Dallas, and Lord & Taylor in New York. One anonymous buyer for a large store was quoted as saying: "We will not promote it or display it. If a customer asks for it, we will take her into a fitting room and show it to her."

Gernreich said: "I'd do it again because I think the topless, by overstating and exaggerating a new freedom of the body, will make the moderate right degree of freedom more acceptable."

Women were arrested for going barebreasted on beaches. A 19-year-old Chicago model, Toni Lee Shelley, was pinched after emerging from a dip in Lake Michigan and charged with "improper attire." She stayed at the police station because as she explained, she "didn't know whether the cops could pin anything on me."

Esquire, however, had the last word. In its annual dubious achievement awards for 1964, the magazine called the topless bathing suit "the dumbest controversy of the year."

Still, the topless suit was one of the few '60s items that was ahead of its time then and is still ahead of its time—no matter how skimpy modern-day swimwear may be.

Gernreich made another contribution to the cause: the No-Bra Bra, molded nylon cups attached to shoulder straps and a narrow elastic band encircling the rib cage, and the "Body Stocking," which also hastened the acceptance of nudity. Later, he created stick-on vinyl patches with which the bikini wearer could decorate her nearly-naked body.

Comics had a field day about the topless bathing suit. "Instead of *Playboy,* the guys will be buying the *Ladies Home Journal.* It leaves nothing to the imagination, and at my age, it's good to have an imagination," said Bob Hope. "The police are apprehensive of what these suits will reveal. I'm apprehensive they'll reveal nothing," admitted Mort Sahl. Said Phyllis Diller: "When I wore one, everyone thought I was Albert Schweitzer."

Twiggy

If the '60s had been anywhere near a normal decade, then the only modeling an English teenager named Leslie Hornby would have done would have been for those public-service ads depicting starvation in some exotic country. She looked like she got along on a diet of shoelaces and gruel. She was 5 feet 6 inches tall and weighed 91 pounds, with dimensions that read like a typographical error: 31-22-32.

But the '60s were not a normal decade. Boys looked like girls. Girls looked like boys. The public ate up anything and because of that, little Leslie—better-known as Twiggy—ended up modeling all kinds of groovy threads, making much bread, and being hailed as the ideal of the new woman.

Close-cropped hair, matchstick-thin, flat-chested, staring from baleful, thick-lashed eyes: this was Twiggy, a Cockney comet who blazed across the media sky in 1967.

Here's how the Twig sprouted.

She was born in 1949 in a working-class suburb of London. Her classmates called her "Sticks." When she was 15, she began dating a 25-year-old hairdresser named Nigel Davies, who preferred to use the more sophisticated name, Justin de Villeneuve.

When Justin, who had a hustler's instincts, heard about Leslie's desire to model, he decided to guide her career. He became her Svengali—as well as boyfriend and bodyguard—zealously and shrewdly marketing her. Dubbing her "Twiggy," he took her to a London hairdresser who cropped and lightened her long brown hair. The hairdresser, the well-known Mr. Leonard, placed a photo of her in his window. In February, 1966, the picture was featured on the fashion page of a London newspaper with the tag: "This is the face of 1966."

Twiggy soon began modeling in London; then Justin took her to Paris, where she appeared on the cover of *Elle.* As she became better known, a line of Twiggy sportswear was created (one fashion writer said "they were cut as if there was a fabric shortage raging through the British Empire"). Twiggy never actually designed the dresses, made them (that was done by two young women from the Royal Academy in London), or sold them— she just put her stamp of approval on them. Twiggy Enterprises was started to handle her business. The odd thing

Even Snoopy had a crush on Twiggy.

PEANUTS
I DON'T UNDERSTAND IT...

I'VE NEVER FELT LIKE THIS BEFORE..

✳ SIGH ✳

I THINK I'M IN LOVE WITH TWIGGY!

is that the Twiggy clothing was, pardon the expression, a big bust here. American girls weren't about to starve themselves to those proportions.

On March 20, 1967, she hit America, creating media madness of a kind which hadn't been seen since the arrival of the Beatles three years earlier. The press dutifully wrote down every Cockney-accented word that poured from her lips. The press reported her major goal, which was to meet two people: Cassius Clay (now Muhammad Ali) and President Johnson. We learned she was just a shy girl, who still lived with her mum and dad, whose hobbies were sewing and listening to rock 'n' roll records. She seldom read ("It takes me six months to read a very short book.") Just about every major magazine did features on her. She modeled for photographer Richard Avedon. Her fee for other modeling sessions was $240 per hour.

In June, 1967, ABC did a three-part special on her, including a segment called "Twiggy, Why?" Then came all the Twiggy products—Justin insisted on complete control over every product to which she lent her name. Yardley peddled Twiggy eye makeup and false eyelashes; Mattel pushed a Twiggy doll, complete with such accessories as a mini-purse, treasure box and fashion tote. And let's not forget the Twiggy lunch box, ball-point pen, board game, T-shirt, sweatshirt, poster, and trading cards. All this merchandising was expected to gross between $1 and $3 million. Her likeness was built for Madame Tussaud's.

Twiggy became engaged to Justin in 1968 but never wed him. The couple split in the early '70s and in 1977 she married actor Michael Whitney. They had a daughter, Carly, born in 1979. The couple separated, and Whitney died in 1983.

She retired from modeling in 1969

but soon recast herself as an actress, dancer, and singer, beginning her career change with a role in the 1971 movie *The Boy Friend,* a campy Ken Russell musical which was surprisingly well-received. She also made two LPs in the mid-'70s and appeared in TV and stage productions, most memorably with Tommy Tune in the early '80s in *My One and Only.* She has also filled out to 32-24-34 and now weighs 110 pounds.

Quotes About Twiggy

"This business about flatness I find very offensive, smutty and dirty. Twiggy's my girlfriend. We're not competing with film stars. We're not trying to sell her as a sex symbol. She's the first girl idol the teenagers have had."—Justin, replying to questions about Twiggy's chest dimensions.

"Women move in certain ways that convey an air of the time they live in, and Twiggy, when she's in front of the lights, is bringing her generation in front of the camera."—Richard Avedon.

"She might become the first topless waiter."—An inside joke, 1967.

"Twiggy will be the greatest thing to hit the screen since Monroe...the whole world will be staggered. Your Julie Andrews and Julie Christies will seem pale and insignificant compared to this girl."—Ken Russell.

"Everyone assumed we were a put-on. But it wasn't an act at all. We didn't have to arrange anything; it all just happened. And I had known it would. I knew the Americans were barmy and would go overboard. All they wanted to do was look at that face and scream."—Justin in Twiggy's autobiography, 1975.

"She is a magic child of the media—the year's most radiant and evocative new image."—*Newsweek.*

Men's Fashions

Mod fashion was a crusade to brighten men's clothes. When one is young and feels everything is grey and drab, you know they want something new and exciting. It wasn't a matter of being in the right place at the right time. I made it happen."— The Merchant of Mod, John Stephen, in *Gentleman's Quarterly,* 1966.

The arrival of Mod clothing for males in 1966 coincided with my entry into the ninth grade. Ninth grade, if you'll recall, is a key year of adolesence—you make the transition from junior high to senior high. To impress those upperclassmen, it helps to have an image that wouldn't result in having your books kicked out of your arms by a deranged hall monitor. I wanted an image change. Mod man it would be. No more nebbish.

A week before school started, I headed to the place for Mod gear if you lived on Long Island—R&G Clothiers ("in the heart of swinging Hempstead," the radio commercials proclaimed), our area's hippest clothing store. It was rumored that this was where the Hassles—which was Billy Joel's first band and Long Island's coolest—bought their clothes.

R&G was no Robert Hall-goes-hip: cards from local rock bands lined the walls and the salesmen looked like they were members of the Blues Magoos. The shelves were brimming with Mod gear, whose labels proclaimed "direct from Carnaby Street." Supplies were rapidly being depleted; it looked as if every teenager on Long Island was in the joint.

Twiggy dressed as Bonne *and* as Clyde

I selected a pair of stovepipe pants with wide belt loops, a Garrison belt, two polka-dot shirts, and one paisley shirt. Was that really me staring back from the mirror? Slouching, fingers jammed through the belt-loops—that's how the cool guys were supposed to pose.

The first day of school was always the day for showing off what weird changes you went through that summer, so I chose that as my coming-out party. I wore the yellow-and-green polka-dot shirt, the stovepipes, and a pair of pointy-toed Beatle boots. As I walked into school, the metal taps beating their tatoo on the tile floors, I thought I saw Mary Gina checking me out through the corner of her eye.

First class, Social studies. Mr. Perry. Ex-marine (he killed a man with his bare hands in Korea, the school grapevine reported). White shirt, narrow tie. He stared at my ensemble the way he might have stared at a North Korean on Pork Chop Hill and proclaimed: "Don't you know that those outfits have been banned by the school board this year? I don't want you ever to wear them again."

Like a schmuck, I listened. And the next day I was back to wearing tab collars (and fag tags), chinos, and penny loafers.

Of course he was just trying to scare me. There was no such edict. A thousand paisley shirts bloomed in the halls of Carey High, at least until the spring of 1967. That's about as long as the Mod fad lasted; Mod clothes in the U.S. had about as much success in the United States as I did the first day of high school.

SOME BACKGROUND

In the '60s, the ferment in men's fash-ion occurred in London, the tradition-al capital of male elegance. For the first time, fashion was starting at the bottom of the social ladder and work-ing upward rather than the reverse.

The Mod look that hit here in 1966 was the culmination of a British youth movement that began in the early '60s. The Mods—for Modernists—were enamored of American R&B, Lambretta motor scooters, purple heart amphetamines, and especially with dressing stylishly.

Mod was, above all, a fashion state-ment. The movement came from the kids themselves, and they created their own clubs, music (Mod faves included the Who and Small Faces, and such performers as Rod Stewart and David Bowie had their roots in the Mod movement), lifestyles, and clothes shops. The true Mods had little to do with the brawling "Mods" who fought the rival "Rockers" (older, greasier, leather boys) in a series of brawls that was blown out of propor-tion by the press in 1964.

The center of Mod fashion life was Carnaby Street, an obscure alley behind the elegant Regent Street. Here, at stores like Hung on You, was where Mod youths bought their low-slung hipster pants (based on the American blue jean), patterned or printed shirts, fitted jackets, which were four-buttoned and vented to the waist, high-heel boots, and peaked caps.

John Stephen, a grocer's son from Glasgow, was the tycoon of Carnaby Street. Before he was 30, he owned ten shops on the shabby street and anoth-er fourteen in the London area. "When I started, I had to fight to sell our clothes," Stephen said. "People laughed at pink-and-red slacks. Frilly shirts. They said they were clothes for women and were effeminate. Word of mouth really made us. Some boy would buy a colorful shirt or tie and some friends would see it and ask 'Where'd you get it?' "

John Stephen Boutiques came to America in 1965. The Dayton Company of Minneapolis featured one, and Stern's of New York renamed its men's department, John Stephen of Carnaby Street. The boutiques were characterized by eardrum-piercing pop music and striped plastic tents for fitting rooms.

By the time Mod came to America, the original English scene had become touristy and silly. By early 1967, it was clear that American Mod had bombed. The American menswear industry said it stood for "Mark Ours Down." At one Minneapolis store, hip-huggers that went for $15 only three months earlier, were on sale for $2.99. In Washington, D.C., shaped, epauletted jackets were down to $4.99 from $25. It was a rapid fall. Only the previous summer, twenty percent of the clothes manufactured by MacGregor and forty-five percent of pants sold at Dayton's had been in the new styles.

Why the decline? Menswear Retailers of America head Lawrence Nathan said: "Mod was killed by the same thing that made it acceptable in the first place—it stopped being different. When these kids decide they don't want something, they won't take it at any price."

But more signifcantly, American kids did not have to overspend on outrageous garb to show the world a sense of social injustice that the lower-class British kids did. It wasn't part of their lifestyle. Besides, a homegrown youth movement—the hippies—had come along and captured imaginations better. Most fashion businesspeople were unprepared for the fact that men could be fickle, too.

Even though some Mod elements—notably the double-breasted suits and checked slacks—held on for awhile, Nathan observed: "Hysteria will not soon return to the youth market. When something like Mod comes along, it should be sampled, tested, and handled gingerly. I think the retailers have learned their lesson." Still, Mod paved the way for a general loosening up of men's fashion—the so-called peacock revolution—which would hit its peak around 1971.

Everybody had an Uncle Sid who ran around wearing aqua shirts and wide, colorful ties, the likes of which hadn't been seen since those 1949 beauties featuring hand-painted scenes of the Atlantic City boardwalk. Most adult men looked ridiculous, of course. Especially Mr. Perry. Two years after he nixed my Mod gear, he showed up in his classroom wearing a powder-blue Nehru jacket and a yellow turtleneck. I had lost the battle, but won the war.

And let us not forget these other hip items.

THE NEHRU JACKET

Butt of many jokes, the Nehru shirt caught on in late 1966 and died out less than two years later. It was inspired by the workaday garment of Indian bigwig, Jawaharlal Nehru. The garment first appeared on the international scene when salesmen in the Paris shop of Pierre Cardin started wearing gray flannel Nehrus after Cardin made a trip to India and liked the jacket.

The jacket was an exact copy of the Indian original, close-fitting with a shaped back, buttoned front and a 1½-inch standing collar. It came in a variety of colors, and paisley was the

A Mod man displays the grooviest Carnaby Street threads (1966).

favorite pattern. It could be worn for business or evening wear and was favored by celebrities. When Johnny Carson wore a businessman's Nehru with turtleneck on "The Tonight Show," within twenty-four hours retailers reported a huge surge in Nehru suit and jacket sales. But the fad disappeared quickly. The garment can still be seen on "Laugh-In" reruns.

TURTLENECKS

Previously worn only by beatniks and Illya Kuryakin, the turtleneck sweater became adopted into the mainstream, ushered in on a wave of publicity that peaked in early 1967.

The turtleneck was the favored accessory to wear with the Nehru jacket. When that garment sputtered, it became fashionable to wear a turtleneck with a sports jacket, and was for those cats who didn't want to wear a tie—like all the groovy young swingers hanging out on "Love, American Style." As *Playboy* noted: "First-rate restaurants and night spots, including the Playboy Club, are now

opening their doors to gentlemen who have tastefully coupled a suit or sportcoat with a turtleneck."

Pierre Cardin, the designer most responsible for the trend, said the turtleneck was appropriate for any occasion, provided that the suit it was worn with was "modern." Pierre dished out a model at $37.50, favored by such tastemakers as Paul Newman, Steve McQueen, and Jason Robards.

Men wearing turtlenecks freaked out fancy headwaiters, who were still freaking at women wearing pantsuits. In fact, Lord Snowden, Princess Margaret's then-hubby, scandalized the British press by wearing a black wool turtleneck under his velvet dinner jacket to a first-night supper party. Medallions and beads were worn with the turtleneck only at the men's own risk.

Long Hair

A DIS-TRESSING TALE

Someday I will have a son who will look at a photo album of me and see me as I was in the late '60s—with a thick moustache and shoulder-length hair. "You really thought that by growing your hair long, you would be able to change the world?" he will ask. And I will dread the question. But I will thrust him upon my knee, and I will tell him the following tale.

Once upon a time in a land across the sea lived four fab lovable prophets with hair that crawled down over their collars. One day in the middle of a dark winter, a huge winged bird bore them to a Great Country. After they landed, the men of that Great

Country began letting their hair grow, too.

Now, the people of this great land had not seen their men with hair so long in many years, not since the days of Millard of Fillmore and Abraham of Lincoln. But that was a long time ago, and few people remembered. Many people didn't like what they saw. An evil cabal of gym teachers, principals, and policemen vowed to fight the menace and tried to slay this modern-day dragon. Armed with scissors, clippers, detention threats, and traffic citations, they tried, but it was too late.

They couldn't stop it. Slowly, month by month, year by year, the hair kept creeping down—over the forehead, over ears, over the collars. Then, in the third year of the Invasion, the same lovable prophets decreed that moustaches and beards and long sideburns should also grow. Let a thousand FuManchus bloom, said the prophets. Let all would-be groovies grow their sideburns into muttonchops.

The forces of darkness were in retreat. But the hair continued to grow even longer. In a city of many hills, a group of elves declared that no longer would combs rush through their hair; no longer would shampoo cleanse their scalps. That shoulder blades should no longer be where hair stopped. And thou shalt bind thine hair like the tails of ponies.

Into the most hidden recesses of the land the menace crept. Into bowling alleys and laundromats and K-Marts, and even into the rosters of major league baseball teams. Even the king and his counselors threw away their Vitalis.

All this should mean something, declared the prophets. Did it? Pundits pontificated; sociologists socialized, and anthropoligists anthropomorphized.

Until one day another wind rustled the peacefulness of the land. The king had been toppled, and the prophets had dispersed to the corners of the globe. And the men of the land, not knowing what to do, began baring their collars, their ears, and their upper lips. They're still waiting for

After he left the Presidency, even LBJ grew his hair long.

another huge winged bird to rescue them.

COMMENTS ABOUT LONG HAIR

1. "It isn't right that people should stare at boys with long hair. Grown-ups who do this are living ten years in the past."
2. "After all, there's nothing new about boys wearing long hair. Two hundred years ago, no one thought anything about it. But just because boys are wearing their hair long again, many adults think it's terrible."
3. "Even my teacher at school criticizes me for the length of my hair and is always telling me to get a haircut."
4. "I'd like to know if the top American longhaired groups like the Lovin' Spoonful and the Young Rascals also have this problem—about people criticizing the length of their hair."—Letter from a Bronx teenager named Howard Stern in the May 6, 1966 "Sound off!" column of *GO* magazine.
5. "It's a passing fad—just a wave. I see no deep-rooted behavior disorders in the present tendency of boys to look like girls. It's not psychiatric. It's not neurotic. It is rebellion—rebellion of the youngsters against their parents and society."—Dr. Wladimir G. Eliasberg, past president of the American Society of Psychoanalytic Physicians.

6 HAIR-RAISING SONGS

1. "Laugh at Me"—Sonny Bono gets mad at the world because they don't dig that he looks like Prince Valiant as costumed by Fred of Bedrock.
2. "Are You a Boy or Are You a Girl?"—The Barbarians asked one of the most popular questions of 1964 and 1965. The answer: You're either a girl, or you come from Liverpool.
3. "Home of the Brave"—Jody Miller's boyfriend is persecuted by school authorities because of his hair length. She learns that everything they taught her about America in her social studies class is not necessarily true.
4. "Hair"—The Cowsills go hip with their peppy version of the theme song of America's tribal love rock musical. Streaming, gleaming, flaxen waxen. Shoulder length or longer.
5. "Back When My Hair Was Short"—A one-shot band, Gun Hill Road, from the Bronx reminisced in the early '70s about social conditions of the early '60s. The same band should have cut a record today called "Back When My Hair Was Long," but still haven't.
6. "Almost Cut My Hair"—Balding David Crosby's (of CSN&Y) defiant statement on why he is going to keep his locks long. He's going to keep his freak flag flying—until a better offer comes along.

3 HAIR-RAISING TALES OF 1965

1. In Cleveland, a distraught gym teacher ordered his shaggy students to wear hair nets.
2. In Los Angeles, a jury convicted a boy of disturbing the peace for refusing to cut his hair.
3. In Kentucky, a father bought his longhaired son a dog license, complete with tag.

I n 1968, these students at Brien McMahon High School in Norwalk, Connecticut protest over suspension of 53 male students whose hair was deemed too long by school authorities.

1966: Orlando, Florida— Eleventh graders Mike McCann, Mike Odle and David Rohr use a yardstick to check the length of classmate Charles Spillner's hair after they were refused admission to school because of "improper hair styles."

STUDENTS OF NORWALK BEAUTIFY AMERICA get a haircut

Alan T. Pearce

A **billboard that says it all**

Hippies

Pity the poor hippie. Here in the mid-'80s, it's difficult to even say the word "hippie" with a straight face, so much has the term become the object of derision. Today, the whole world looks at hippies approximately the same way as Peter Boyle did when he played Joe, the bean-brained construction worker in the classic anti-hippie film—as foolish parasites, dirty longhairs, naive, unambitious slugs. The worst critics of all are lapsed hippies, those over 35, who have long since renounced their mindblown pasts and who only tend to talk about it in the privacy of their co-op lofts after draining several liters of Chardonnay.

But looking back, the original hippies, those that flourished in San Francisco's Haight-Ashbury (Hashbury, to the media) between, say, 1965 and 1966, were really on to a good thing. They really thought they could shuck the American dream—live cheaply, communally, unhypocritically, wear their hair as long as they wanted, and wear as freaky an outfit as they wanted. Armed with slogans —Love Is All You Need, Flower Power, Do Your Own Thing—they thought they would change the world.

Unlike their Bohemian predecessors, the Beats, the hippies lived in a world of day-glo colors and rock 'n' roll, not of black and white and jazz and poetry. They didn't have as many intellectual pretensions, but rather a more childlike view of the world.

For a while their lifestyle worked. But by 1967, the media got wind of the phenomenon and invaded Haight-Ashbury, announcing it to the world, and spreading the vibes into every hamlet and suburb across America, where it found a receptive audience among the restless, spoiled youth of America like myself. Once an hour, Gray Line buses motored out to the Haight from the ritzy downtown hotels. "The Hippie Hop" at $6 a tourist was advertised as a "safari through psychedelphia" and the only foreign tour within the continental limits of the United States. Sometimes, the buses would be met by hippies holding mirrors to have the gawking straights actually look at themselves.

During 1967's Summer of Love everyone began thumbing their way to San Francisco, if not on the highway, then in their own minds, lured by the siren song of Scott McKenzie: "If you're going to San Francisco, be sure to wear some flowers in your hair." San Francisco police claimed that in 1967 there were no more than 5,000 full-time hippies, not counting the plastic or weekend hippies, who swelled their numbers.

Hippies became many adults' nightmares, many teens' dreams. But the mythology proved too overwhelming. In October, 1967, a group of hippies held a Death of Hip ceremony in Golden Gate Park. They burned a coffin containing orange peels, peacock feathers, charms, flags, crucifixes, and a marijuana-flavored cookie. They sang "God Bless America" and "Hare Krishna," and shouted "Hippies are dead! Now the free men will come through."

Things didn't get much better. There were murders, speed freaks, bum trips. Still, hippie communities continued to function in American cities. If anything, their legions swelled and grew stronger. On impressionable youth is where the hippies may have made the most important impact. "We are everywhere" was the new slogan. But somewhere between then and now, the last hippie grew up. And if the cults didn't get 'em, the corporations did.

Drugs

Drugs were the things your parents told you not to take. ("Why do you think they call it dope?") That in itself was probably a good enough reason for drug-taking to become probably the major participant activity of the '60s. Along with blue jeans, casual drug use could be one of the most enduring legacies of the decade. Walk along Wall Street any day at high noon, and chances are you'll be able to spot pinstriped brokers blowing their minds higher than a bull-market Dow-Jones average.

In the '60s, marijuana (a.k.a. grass, wacky weed, pot) use was anything but casual. It was still primarily associated with beatniks, jazz musicians, and misfits, and had outlaw status. Today, it is status quo. Today, no longer do you have that sinking feeling in the pit of your stomach when you're cruising in your folks' smoke-choked car and in the rearview mirror you spy a blinking light. No longer do you have to suddenly throw $100 worth of Lebanese hash down the crapper because you hear a knock on the door at 2 A.M., and you weren't expecting anybody.

Yes, progress is wonderful. Really, you have to be reminded that marijuana is still illegal. I do miss the paranoia, though. In fact, I'm convinced that the paranoia actually triggered a chemical reaction in your brain, which made the dope seem

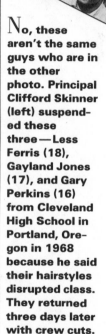

No, these aren't the same guys who are in the other photo. Principal Clifford Skinner (left) suspended these three—Less Ferris (18), Gayland Jones (17), and Gary Perkins (16) from Cleveland High School in Portland, Oregon in 1968 because he said their hairstyles disrupted class. They returned three days later with crew cuts. Principal Skinner was pleased.

better. That's one reason why getting high has lost its cachet in my set.

And what of LSD? No one trips anymore. Today's kids think microchips are hipper than microdots. LSD was the drug that was supposed to change the world. Such misplaced trust we high-flying fools showed, however. Here, kid, take this piece of paper, chew it, and in just a few minutes you'll see enough visions to fill Lourdes for a month.

Old '60s hands now tell trip stories the way their daddies told war stories. Remember the time we went to see the Dead, and they changed before my eyes to a bunch of cavemen playing volleyball? I know one guy in 1968 who tripped and said he saw the future, hallucinating women pumping iron, people with blue mohawks, and gas that cost $1.50 a gallon. We were convinced the guy was a lunatic.

Ah, colorless, odorless, tasteless lysergic acid diethylamide. It had first been synthesized during the '30s in the laboratory of Dr. Albert Hoffman, a Swiss chemist working for Sandoz, a pharmaceutical company. It was the first hallucinogenic drug produced in a laboratory since 1799 when Sir Humphrey Davy developed nitrous oxide (laughing gas). But it wasn't until the early '60s when two Harvard eggheads—Timothy Leary and Richard Alpert—began swallowing it at regular intervals, convinced of its theraupeutic and religious value, that the drug became known to the public. Tim and Dick roamed around Harvard Yard proselytizing on behalf of LSD and occasionally slipping a spare sugar cube into a student's malted milk.

After being dismissed by Harvard University, they went on the road as full-time psychedelic salesmen. Leary—a West Point dropout and former Army psychologist—set up shop in Millbrook, New York with his own church, the League of Spiritual Discovery. Leary said that if you took LSD you'd be able to speak to God. Since one of the catchwords of the '60s was that God Is Dead, this sounded as though Leary was pulling your chain — unless he had a special connection. The church's services were occasionally disrupted by the local G-man, G. Gordon Liddy, then a Duchess County Assistant District Attorney. Fifteen years later, the pair kissed and made up so they could tour college campuses together, reminiscing about the good old days.

Up until 1966, in fact, acid was still legal in the United States. But after it was outlawed, LSD became a pretty popular recreational activity among college students, who knew the right "chemists" who could concoct the substance for them. Even during the great airplane strike of 1967, plenty of people were still flying—on the ground. Unfortunately, a handful of LSD users flew right out of windows, believing they could walk on air, and ended up in the hospital or in hippie heaven.

These sad consequences helped contribute to the negative publicity about the drug. Rumors also abounded that LSD allegedly caused chromosome damage, and consequently, kids of tripsters would have three heads. That hasn't happened, although there

does seem to be a plethora of modern babies named Jennifer and Jason. We're still waiting to find the connection.

What happened to the dynamic duo of acid?

Leary spent the early part of the '70s as a fugitive, sprung from jail (where he was serving 1 to 10 on a pot rap) by the Weathermen. He fled to Algeria, hung out for awhile with Eldridge Cleaver, and was finally nabbed by narcs in Afghanistan in 1973. Three years later, he was paroled—under suspicion that he sang to the feds. Since then, he has tried stints as a nightclub comedian, author and lecturer, including holding debates with Liddy, his former nemesis.

Alpert, a nice Jewish boy, who at one time advocated government-run centers where responsible adults could take LSD in a safe, pleasant environment, changed his name to Baba Ram Dass and moved to India. During the '70s he developed more of a cult following than Leary had during the '60s.

QUOTES ABOUT LSD

"I have taken LSD 300 times, but I want to tell you that it is no business for neurotics to play around with. It is like a religious experience. It makes you see the most vicious things about yourself—that you're a liar, that most people are robots, that men are blind to the wisdom that is within their grasp. It's a ruthless microscopic view of how really ridiculous we perceive ourselves. LSD pulls the rug right out from under you. If you're not ready to look at the most unpleasant aspects of reality, stay away.—Timothy Leary.

"It is so seductive, it is such a glorious, rapturous, blissful experience. A good trip is not going to go the way of

goldfish eating."—Dr. Sidney Cohen of UCLA, chief of psychomatic medicine at the Los Angeles VA hospital, and author of *The Beyond Within,* a study of LSD.

THE GREAT BANANA HYPE

This was among the best rumors of the '60s—ranking right up there with Paul Is Dead, President Kennedy is alive, and the V-sign means you have pot.

In 1967, some amateur chemist said that the scrapings of the inner skin of a ripe banana, dried slowly in a 200-degree oven and smoked in a pipe or cigarette, could get you high. The underground papers, then the straight press, spread the news.

"Banana, banana, banana!!" shouted hundreds of hippies at a Central Park be-in. "Everybody's turning onto bananas now," a 28-year-old welfare department worker said to the *New York Times.* "It's not as good as a pot high, but, what the hell, the cops can't arrest you." A group of San Franciscans started the Mellow Yellow Company to research, develop, and market the banana high.

Meanwhile, scientists at the Federal Food and Drug Administration began investigating the phenomenon and announced that, yes, these damn

I n 1966, wondering whether a longhair was a boy or a girl was a popular pastime. From the shoulders up it looks as if these two are a couple of girls. But surprise! When they turn around it's a guy and a gal.

hippies may be right. Banana skins were rich in serotonin, a chemical which might, when heated, acquire a dimethyl ring, changing it into bufotenin, a hallucinogen used by South American Indians.

Eventually it was all revealed as one big put-on. The electrical banana, despite what Donovan said in "Mellow Yellow," was not going to be the very next craze.

ACID TEST

1. How did STP compare with LSD in strength?
2. What was the drug, MDA's, nickname?
3. What was THC?
4. What year did the Great Marijuana drought occur?
5. Name five songs that have real or imagined drug-related lyrics.
6. Name three types of LSD.
7. What was the accepted per-ounce price of marijuana in 1968?
8. What does "to bogart" mean?
9. Where are drug peddlers most likely to hang out?
   a. bowling alleys
   b. hot dog stands
   c. shopping centers

ANSWERS

1. It was more powerful than LSD
2. "The Love Drug"
3. Synthetic marijuana
4. 1969
5. "White Rabbit" (Jefferson Airplane); "Shapes of Things" (Yardbirds); "Lucy in the Sky with Diamonds" (Beatles); "Eight Miles High" (Byrds); "Rainy Day Women #12 & 35" (Bob Dylan)
6. Orange sunshine, window pane, Mr. Natural
7. $15
8. To hold onto a joint longer than is socially correct
9. Whoops! I got this one off a hygiene class from senior year. It just kinda slipped in here.

The Sexual Revolution

A SIXTY-SECOND SWINGER'S TOUR OF THE SEXUAL REVOLUTION

1960
First Playboy Club opens — a bunny for your thoughts.
Birth-control pill approved by FDA.

1962
Helen Gurley Brown's *Sex and the Single Girl* is published. Nice girls should do it, too, advises the *Cosmopolitan* editor.
The pill becomes available at drug stores by prescription.
Grossinger's holds its first singles weekend.

1964
One-time prune picker and file clerk, Carol Doda, becomes the world's first topless waitress at San Francisco's Condor, a North Beach club.
Gael Greene's *Sex and the College Girl* is published. One memorable passage described a sorority girl attempting to climb a wall in mock agony, while crying out in frustration: "You don't know how long it has been

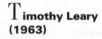

Timothy Leary
(1963)

since I got screwed!"

1966
Computer dating sweeps college, and then, high school campuses.
Masters and Johnson publish *Human Sexual Response.* Among their research equipment: an artificial phallus, an electrically-powered plastic penis with a tiny camera and illuminator inside to record what was happening in the subject's vagina. It could regulate depth and speed of the thrust.

1967
First singles bar opens, "Friday's," on the Upper East Side of Manhattan.

1968
Co-ed dorms become popular on college campuses.

PLAYBOY

Playboy was actually started in 1953, but its popularity accelerated in the '60s. It was the magazine in which such literary giants as Fleming, Malamud, Bellow, and Singer were published; where you learned what records to buy, wines to drink, clothes to wear. Cut it out. You read it for the girls. The real women. Mamie Van Doren and Jo Collins and all those women who didn't look like your mother or even your fourth-grade teacher.

The word "playboy" was one of those intrinsically cool '60s words that has lost all meaning today. To have a girl call you a playboy was the ultimate compliment-cum-warning-sign of respect. The Marvelettes wrote a song about one, "You Beat Me to the Punch." Mary Wells found out too late that her boyfriend was one. Gary Lewis, Jerry's boy, thought it would be a cool name for his rock 'n' roll band; so did John Fred (John Fred and His Playboy Band: "Judy in Disguise

with Glasses").

That was the fantasy, and what a good one it was: living in a Playboy pad, a penthouse high above the city streets, pitchers of martinis in the fridge, 'Trane on the hi-fi, white llama wall-to-wall carpeting, automatic light dimmer, a round vibrating bed — just like Hef.

These were fantasies fueled by purloined copies of *Playboy* from the half-blind, fully-deaf candy-store owner or from a steamer trunk owned by a 19-year old Brooklyn College sociology major working as a summer camp counselor. To be a playboy meant to be a swinger. Now there's a truly '60s word — before it became the name of a Polaroid camera or referred to the practice of wife-swapping. To be a swinger was cool, hip, all-knowing, like Frank, like Dino, like Hef.

To score with chicks, you had to live in a raunchy pad, with mattresses on the floor, posters of Che Guevara on the wall, loose joints, and a hookah. A playboy was an incredibly hung-up cat, you know? When Hef began dressing his bunnies in headbands and unbuttoned fringed jackets, you knew the age of the swinger was over.

It became time for the *Cosmo* girl and for *Playgirl* and Alan Alda. Many are still wondering what kind of man still reads *Playboy.* The magazine seems a relic of another era. All you have to do today is turn on the cable box or pop in an X-rated videocassette or walk to a newsstand and purchase an issue of *Beaver* as easily as *Boys' Life.* You get more titillation than Hef ever printed in a year. The thrill of it is most definitely gone.

TELL IT LIKE IT IS, HEF

"A lot of people are starved for fresh air and there's pure oxygen coming

Timothy Leary
(1969)

Andy Warhol and his companion, Edie Sedgwick

from this corner. It's no wonder people are pressing close to the ventilator." — This is how he explained the success of *Playboy,* "an empire built on sex," to *Life* magazine in 1965.

The Art Scene

POP ART

All that other stuff—it's old, it's old, it's antique. Renoir? I hate him. Cezanne? Bedroom pictures. It's all the same...Pop is the art of today and tomorrow and the future. These pictures are like IBM stock, don't forget that and this is the time to buy, because Pop is never going to die." — Leon Kraushar a Long Island, New York art collector, who had Tom Wesselman's *Great American Nude* in the bathroom of his seven-room house. Also in the bathroom were Brillo boxes and a statue of a jazz combo; the bedroom featured silkscreens of Jackie, Liz, and Marilyn.

Pop art was the perfect style for the '60s — a decade which glorified consumerism and kitsch. It was a form that displayed a sense of humor in a decade when nothing could be taken seriously.

Pop Art used the objects of the ordinary world as art — a radical idea for the art world, whose most-favored paintings had become increasingly complex. Pop Art gave people a new way of looking at things, to notice the world around them—as well as changing one's notion of what taste is. Said the popsters: advertising, TV, movies, cars, and supermarkets should now be considered as art.

The "fine" artists couldn't understand what was going on. "It is the want of imagination, the passive acceptance of things as they are that makes these pictures dull and unsatisfactory," said Peter Selz, curator of New York's Museum of Modern Art. "It is as easy to produce as it is to consume."

The impetus for Pop Art (a term coined in the '50s by critic Lawrence Alloway) came from people outside the art establishment. But acceptance by insiders, like Jasper Johns, helped hasten acceptance. Roy Lichtenstein's 1961 stylistic switch to comic-book paintings from Abstract Expressionism further legitimized Pop Art.

Pop's most visible proponent was a silver-haired, media-conscious former commercial artist named Andy Warhol. He became famous by painting Brillo boxes and silk-screening multiple images of Marilyn Monroe, later branching into underground films and magazines.

Pop Art became accepted by the New York in-crowd at the same time this clique was embracing pop music. Pop became highly collectible as well, with Warhols being hung on apartments where not long before were Matisses. Ethel and Robert Scull were *the* Pop Art couple, who used their patronage of the new form to work their way into New York society, as wittily chronicled in one of Tom Wolfe's essays. Scull, a New York cab-fleet owner, who helped support artists he admired, paid $60,000 for James Rosenquist's *F-111,* an 85-foot long depiction of a jet fighter from which hung such objects as a hair dryer and a light bulb. But even this was too big to hang in the Scull residence, so it was donated to a Manhattan museum.

Ethel "Spike" Scull commissioned Warhol to paint her portrait. He took her to one of those quarter, shoot-yourself booths, got dozens of photos, made silk-screens of them, and then produced the multiple portraits of Mrs. Scull. Their kitchen featured a Claes Oldenburg Pop Art stove with painted-plaster food and a Jasper Johns painting of an American flag on the wall.

The Sculls had a much-celebrated divorce in the '80s, with dispensation of their Pop Art collection a source of contention.

FOUR COOL POP ART MOMENTS

1. By 1968, even Brillo had gotten into the act. They offered a Brillo Pillo—an inflatable vinyl pillow with the Brillo logo. Said the promotional ad: "The latest in groovy Pop Art."

2. In 1967, "The Man from U.N.C.L.E." offered its viewers a tidbit called "The Pop Art Affair." Illya played a beatnik who must trace the source of a gas that causes people to hiccough to death. The episode contains much flip chatter.

1964 Mustang

3. In a mid-'60s *Batman* comic book, one panel said "At the Gotham City Museum, Bruce Wayne, millionaire sportsman and playboy, and young ward Dick Grayson attend a sensational 'Pop Art' show."

4. Supermarket art. In 1964, there was an exhibit of food in a Manhattan art gallery. The gallery was decorated to resemble your local A&P. Patrons couldn't tell what was real and what wasn't. Warhol's famous Campbell's soup cans sold for $1,500; underneath were normal 2-for-35-cent cans, autographed by Warhol, which sold for $6. Typical prices: $27 for a hunk of Swiss cheese; eggs for $144 a dozen; pork loins, $49. It sounds like a preview of food prices in 1992.

Wheels

Twenty-six mpg city? 35 highway? Wash your mouth! You'd never hear anything like that in the '60s. The only people who were concerned with automobile gas mileage probably wore leather patches on their jackets, weren't impressed by the Green Berets, and drove strange-looking things made in some country that used to be our enemy. Volkswagens weren't for driving, they were for stuffing college students into, like in those good old '50s college days. No, the numbers you heard in the '60s were things like 396 cubes, zero-to-60 in 4.6. Numbers to inspire fear and awe, not frugality.

You talk '60s cars, and you're talking muscle cars and Pony cars. The '60s were the last decade of big, powerful, snazzy machines; the last decade for cars to inspire rock 'n' roll songs ("GTO" by Ronnie and the Daytonas; "Hey Little Cobra" by the Ripchords; "409" by the Beach Boys). It was also the last decade when you could cruise without guilt; when driving far and fast was not only fun, but patriotic — in fact, it was your American duty to burn up all those spanking-new interstates the government had asked you to shell out your tax dollars for.

And when you were low on fuel, you'd stop at something called a gas station—they were everywhere, always open, and they sold only gasoline, not milk and eggs. You'd splurge $5 for a tankful, and you'd also get to play all kinds of fun games like Dino Dollars or Flying A Win-a-Check, where you matched halves of tickets to win big bucks.

And what would you be burning up those interstates in? Not in the chrome-and-finned beauties of the '50s (the last tailfin straightened up around 1961), but cars that drew adjectives from teens like boss, tough, and bitchen.

Here are some of them.

FORD MUSTANG—Sonny and Cher drove matching versions; Steve McQueen was chased up and down the hills of San Francisco in one in *Bullitt*. The Mustang was sporty, sexy, and affordable — and the greatest single automotive success of the '60s. The car raised Ford volume and set an all-time record for first-year sales of any new model to date. Between its introduction date in April, 1964 and January, 1965, a total of 680,989 Mustangs were sold. Dealers auctioned them off because buyer demand exceeded supply by fifteen to one.

The genius behind the car was Lee A. Iacocca, now president of Chrysler. He was an engineer-turned salesman who worked his way from an obscure sales position to Vice-president and General Manager of Ford Division in five years. He later would become president of the corporation, largely because of his success with the Mustang.

His idea was a new "personal car." As a salesman, he had noticed how many customers still pined for the two-seat Thunderbird. He kept trying out ideas and by 1961, he had developed a plan: a youth-oriented sports car that would be inexpensive to build, but peppy and sporty-looking. It would sell for less than $2,500. Three years later, the Mustang came roaring out of Dearborn.

CORVAIR — The first of the Big Three's compacts, it was revolutionary when it was introduced in 1959 because of its air-cooled aluminum-block engine mounted in the rear. The car got off to a quick start. In 1960, the first full year, 229,985 people bought the Corvair. The initial success of the Corvair boosted its creator, Edward N. Cole, to the presidency of General Motors.

Ten years and 1,710,018 cars later, the last one rolled off the GM assembly line in May, 1969. It was killed by foreign competition, the Mustang (which was peppier), but mostly by Ralph Nader's 1965 book, *Unsafe at Any Speed,* which pointed out the potentially fatal defects in the Corvair. Nader charged that the Corvair suspension system was faulty and could, in certain circumstances, cause the car to flip over. (We'd eventually get used to such warnings, but this was the first widely-publicized attack against cars.) In 1966, sales plummeted to 88,951; In 1968, only 12,977 were sold; by mid-1969, a mere 4,511.

Corvair owners filed 150 lawsuits against GM. The 4,511 owners of the 1969 Corvair were issued certificates by GM worth $150 redeemable on the purchase of any other Chevy up through 1973. Let's hope none of them spent that money on a Chevy Vega.

Today, a lot of naysayers to Nader have made the Corvair a collector's item.

DODGE CHARGER — This was the Arnold Schwarzenegger of muscle cars, a thunder-powered, sexy machine. The 1967 variety was most recently seen tearing up the countryside as the "General Lee" on "The Dukes of Hazzard."

CORVETTE STING RAY — The ultimate sports car was the revolutionary '63 'Vette with the split rear window. It looked mean and ominous and it was.

BARRACUDA — It was originally introduced in 1964 as Plymouth's answer to the Falcon and Corvair, but unlike them, was built for high performance; it could go from 0 to 60 in eight seconds. It was the first car to sport the "fastback" — acres of sloping glass which gave the 'Cuda its sleek, sexy look. The car became the best-selling Plymouth for 1965. Buffs go for the 1967-69 models.

GTO — (for Gran Turisimo Omologato) — Introduced in 1964, this car helped Pontiac change its image from the family car of the '50s to the high-performance car of the '60s. Hurry on down to wide-track town, and for $3,800 you'd get a monster with all conceivable options. The GTO was the first of the muscle cars, and the one that *Car and Driver* claimed could beat the Ferrari in a drag race. Three hundred and sixty horses all charged up and ready to go. Shut 'em down.

1963 Corvette

Skateboards

During the spring of 1965, American doctors reported an increase in the number of scrapes, and broken arms and wrists in their under-18 patients. The reason for the rash of injuries at this particular time can be traced directly to the popularity of skateboarding, which then was at its peak.

The craze even had its own anthem —Jan and Dean's "Sidewalk Surfing," which borrowed its music from the Beach Boys surfing hit "Catch a Wave." During their concert appearances, the duo would arrive on stage via skateboards. That was just one tangible example of the link between skateboarding and surfing.

In the late '50s and early '60s, skateboarding was a dry-land extension for Southern California surfers to stay in shape when the surf wasn't up. The first skateboards were primitive, little more than skates attached to planks. At the time, it was really a cultish, amateur phenomenon. By 1962, the hobby had grown enough so that enthusiasts called it "terra surfing."

In 1963, the fad became more popular—the first surfboard-shaped boards went on the market, at prices ranging from $1.79 to $14. The first formal competitions at a junior high in Hermosa Beach and a high school in Pacific Palisades drew about 100 spectators, which was considered a large crowd. At these competitions, some of the famous skateboarding tricks began developing—wheelies, handstands, headstands, 360s, and high jumps.

But the years of skateboarding's biggest popularity were 1964 and 1965. In 1964, there were ninety-two manufacturers of skateboards, creating such wonders as a thirty-inch "full precision board" with fiberglass wheels and special bearings ($29.95) and a motorized skateboard ($49.94). Fifty million skateboards were built during this boom period.

On May 22 and 23, 1965, the first annual National Skateboard Championships were held before a capacity crowd of 10,000 at La Palma Stadium in Anaheim, with teams from Mexico and Japan competing. All three TV networks covered the event, which featured standing, jumping, and twirling while on the boards, and it was later rebroadcast on "ABC's Wide World of Sports." In May, 1965, *Life* featured skateboarding on its cover.

Most tyro skateboarders weren't as agile as the competitors. In fact, most found that falling off a skateboard reacquainted you with the scientific fact that concrete was hard. Since equipment was not as good as today's freewheeling models, many accidents occurred. Thus began the skateboarding backlash, trumpeted by the media that had just finished hailing the fad.

The California Medical Association called it a "new medical menace." The National Safety Council issued an alert on skateboarding. By August, 1965, twenty cities had banned skateboarding; some municipalities even confiscated the boards. Said *Good Housekeeping:* "Seldom has a sport fad produced as many fractured arms, wrists, and legs, concussions, and lacerations, as skateboarding."

Police in some cities entered department stores and asked that the boards be removed from the shelves as "a public service." In Portland, Oregon, cops chased a dog who had learned to ride a skateboard. New York City officials banned them from Central Park. In Shrewsbury, New Jersey, the police impounded all boards, returning them with a notice which stated that second offenders

Slot cars— electric-powered miniaturized racing cars—were a brief, but big fad among young teens in 1965 and 1966. There were 3,000 slot-car centers in the U.S. in 1965 where kids would plunk down a quarter or so for 15 minutes of racing. "Anyone who has yearned to handle a hot Ferrari or a hairpin turn at LeMans has got to love the slots," said one manufacturer.

would only get back the wooden part of the board, not the skates.

By November, 1965, those booming orders had been reduced to a trickle. We threw our skateboards into our junk closets. But skateboarding would be revived in 1973 with the introduction of the polyurethane wheel, allowing a whole new generation to do dips and spins—this time with less risk of injury. Still, no one has yet written a modern-day ode to skateboarding as cool as "Sidewalk Surfin'."

Barbie Dolls

After school, while I was busy with such adolescent male pursuits as flipping baseball cards and glomming through stolen copies of *Playboy,* my sister would be behaving in typically silly, little-girl fashion. She'd be down in our finished basement with her icky girlfriends playing with dolls. As I ogled pinups, squeals of joy drifted upstairs, followed by such strange statements as "Robin's got the dream house," "Judy has the convertible," "my mother bought me the baby-sitting outfit." Just what all this meant to me was arcane and a bit foolish. Anyway, weren't these 11-year-olds a little too old to be playing with dolls?

Not when the doll was Barbie. She was the world's first teenage doll — "a modern America in miniature, a tiny parody of our pursuit of the beautiful, the material, and the trivial," said one mid-'60s writer, sending a barb at the fashion-plate doll designed by Mattel. Ah, but why be so harsh? Has there been no better role model for today's women? Where do you think these contemporary female

Yuppies first learned to dress for success? Who do you think first instilled the consumer ethic in the hearts of baby-boom girls?

As quickly as fashion changed in the '60s, Barbie was there to reflect it. She had more outfits than Joan Collins wore in a season's worth of "Dynasty." She had special outfits for a lunch date, an after-five date, a Friday-night date, a Saturday-matinee date, a theater date, a country fair, a masquerade. She could be outfitted for hot and cold weather, skiing, skating, skin-diving, shopping; as a cheerleader, majorette, ballerina, stewardess, nurse, or hospital volunteer. Having a daughter with a Barbie doll meant having another child to clothe. In 1964, her complete wardrobe of nearly fifty items cost $136.

More than just an inspiration for fashion, Barbie was an eleven-and-a-half inch primer for sex education. Girls prepared for their first real-life dates by going through the paces with Barbie and her collegiately cool boyfriend, Ken.

Barbie came along at the height of the baby boom in 1958. The little doll was modeled on Barbara Handler, the baby-boom daughter of a Los Angeles couple named Elliot and Ruth Handler. They operated a small toy manufacturing company which had developed the first mass-produced music box, as well as more typical items such as toy rockets. Mrs. Handler would watch young Barbara play with paper dolls and dress them in the cutout fashions. Well, why not create a three-dimensional doll that one could clothe? she thought. Why not make a doll that would be not a baby, but a teenager to serve as a role model?

In 1958, the first Barbie doll hit the market. By 1965, the doll was making $97 million for Mattel.

Barbie spawned an entire world of products. When she babysat, Mattel introduced a Barbie-Baby-Sits outfit,

B arbie Doll (c. 1963)

Courtesy of Mattel

which included an apron, a tiny phone, a soft drink, pretzels, schoolbooks, a baby bottle, and a baby—most certainly not hers and Ken's.

Barbie's still around today and as popular and sexy and contemporary as ever—she even has an aerobics outfit. Yet kids are dating even earlier than ever. One can only imagine what goes on in finished basements today. What lessons can today's young girls still learn?

THROUGH THE '60S WITH BARBIE

1961
Ken is introduced as Barbie's boyfriend after fans wrote letters expressing the need for a male doll. First he is accepted as an escort for Barbie, then as a personality in his own right.

1963
"Fashion Queen Barbie" is introduced and can wear wigs. The same year, Midge is introduced as Barbie's freckle-faced friend; she can wear Barbie's wigs. Barbie begins receiving fan letters.

1964
More new dolls: Skipper, Barbie's little sister, and Allen, Ken's Buddy. For the first time Barbie has bendable knees, and eyes that open and close!

1965
Bendable legs are introduced.

1967
Barbie goes groovy — her hairstyle is changed to long straight hair, plus the twist-and-turn waist is introduced.

1968
Barbie talks for the first time. She gets an English friend, Stacey, with an appropriate accent, and a black friend, Christie. (A black doll named Francie was introduced the previous year, but didn't catch on.) Meanwhile, Mattel introduces the Twiggy doll, named for the stick-like fashion model.

A STINGING BARB AT BARBIE

"A symbol of the American urge to hurry our children into the trappings of childhood, possibly eliminating their youth altogether... We are seeing children who are excited and disturbed by dolls like Barbie and her friends.

"With baby dolls girls can play at being attractive, nurturing mothers and housewives.

"With Barbie, girls learn to expect to be valued by an ever-increasing wardrobe and by their ability to manipulate their fathers, and later, husbands into buying clothes and more clothes. Boys are being seen in the clinic who use Barbie for sexual stimulation, a fact which might trouble the same parents who are scandalized by comic books and pinup magazines, were it not for the fact that Barbie masquerades as a child's toy.

"Both boys and girls are introduced to a precocious, joyless sexuality, to fantasies of seduction, and to conspicuous consumption. This reflects and perpetuates a disturbing trend in our culture, which has serious mental health complications." — Dr. Alan F. Leveton, Director, Pediatrics Mental Health Unit, University of California Medical Center, San Francisco, quoted in *Ramparts,* 1965.

Charles Schulz's "Peanuts"

Is it any wonder the *Peanuts* gang became so popular during a decade full of disappointments, when it seemed as if some meanie was always pulling the football away just as we were about to kick it? Charlie Brown's favorite saying, "How can

I'm a Plainclothes Hippie

we lose if we're so sincere?", perfectly expressed the dashed hopes and aspirations of the counterculture.

But the strip, with its innocent, yet sophisticated kids and intelligent beagle, appealed to all groups. Good Grief! they did. During the '60s, Charles M. Schulz's comic-strip kids were scrutinized by psychologists, argued about by professors, and quoted by theologians.

"*Peanuts* portrayed kids who showed an engaging wisdom beyond their years — simplistic, but impressive understanding of the assorted problems that perplex their elders," said *Time* magazine in a 1965 cover story. "*Peanuts* makes parables about the basic Christian belief in blind faith and love," claimed Robert Short in his 1965 book, *The Gospel According to Peanuts.*

As for Schulz, he could only speculate that "People read a lot into the strip, and I guess what people see in it, that's what's in it. But actually the strip is just about all the dumb things I did when I was little." On another occasion, Schulz said: "Why does the strip appeal to so many people? Well, it deals in intelligent things — things that people have been afraid of. Charlie Brown represents the insecurity in all of us, our desire to be liked. Lucy is the dominating one in the family, the little girl who has no doubts about who is going to run the show."

Schulz never anticipated that the strip would reach the heights of popularity it achieved. When he started syndicating *Peanuts* in 1950, the strip was picked up by only seven newspapers. During the '50s, the strip grew slowly while a series of paperbacks recycled the best panels. In 1960, the characters burst into the national consciousness by appearing in ads for the peanut-sized Ford Falcon (Schulz himself drove a Ford).

In 1962, the *Peanuts* boom began.

An enterprising and visionary San Francisco businesswoman, Connie Boucher of Determined Productions, saw the value in marketing *Peanuts* products. The first product was a book, *Happiness Is a Warm Puppy,* a collection of pithy phrases accompanied by Schulz illustrations. *Happiness Is...*was on *The New York Times* bestseller list for forty-five weeks in 1962 and 1963, and was followed by two other similarly successful books, *Security Is a Thumb and Blanket* and *A Friend Is Someone Who Likes You,* followed by the *Peanuts Projects Book,* and *The Peanuts Calendar-Date Book.*

Non-book products included stuffed pillows, pocket dolls, sweatshirts, Snoopy wristwatches, and sleepwear. Hallmark started a line of greeting cards and stationery. Wilson Sporting Goods made a Charlie Brown baseball. By 1969, *Business Week* estimated that *Peanuts* merchandising was a $50 million-a-year industry. The strip grew accordingly — from 650 in 1961, to 700 in 1966, to 1,000 in 1969.

In the mid-'60s, the popularity of *Peanuts* accelerated. In 1965, the strip moved from print to television (1965's "A Charlie Brown Christmas" was the first of many *Peanuts* specials), film (1967's *A Boy Named Charlie Brown*) and stage. The musical, *You're a Good Man, Charlie Brown,* opened in New York in March, 1967, and ran for four years. *New York Times* critic Walter Kerr praised it: "They have marched clean off that page of pure white light...and into forthright, fuming, explosively funny conversation without losing a drop of the ink that made their lifelines so human."

In Vietnam, combat pilots (one was Captain Charles Brown of Elwood, Indiana) flew off with Snoopy painted on their planes. Buffalo's Westminster Presbyterian church had Schroeder at his piano painted in the same stained-glass window as Albert Schweitzer playing the organ. An obscure rock band, the Royal Guardsmen, had three hits based on the Snoopy-Red Baron confrontation.

NASA adopted Snoopy as a promotional device. Snoopy pins were presented to seven North American Rockwell launch operations personnel for their work on the Apollo program. Snoopy emblems were worn by more than 800 members of the manned space-flight team. In March, 1967, Snoopy doffed his World War I aviator's helmet and replaced it with an astronaut's spacesuit. In the most famous example of the NASA-*Peanuts* relationship, the astronauts aboard *Apollo X* in 1969 used the code names "Snoopy" and "Charlie Brown" for its command ship and lunar module.

The *Peanuts* gang has weathered Vietnam, Watergate, and the Energy Crisis, while maintaining its popularity. *Peanuts* today is now syndicated to more than 2,000 newspapers worldwide. And Lucy's psychiatric help still only costs five cents.

In a 1967 article in *The New York Times Magazine,* Schulz had these things to say of his characters.

Charlie Brown: "Sure he's wishy-washy — but that doesn't mean I don't like him."

Lucy: "She's not as smart as she thinks she is. Behind her surface there is something tender but perhaps if you scratched deeper, you'd find she's even worse than she seems."

Linus: "He's the brightest, most promising, practical. But then there's that blanket. All my kids had their blankets, but only one sucked his thumb."

Snoopy (based on Schulz's childhood dog Spike): "White and black spots. He was the wildest and smartest dog I've ever encountered. Smart? Why, he had a vocabulary of at least fifty words."

PEANUTS TV SPECIALS
OF THE '60S

"A Charlie Brown Christmas," 1965
"Charlie Brown's All Stars," 1966
"It's the Great Pumpkin, Charlie Brown," 1966
"You're in Love, Charlie Brown," 1967
"He's Your Dog, Charlie Brown," 1968
"It Was a Short Summer, Charlie Brown," 1969

SNOOPY SHOULD BITE YOU

A *Life* magazine reader named Kenneth Gunetert of Notre Dame, Indiana wrote to the magazine after its *Peanuts* cover story in 1967: "Your callous portrayal of *Peanuts* as intellectually sound can only be seen as a gross error. Superficially humorous at best, Schulz's philosophy undermines the intellectual fiber of today's youth. His prosaic "theological implications" are completely disregarded with Snoopy, a naked manifestation of the author's own bellicose tendencies (particularly) his endeavors to liquidate the Red Baron."

SNOOPY SHOULD BITE YOU AGAIN

"Lucy is a Fascist and all the *Peanuts* characters are sad, little alienated Americans." — Rome's communist newspaper, *L'Unita*, 1963.

MIXED *PEANUTS*
FACTS

Did you know?
Mia Farrow called her hubby, Frank

Sinatra, "Charlie Brown" because, she said, "when he furrows his brow, he looks just like Charlie Brown."

One *Peanuts* '60s character who you'll never see again: José Peterson, who Schulz called the "world's greatest baseball player." — He just didn't belong, so out he went.

Johnny Carson had a best-selling book answering *Happiness Is a Warm Puppy* called *Happiness Is a Dry Martini. Mad* magazine parodied the *Peanuts* books with two articles: "Misery Is a Cold Hot Dog" and "Insecurity Is a Pair of Loose Swim Trunks."

The strip's original title when it appeared in 1947 in the weekly *St. Paul Pioneer Press* was "Lil folks." At first, Schulz didn't like the name *Peanuts.* He preferred "Good Ol' Charlie Brown."

AN INTERVIEW WITH
CHARLES M. SCHULZ

Question: Was there anything special about the '60s that helped make *Peanuts* more successful?

Schulz: I never thought there was anything special about it. I was just drawing the comic strip, which had started in the fall of 1950. I think you have to realize that we looked at all these things from different points of view. This was just my career, something I had looked forward to my whole life and planned — the way someone had wanted to plan to be a teacher. Had nothing to do with the time period. It was influenced by the times to a certain extent, but I didn't do the strip because I had something to say or anything like that. It's what I wanted to do.

I just did what I wanted to do. I kept trying to make it better. I don't know why it succeeded; I guess it's just a good comic strip. I was just someone living at those times and observing some of those things that were happening.

Question: There are those who say that during the '60s Americans were having a crisis of confidence and identified with Charlie Brown, the kid who was always getting kicked around.

Schulz: These are just things people say, doesn't mean much. Just because they said it in a magazine or some pop star gets on Carson and starts talking about it.

Question: Was there a problem naming the Apollo command module after Charlie Brown, who was such a lovable loser?

Schulz: There was always worry that if something went wrong with the flight, they might make that connection. But what they were doing was far more important than a comic strip.

Question: What was your reaction to the Royal Guardsmen and their "Snoopy" record?

Schulz: I first heard that one morning when I was getting ready to take the kids to school. One of the other kids said they just heard the "Snoopy vs. Red Baron" song on the radio, and I didn't know what she was talking about. And then, that very day, the business manager of UFS, Jim Hennessey, said he had just heard about it so he checked into it and he found out that the song had become a real hit, so we had to contact the producers of the LP to remind them they had done something without getting proper permission. And that we would have to get royalties on it.

They never were very proud of that, they thought they were doing things that were more important, more serious. But that was their biggest hit.

Charles M.
Schulz

WORDS

THE '60S IN PRINT

INTRODUCTION

The printed word took a battering during the '60s: Marshall McLuhan predicted its demise, Tom Wolfe stretched it like a piece of Turkish taffy, Jackie Susann rediscovered that the best color for prose was purple.

All this shakin' rattlin' and rollin' in the "Gutenberg Galaxy" was a response to the zeitgeist of the '60s. New forms were needed because the old forms weren't working—hence the New Journalism, the underground press and publications, like *Rolling Stone,* which took rock 'n' roll seriously. Interest in literature waned; why read *Robinson Crusoe,* when you can watch "Gilligan's Island"? Why read Shelley when you can read Rod McKuen?

But it wasn't that bad. The printed word has survived—and looking on the bright side, the '60s was the last era before *People* magazine, celebrity workout books and one-minute advice books.

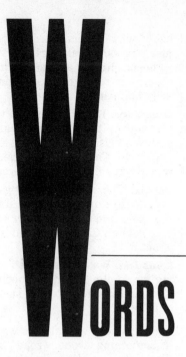

Ian Fleming

"VERDICT: Excellent book by a genius who will do anything to get attention."

—Kurt Vonnegut, Jr. THE NEW YORK TIMES BOOK REVIEW

the Kandy-Kolored Tangerine-Flake Streamline Baby by Tom Wolfe→

Reproduced with permission from Pocket Books

Tom Wolfe and The New Journalism

Tom Wolfe was the stylistic madman of American letters in the '60s. The greatest press agent for the decade, he trumpeted its bizarre subcultures, fads, and follies with a grasp of American and world history, sociology, and anthropology far beyond that of mortal newspapermen. Phil Spector, surfers, Baby Jane Holzer, the Merry Pranksters, Murray the K, custom cars, stock cars — subjects that he maintained would not or could not be adequately covered by traditional journalism — all came under Wolfe's eye.

Out of his freaked-out Underwood came a breathless prose full of ellipses, capital letters, exclamation points, points of view, interior monologues. Someone came up with the term New Journalism to describe this lunacy (Para-Journalism by fuddy-duddies who insisted on the old maxims).

Wolfe says his style started quite unintentionally. It was in 1964, and he had an *Esquire* deadline to meet for an article about custom-car shows. He just couldn't get his act together (he had a full-time job as a reporter for the New York *Herald Tribune)*, so with the deadline staring him in the face, he collected his notes and frantically began typing them as a memo to editor Byron Dobell. Finishing the memo early the next morning, he took it to Dobell, who loved its prose style. Strike the "Dear Byron," he said, and we'll run the memo as the article.

The story appeared as the "Kandy-Kolored Tangerine-Flake Streamline Baby," which became the title piece of Wolfe's first book, a superb tour-de-force of '60s pop culture and the best on-the-spot reportage of the pop madness of 1964-65. Newsweek said: "This is a book that will be a sharp pleasure to reread years from now, when it will bring back, like a falcon in the sky of memory, a whole world that is currently jetting and jazzing somewhere or other." And they were right.

The best of Wolfe ran in *Esquire* and in *New York* magazine, then in the innovative Sunday supplement of the late New York *Herald Tribune,* edited by Clay Felker.

People argued whether the New Journalism was new or not, but that wasn't really the issue. The sensibility of the '60s demanded that reporters abandon their pose as "the gentlemen in the grandstand" and immerse themselves in their subjects. Take the point of view, get inside your character's head, make it read like fiction. A cocky and self-assured Wolfe briefly ballyhooed the theory that the New Journalism had replaced fiction as the preeminent literary form of the decade.

Among the New Journalism's finest works are Gay Talese's *Esquire* profiles, which read like short stories; *Paper Lion,* the first-person accounts of George Plimpton, who played quarterback in one game for the Detroit Lions; *Hell's Angels: A Strange and Terrible Saga,* by a pre drug-crazed Hunter Thompson; Truman Capote's best-selling "non-fiction novel" *In Cold Blood;* and Norman Mailer's *Armies of the Night.* The latter two put the New Journalism on the best-seller lists.

Rising publishing expenses, Watergate (everybody wanted to be investigative reporters), the legitimizing of gossip in *People* magazine, and the rise of self-help magazines killed the New Journalism. Who, nowadays, has the time to read these lengthy pieces anyway?

Best Sellers

At the beginning of the decade, the best-seller lists boasted names like O'Hara, Salinger, and Faulkner. By the end of the decade, it was Susann and Puzo people were clamoring for. The novel — as in the Great American — was losing popularity, except for the perennial best-sellers such as James Michener, Leon Uris, and Irving Wallace. The G.A.N. was being replaced by what Tom Wolfe called the "non-fiction novel" (i.e., Truman Capote's *In Cold Blood* or Norman Mailer's *Armies of the Night),* or by the experimental fiction of Thomas Pynchon and John Barth, which proved too obscure for the average reader.

Spy books and thrillers had their day as the world seemed to get more dangerous. Black humor became a popular literary genre, as shown by the success of Joseph Heller's *Catch 22* and Philip Roth's *Portnoy's Complaint.* Still, the majority of readers seemed to prefer non-fiction to fiction.

Here's a quick tour of some of the more notable best-sellers and authors of the '60s.

CATCH 22 (Joseph Heller) — This classic black humor antiwar book was originally published in 1961, but its popularity — especially in the paperback version — increased in the late '60s as the United States became increasingly mired in the Vietnam War. Heller's book received mixed reviews. *The New Yorker* called it "a debris of sour jokes, stage anger, dirty words, synthetic looniness, and the sort of antic behavior children fall into when they know they are losing our attention" while writer Nelson Algren in the *Nation* said it was "the

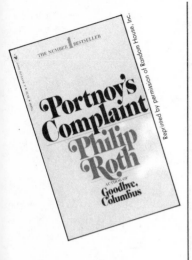

strongest repudiation of our civilization to come out of World War II."

Heller spent eight years working on the novel, most of the time while he was working as a promotion writer for *McCalls*. The novel concerns the befuddled Captain Yossarian, who is trapped on his island with his Air Force bomber squadron and can't get off because of the Kafkaesque Catch 22. Yossarian finally deserts. "Yossarian's choice to break out is a completely moral one," Heller said. "His last loyalty has to be to himself."

And what was the infamous "Catch 22"? A man is considered to be insane if he continues to fly combat missions, but he must put in a formal request to be relieved from such missions. But the act of making these requests proves he is sane, and, therefore, he cannot be relieved.

DIET BOOKS — The hottest diet book of the early '60s was *Calories Don't Count* by the formerly fat Dr. Herman Taller. His elixir was safflower oil, which was said to help reduce fat. His formula was to take two daily CDC capsules (for "Calories Don't Count") containing safflower oil and then eat as much as you want, as long as the diet contained sixty-five percent fat, thirty percent protein, and fifty percent carbohydrates.

The FDA thought something wasn't kosher with Taller's diet. They seized 1,600 copies of the book and 58,000 CDC capsules saying the book made false claims, and the pills bore misleading labels. The FDA later charged that Taller had written the book to promote the sales of the capsules, and that he and two vice-presidents of Simon & Schuster, who published the book, had acquired financial interests in the company that manufactured the capsules.

The case finally went to court in 1967 with Taller facing a forty-nine-count indictment. He was found guilty

on twelve counts of mail fraud, conspiracy, and violation of the Federal Food, Drug, and Cosmetic Act. He was fined $7,000 and given a two-year probation.

GAMES PEOPLE PLAY — In the '70s, the best-seller list would be glutted with self-help and pop psychology tomes. But in the mid-'60s, Dr. Eric Berne's book helped spread the gospel of transactional analysis and turn it into a middle-class neurotic's parlor game. People debated whether they were living out their life-scripts as frogs or princes when they played such games as "Kick Me," "Ain't It Awful," and "Doctor."

Berne was a poker-playing, California psychiatrist, who drove a Maserati that he called a "mazel tov." Said *Life* of this satisfied shrink: "He acts and talks as though his M.D. had been conferred in a moment of great hilarity by James Thurber."

KENNEDY-MANIA — The year after JFK died, the best-seller list contained several Kennedy books — *Profiles in Courage, Four Days,* Jim Bishop's *A Day in the Life of President Kennedy,* Bill Adler's *The Kennedy Wit,* and Mark Shaw's *The John F. Kennedys.*

THE DEATH OF A PRESIDENT CONTROVERSY — In 1964, the Kennedy Family commissioned veteran political writer William Manchester to author a book about the events surrounding the assassination of the president. Manchester was flattered by the request, and then went about his business doing numerous interviews. The family balked at what Manchester might report. Jackie Kennedy sued, not over the issue of truth or accuracy, but because of what she termed a "breach of faith." They settled out of court, and in the end, only 1,600 words were deleted. The publicity of course helped create a huge demand for the book. When *Death of a President* was serialized in *Look* in early 1967, newsstand sales of the magazine increased fourfold, and the book rapidly climbed the best-seller list.

Other Kennedy-related best-sellers included *Rush To Judgment* by Mark Lane, the most prominent of the books challenging the findings of the Warren Commission, and *A Gift Of Prophecy* by Jeanne Dixon and Ruth Montgomery. Psychic Dixon's crystal ball shone brighter than her fellow seers' because of her prediction about the Kennedy assassination, and the book became a best-seller in 1965.

PORTNOY'S COMPLAINT (Philip Roth, 1969) — After his modest successes with *Letting Go, When She Was Good,* and *Goodbye Columbus,* Roth became a household name as the author of 1969's top-seller about Alexander Portnoy, the man who wants to put the id back in Yid. *Portnoy* was a rollicking monologue delivered from a shrink's couch by the book's protagonist, a liberal, 33-year-old American Jewish prince. A chronicle of angst and kvetching, *Portnoy* created a stir because of its sexual explicitness and for what some might say was an unsympathetic portrayal of American Jewish life.

SPY STUFF — With the success of James Bond in the movies and TV's "The Man from U.N.C.L.E.," espionage and spy novels became increasingly popular in the mid-'60s.

Ian Fleming, a former Naval Intelligence officer and British journalist, was the most well-known writer of the genre. His sexy, violent novels featuring the adventures of Her Majesty's Secret Service Agent 007 enjoyed a cult following even before the films were released. But it was the films — as well as raves from JFK and serializations in *Playboy* —

that really made the world stand up and notice Bond.

Fleming took the name of his hero from the author of a book that was always on his coffee table, *Birds of the West Indies,* by an ornithologist named James Bond. Fleming's Bond was said to be a combination of Fleming himself (he liked dry martinis and caviar; disliked flowers), Dusko Popov (a British double agent), and Sidney Reilly (an ace British spy who disappeared in Russia in the '20s).

Jacqueline Susann and Judy Garland, who was almost cast in the lead role of *Valley of the Dolls*

His first four books, published in the '50s, were *Casino Royale, Live and Let Die, Dr. No,* and *Goldfinger.* In the '60s, his books included *For Your Eyes Only, Thunderball, The Spy Who Loved Me, On Her Majesty's Secret Service, You Only Live Twice, The Man with the Golden Gun,* and *Octopussy and the Living Daylights.* Fleming died in August, 1964, after suffering a heart attack on a golf course.

John Le Carré's gritty, realistic cold war dramas, *The Spy who Came in from the Cold* and *The Looking Glass War,* were among the top-sellers of the '60s. Le Carré was the pseudonym of David John Moore Cornwell, a former British Foreign Service agent in Germany. He chose the pen name because he was still working in the Foreign Service while writing his earliest books.

Le Carré brought style and literary quality to the spy-novel genre. His British hero, agent Alex Leamas, was a decidedly unglamorous antihero. He rode buses and had a love affair with a lonely librarian. Not surprisingly, Le Carré didn't like James Bond. "The really interesting thing about Bond is that he would be what I call the ideal defector," he once said. "Because if the money was better, the booze freer, and women easier over there in Moscow, he'd be off like a shot. Bond, you see, is the ultimate prostitute."

Len Deighton created another un-Bondian hero, Harry Palmer, a working-class agent moving in an unfamiliar upper-class environment filled with distrustful people. Michael Caine captured this sense perfectly in the movie versions of *The Ipcress File* and *Funeral in Berlin.* Deighton used appendices and footnotes in his books and was accused of being deliberately obscure.

Deighton was a bit of an eccentric. To reach the writer on the phone would be impossible; he could only be reached by using a teleprinter machine. A cooking expert and illustrator from a working-class background, he enjoyed putting people on. On his paperback jackets, he would describe himself thusly: "He was the son of a governor of the Windward Islands, educated at Eton and Worcester College and his subsequent jobs included being a deckhand on a Japanese whaler."

VALLEY OF THE DOLLS (Jacqueline Susann, 1966) — Susann ushered in the era of writer-as-media-hyped celebrity. Her book, a sordid tale of pills, booze, and debauchery among would-be Hollywood starlets, kept readers guessing about the true identities of her characters. *Valley of the Dolls* was at the top of *The New York Times* best-seller list for twenty-eight straight weeks and was near the top for sixty-two weeks.

By the spring of 1969, more than ten million paperback copies of the book had been sold. "The hell with what critics say," she said in 1966 about the less-than-enthusiastic notices the novel had received. "I've made characters live so that people talk about them at cocktail parties and that to me is what counts...The day is over when the point of writing is just to turn a phrase that critics will quote."

Susann, herself, had been a fairly successful actress (from 1953-57, she was named Best Dressed Actress on TV) before she took up writing — spurred on by Irving Mansfield, her promotion-minded husband. With her falls and fake eyelashes, and her penchant for appearing on any and all talk shows, autograph parties, and at in-store promotions, Miss Susann became as well known as the actresses she wrote about in this incredibly successful roman à clef.

The Message of Marshall McLuhan

Marshall McLuhan, what're you doin'?" asked Henry Gibson in one of those microsecond gags on "Laugh-In." Gibson's couplet not only rhymed, it also summed up the attitude of many people who encountered the strange theories cooked up in the Great White North by this English professor who became head of the University of Toronto Center for Culture and Technology.

McLuhan spouted lots of aphorisms about the media and its impact on society that made people seek him out. He became that distinctly '60s phenomenon: the pop philosopher, or as *Life* dubbed him, "The Oracle of the Electric Age." He wrote in long, complex, elliptical sentences, expounding a theory that many are still trying to decipher. And the more complexly he wrote, the more the media hailed him as a genius. He even had his own TV specials. But sifting through the hundreds of thousands of words McLuhan wrote (*The Gutenberg Galaxy, Understanding Media, The Medium Is the Message*) and putting them through a strainer, you might emerge with something like this.

The invention of movable type in the fifteenth century revolutionized the transmission of information. Before the introduction of movable type, the ear had been the main organ of reception; after print, it was the eye. But the development of electronic media brought forth a new sensory

awareness, combining aural and visual elements. Print segregated people; TV and other electronic media brought them together in a new tribal pattern. Because of this, print is on its way to becoming obsolete.

To understand McLuhan's theory, one must also know these key phrases:

Global village. We are now in an age where electronic technology links all the citizens of the world together.

Cool media. TV and movies are cool because they take less energy. TV requires "depth involvement" of the viewer to fill in the image. Hot media (i.e., newspapers and books) constantly demand your attention — and are becoming increasingly archaic.

The medium is the message. Certain media — especially TV and movies — have the ability to work us over completely — massage us, as it were.

That's all you need to know. Really. If someone challenges you, wing it. McLuhan's been dead since 1980, so there's no chance of him popping up behind you on a movie line as he did in *Annie Hall* to dispute your beliefs.

What you're holding in your hand by the way is proof that McLuhan's theories haven't panned out just yet. But give us time. As Tom Wolfe noted in his profile of this "electronic Socrates": "Suppose he is what he sounds like, the most important thinker since Newton, Darwin, Freud, Einstein, and Pavlov — what if he is right?"

The Pop Poet— Rod McKuen

Rod McKuen was the Alan Alda of free verse, a sentimental pop poet or "king of kitsch," as *Newsweek* dubbed him, who found a receptive audience among the same people who became dewy-eyed listening to Joni Mitchell and Judy Collins. He preached his message — "Don't fear to bare your emotions" — in person at nightclubs and on records. He was gravelly-voiced and cloying, but effective.

A former cookie puncher, lumberjack, horse wrangler, shoe salesman, movie actor, and disk jockey, McKuen first tried to make it as a singer and actor. But it was in Paris, in the company of Jacques Brel and Charles Aznavour, that he developed his style of poetry. When he returned to the States, his poems and songs started to catch on. His free verse in book form sold unexpectedly well (more than a million copies) and he became wealthy.

His '60s books — *Lonesome Cities, Stanyan Street and Other Sorrows,* and *Listen to the Warm* — were among the top books of each year. He wrote the score for the film version of *The Prime of Miss Jean Brodie* and six songs for the film *A Boy Named Charlie Brown.*

The Canadian-born, sneaker-wearing animal lover called himself an anti-poet. "I'm not a poet. I'm a stringer of words," he said in 1968. "My stuff is conversational, one man saying as simply and honestly as he can how he feels about people and about himself. It's a tremendous outlet for people. They tend to think in this country if you show any kind of deep emotion, you're suspect — a faggot, a sissy, or a crazy mixed-up kid. Today, I'm the only one doing what I'm doing, but hopefully not the last. I don't think I will be. I'm convinced we're on the verge of another Romantic era."

The man had lasting impact. Just check out Woody Allen's film *Sleeper* — when admirers praise half-baked 22nd-century poet Diane Keaton as being "so deep, so McKuen." Man, that is praise.

The Lord of Fantasy — J.R.R. Tolkien

J(ohn). R(onald). R(euel). Tolkien, an Oxford Don (and language expert) then in his '70s, known as the author of a critical study of *Beowulf,* wrote adult fairy tales which were popular on college campuses during the middle-to-late '60s. Tolkien always denied he wrote the stories for children.

How popular was Tolkien? Well, one student was quoted as saying: "To go to college without Tolkien is like going without sneakers." A girl in my college dorm had a cat named Frodo. Dorm walls were plastered with maps of Middle Earth. Another guy I knew, a spacy, "sensitive" high school senior, changed his name to Frodo Godot, when he entered college.

Tolkien was favored by soulful chicks (the ones who ironed their hair) or by guys who wore round, wire-rimmed glasses, wore buttons proclaiming "Go, Go Gandalf," and got A's in English Lit. Fan clubs existed at Harvard and Berkeley to discuss the history and linguistics of Middle Earth. A highbrow Tolkien Society of America debated the essence of Tolkien. He fit right in with the escape from rational thinking and fas-

Rod McKuen

cination with mysticism that gripped many young Americans in the late '60s.

The Lord of the Rings, written during a fourteen-year period, is a 1,200-page trilogy consisting of *The Fellowship of the Ring* (1954), *The Two Towers* (1954), and *The Return of the King* (1955). It was at the top of the 1966 paperback best-seller lists. (*The Hobbit* was written in 1938.)

During the '50s, the Tolkien stories were principally cult items, a cult that included W.H. Auden and C.S. Lewis. In the '60s — with a little help at first from the publisher — Tolkien became a campus best-selling author. By 1967, worldwide sales of Tolkien had reached three million copies.

The story takes place in an imaginary world called Middle Earth and tells of a conspiracy by an evil wizard called Sauron to take control of a ring, the One Ring, which would enable him to dominate everything. Frodo Baggins, a hobbit (a peaceful little creature about three feet tall, humanlike except for hairy feet, who eats six meals a day), has come into possession of the Ring. His mission is to carry it across Middle Earth into Mordor, Sauron's new home, where it must be thrown into the fiery Mt. Doom and destroyed. The only problem is: The ring corrupts anyone who possesses it, including our hero, Frodo.

Many readers found a deep religious meaning in the hobbit's quest. Additionally, in the sense of the moral absolutes that pervaded the '60s, the issue of good guys vs. bad guys was clearly spelled out. For an intellectual patina, Tolkien included pseudo-scholarly material: tables, charts, family trees, alphabets, guides to pronunciation, and a special language, Elvish, supposedly not dissimilar to Finnish, a tongue with which Tolkien had been fascinated.

The Beatles were among those taken by *The Lord of the Rings.* At one point, they were considering adapting it as a movie. A British music periodical speculated that Paul would be Frodo, with Ringo cast as Sam, Frodo's servant. George would play Gandalf the Wizard, with John as the creature named Gollum.

Tolkien died in 1973. His *The Silmarillion,* published posthumously in 1977, sold well, but nowhere near as well as *The Lord of the Rings.*

The Magazines

Magazines were bigger in the '60s, and here's a look at two of the best.

Esquire — The quintessential cool '60s mag. Under the stewardship of editor Harold Hayes, it projected a detached attitude — a combination of put-on, cynicism, and sophistication — that seemed to position them far above the fray. *Esquire* viewed the social conflict of the '60s as if it was some demented spectator sport, like a demolition derby, for their bemused eyes.

Give them points for breaking the journalistic mold. They were home to the New Journalism; Gay Talese and Tom Wolfe made their mass-magazine debuts here. And what about those George Lois covers?—Sonny Liston as Santa Claus, Cassius Clay as St. Sebastian, Lieutenant Calley posing with Asian children on his knee. (They never ran the Lois cover on black militancy: Aunt Jemima holding a meat cleaver in her hand and the line: "Aunt Jemima...what took you so long?") The magazine also had great cover lines: "This is Nixon's last chance: This time he'd better look right"; "If you think Vietnam is Hell, you should see what's happening on campus, baby" (annual college issue in September, 1967).

To get a good sense of all this, one couldn't do much better than to check out the thick book *Smiling Through the Apocalypse,* a superb collection of articles from this period of *Esquire's* history.

Life — Henry Luce's American century was rapidly disintegrating, but in the '60s, *Life* was still required reading at most suburban homes. Its arrival in the mail was eagerly awaited, its contents to be discussed among friends the next day in school. It was the last of a breed of a magazines that the whole family would fight over to look at (the fights could occur during "The Ed Sullivan Show," the last of a breed of TV shows that the whole family could watch).

Life was the last gasp of innocent mass-market print journalism before TV, *People,* and the gossip tabloids took over and made us all into cynics. *Life* was notable for boosting the astronauts as mythic heroes (1959-62), printing photographs of an unborn fetus (1965), and putting the Jefferson Airplane on its cover (1968). The *Life* we knew and loved died in 1972, joining *Look* (1971) and the *Saturday Evening Post* (1969) in the mass-market magazine pavement discard pile, although all three were revived in scaled-down editions in the mid-'70s.

Mad-ness

Mad, more than any other publication, really got me through the '60s. It helped give me the skeptical, critical eye to see that life really is full of fershlugginer things. Its creators were able to see and shoot down cultural come-ons and gimmicks. Among all the Finsters,

ESQUIRE

THE MAGAZINE FOR MEN

FEBRUARY 1969
PRICE $1

"Chicks up front!"

How troublemakers use girls to put down the cops. See page 86

Reprinted with permission from *Esquire.* Copyright © 1969 by Esquire Associates

210

Furds, axolotls, and Potrzebies found in every issue was dead-on humor.

Although *Mad* started in the '50s, it really hit its stride in the early '60s. Bob Dylan would soon say "don't trust leaders" and everyone would hail him — but the *Mad*men had been saying that for years. At the time, few publications were actively dissecting the frauds of the world. *Mad* nurtured a healthy skepticism in kids which may have helped contribute to the upheavals of the latter part of the decade.

Every month you'd plunk down a quarter and what you'd get was the world — torn into little shreds by "the usual gang of idiots." Few phenomena of the '60s escaped their scalpel. There was James Bomb, Balmy and Clod (whose producers decided to make a sequel about another swinging couple of the '30s: "Adolf and Eva"), Hullabadig a Go-Go (a satire of rock shows in which cages of mice were let loose by stagehands to get teenage girls to scream), Batsman, Dr. Killjoy, 201 minutes of a Space Idiocy, Hippie magazine, Sik-Teen magazine.

Mad was one of the first publications to deal with political satire following the uptight '50s. *Mad* reduced the cold war to a comic gangwar. One of *Mad's* most memorable articles, "East Side Story," featured leather-jacketed leaders of the Free World duking it out with the Reds on the turf of the United Nations. The Reds got their comeuppance at the end of the story when the real boss of the Commie world — Nina Khrushchev — came by and grabbed her tubby hubby by his ears, excoriating him for acting like a common hoodlum.

By the late '60s, *Mad's* put-downs of "hip" items like Woodstock, the Maharishi ("Swami, how I luvya"), and hippies seemed like a condescending look by adults who didn't understand. But reading through these articles sixteen years later, you get the feeling that these guys were right on the mark.

In the '70s, their brand of humor was surpassed by the taboo-breaking *National Lampoon.* By then, there was less to make fun of, anyway. Today, *Mad* is over 30, but the usual gang of idiots are still skewering the world for an even more skeptical generation.

Underground Newspapers

The editorial format of the underground press calls for a Marxist message blanketed in sex and drugs. This is kneaded with four-letter words malapropped with polysyllables and stirred with Communist revolutionary slogans that would have embarrassed an East Side anarchist of 1910. It is mixed in with hip language taken from the lexicons of Marx, Lenin, and Mao, along with the weird vernacular of Hindu mystics. Served with a quart of self-righteousness, the above recipe produces the nicest little revolutionary stew you ever saw." — American Opinion, published by the John Birch Society, on the underground press of the '60s.

The New York Times may call itself the Paper of Record — but to many alienated young people in the '60s that record may have seemed a bit scratched. If you preferred to get the news from a peasant-bloused hippie chick rather than the Good Gray Lady, where could you turn?

The underground press, a loose confederation of publications, chronicling

the counterculture, was created in response to its editors' mistrust of the so-called establishment newspapers. On their pages, you'd find lots of talk about drugs, revolution, rock, sex, and radical politics, plus weird advertising (sample classified ad: "Groovy, free-spirit chick wanted to share West Village apt. with guy, 27. No rent").

These magazines also had weird layouts (tilted columns or columns that didn't run into each other), and weird typography (bright-colored pages in Hindu patterns). Spelling didn't count, except the four-letter words which were always spelled correctly. "Amerika," "Amerikka," or "Czechago" were favorite misspellings. Like many artifacts of the counterculture, the underground press had a self-righteous tone, a self-proclaimed monopoly on the truth.

"The *Oracle* was an attempt to break the lie of our linear habit," said editor Allen Cohen of the pioneering San Francisco underground newspaper. "It was a contrast to regular papers, intended to show that most newspapers' objectivity was ugly and a lie. It was a judo on the newspaper format."

Unlike underground newspapers of other times, such as those published by French resistance fighters during World War II, the modern versions were sold aboveground, although there was some element of risk involved in handling them. Vendors, who stood on street corners like Jehovah's Witnesses, were often busted by the police for peddling them.

The papers themselves ranged from crude and embarrassing scandal sheets to more respectable publications involved in solid investigative reporting of undesirable conditions, such as when the *Berkeley Barb* documented charges of racial discrimination by the management of a scaffolding factory owned by the mayor. The more politically-extreme papers printed telephone company credit-card numbers of prominent people so that readers could charge phone calls to them, or to the home phones of local narcs. They also printed unusual drug-filled recipes.

The Big Four of the underground movement were the *Los Angeles Free Press, The Berkeley Barb,* New York's *East Village Other,* and San Francisco's *Oracle.* The politically-oriented *FREEP* was the first of the new underground papers when it appeared in 1964. An *Esquire* article in 1967 said it was the best, an "underground version of the New York *Herald Tribune.*"

The *East Village Other* was created in 1965 in response to the original underground paper, the *Village Voice,* which by then was considered out of step with the emerging radical-hip community. Less gentle than some of its sister papers, the *Other* had a sense of sick humor and lots of bizarre cartoons (an example is Joe Brainard's "Believe It or Not": "W.W. Loo taught school in Lien, Minn. — although he had no hands, he frequently whipped unruly youngsters with his empty sleeve").

The *Berkeley Barb* reflected the leftist political culture of the California university town, featuring a radical-political columnist known as the "Roving Rat Fink." Across the Bay, San Francsico's *Oracle* used rainbow-colored graphics, reflecting the psychedelic excitement of Haight-Ashbury. Their calendar of events was called the "Trips Page," and it featured a gossip columnist called the Gossiping Guru. He asked in 1967: "Many of us are waiting eagerly for the next edition of Tim Leary's *Psychedelic Prayers* to come out. It's an ideal gift in view of the number of friends and acquaintances of us who are planning their voyages."

Every major city had at least one underground paper or more: New York's *Rat,* Chicago's *Seed,* Detroit's *Fifth Estate,* Philadelphia's *Different Drummer.* In 1966, thirty of them banded together to form the Underground Press Syndicate, for free interchange of articles and ideas between the various undergrounds.

"We are in favor of evolution, not revolution," said Alan Katzman, the managing editor of the *East Village Other,* and a key force behind starting the UPS. "We hope to transform the middle class by internal and external stimuli, by means of media and LSD."

Unfortunately, we're still waiting for that transformation. The breakup of the counterculture as well as rising costs put many undergrounds, including the *Other,* out of business in the early '70s. Those that survived decidedly went aboveground, becoming by the mid-'70s, something called "alternative weeklies," specializing in high-brow articles and with advertising designed to attract an upwardly-mobile readership who, they hope, will buy the paper each week, along with *The New York Times* and the *Wall Street Journal.*

Along with the underground newspapers, the growth of the rock 'n' roll press—which treated the music seriously—was one of the more important countercultural journalistic developments of the late '60s. The first serious rock mass were the short-lived *Mojo Navigator News* and the more successful *Crawdaddy,* which featured long-winded, often pretentious analyses of rock music. In October, 1967, *Rolling Stone* issued its first edition and soon became *The New York Times* of the rock press in influence, prestige and circulation. Its founder was Jann Wenner, a chubby 21-year-old former UC student, who was encouraged by his friend, Ralph Gleason.

The San Francisco-based *Rolling Stone* was tuned into the hip subculture, with rock 'n' roll at its core. Wenner shrewdly saw the need for a publication that would fill the gap between the music trade and the fan mass, while avoiding the excesses (both typographical and journalistic) of its cousin, the underground press.

When *Rolling Stone* arrived in the mail, you felt connected to the great American counterculture. Journalistically, RS kept getting better and more provocative. In 1968, it generated considerable outrage by publishing nude photos on its cover of John Lennon and Yoko Ono (street vendors were arrested for selling copies of it) soon followed by a lengthy article about groupies, which revealed their lifestyles to the world. *Stone* hit its apex in 1969 with its powerful investigative report on the tragic incident at Altamont (see the section on the Rolling Stones). But the magazine's influence was tied with the rise and fall of the rock culture.

In 1977, Wenner sensed the winds were changing and he moved the operation to New York, striving to become a would-be tastemaker among a more moneyed set. Although *Rolling Stone* is still an attractively designed and financially successful publication, today's version lacks the bite, conviction and sense of community found in its earlier issues.

Janis Joplin was *Rolling Stone's* cover girl in 1969.

Reprinted by permission of Rolling Stone

Short Takes

A " P O P " - P O U R R I

 p to this point, *The Pop Sixties* has eschewed the mention of politics. But there were some politicians who projected such an aura of coolness and celebrity that they deserve to be called Pop Politicians and merit inclusion in this book.

JOHN F. KENNEDY — George Washington may have been braver, Lincoln more compassionate, FDR stronger, but when it comes to presidents, there was none cooler than JFK. His myth grows stronger, even as tons of tomes try to convince us of what a heel he was. With his bad back, he still had time for affairs of state — and of the heart. Twenty-five years later, American pols still must pattern their act — from their hairstyle, to their family, to their TV gestures — on the Kennedy style if they want to get elected.

John
Fitzgerald
Kennedy

LYNDON JOHNSON — The 36th president of the U.S. (1963-69). He rates because, among other things, he showed the world the long diagonal scar from his kidney-stone and gallbladder operations, and because he pulled the ears of his beagles — two acts of supreme '60s cool. On the other hand, Vietnam wasn't so cool.

ADAM CLAYTON POWELL — Renegade congressman from New York. When Powell wasn't in Congress (which was most of the time) or preaching at the Abyssinian Baptist Church in Harlem, he could be found down in Bimini, the Bahamas, usually with one arm around some babe, the other on the steering wheel of his boat, the *Adam Fancy*. He valued his privacy, once chasing *Life* photographers away with a shotgun when they wanted to snap him at Bimini. Powell coined a key '60s phrase, "Keep the faith, baby," but was ousted from his committee chairmanships by his vindictive congressional colleagues.

NIKITA KHRUSHCHEV — The chrome-domed Russian biggie who looked like he should be a garment center tailor. His achievements included general worldwide mischief-making (1958-64), banging his shoe at the U.N., and being barred admittance to Disneyland during his U.S. tour.

LOUIS ABOLAFIA — This political footnote ran for president in 1968 on the Love-Peace ticket. He posed nude on his campaign posters, declaring: "I have nothing to hide." His platform: free love, nonhostility, brotherhood, and camaraderie. A platform far more appealing than those of his rivals — Humphrey, Wallace, and Nixon.

MADAME NHU — The Nhu wave swept Vietnam in the early '60s. With her teased hair, Ray-Ban shades, and clinging dresses, she looked like she could be a member of a Phil Spector singing group. She was the Dragon Lady who ruled Vietnam with an iron fist, criticizing the Americans and the Vietnamese Buddhists. She was the power, some say, behind her brother-in-law, Ngo Dinh Diem, the president who got his in a November, 1963 coup, an action alleged by many, including Mme. Nhu, to have been sponsored by the CIA. She was in Beverly Hills on an American tour when the coup came.

BARRY GOLDWATER — If you liked him, you said "in your heart you know he's right." If you didn't, then it was "in your guts, you know he's nuts." With his jutting chin and steely eyes, the half-Jewish, ham-radio operating, plane-flying senator from Arizona *looked* like a president. He meant business with his arch-conservative philosophy. And he got wiped out by LBJ in 1964 in a crushing defeat no one thought could ever again be inflicted on a presidential candidate, until a mixed-up liberal named McGovern came on the scene eight years later.

RICHARD NIXON — Unlike the paranoid, tape-loving statesman of the '70s, the Nixon of the '60s was a perennial loser transformed into a surprise winner in 1968. Whatever happened to the "New Nixon"?

SPIRO AGNEW — Rumored to have been vice-president of the United States, sometime in the late '60s.

AND HONORABLE MENTIONS TO: William E. Miller, Kwame Nkrumah, Moise Tshombe, Big Minh, Curtis LeMay, John Lindsay, Patrice Lumumba, Che Guevara, the Chicago 7, Alec Douglas-Home, John Profumo, Everett Dirksen, and Senator George Murphy.

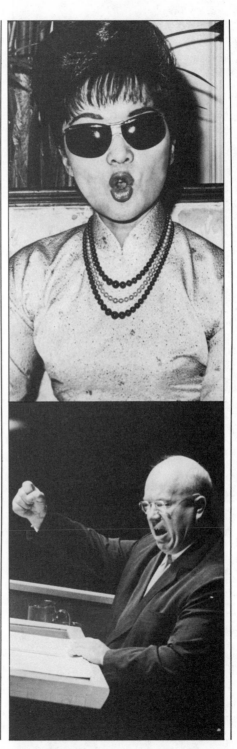

Madame Nhu

Nikita the K

The Comedians

The early '60s was the golden age of stand-up comedy. Not only were comedy LPs in the Top 10 but, from the stages of nightclubs like Mr. Kelly's in Chicago, the Blue Angel in New York, and San Francisco's Hungry I, stand-up comedians attracted a sophisticated audience — unlike today's comedy-club audiences who often seem to resemble those at a heavy-metal rock concert. These smarties came to hear a new group of "hip" (some called them sick) comics poking fun at previously sacred cows and, in the parlance of the day, telling it like it is. Roll over, Myron Cohen.

Among the best were:

LENNY BRUCE — Three years after he died, a record company reissued his material with an ad saying: "You can listen now, he's dead." Death had made safe the man who, in the late '50s and early '60s, was unarguably America's most controversial comedian. Was he a brilliant social satirist or, as his many critics, such as Walter Winchell, maintained, "America's No. 1 vomic" or the "man from outer taste"? He outraged moral sensibilities with his bits, spoken or spritzed rapidly, like a jazz cat blowing bop. This nasally-voiced Jewish hipster assailed the previously unassailable and unmentionable: religion (Christ and Moses go to St. Patrick's Cathedral), race relations ("How to Relax Your Colored Friends at Parties"), sex ("didja come good?").

Yes, he used four-letter words, but he never told a dirty joke. As he once said: "People should be taught what is, not what should be. All my humor is based on destruction and despair. If the whole world were tranquil, without disease and violence, I'd be standing on the breadline — right back of J. Edgar Hoover."

Conventional America wasn't ready for Lenny Bruce. He was busted for narcotics or obscenity seven times between 1961 and 1964, ultimately becoming a paranoid, obsessed man. He died on August 3, 1966, falling off a toilet seat with a needle in his arm. As the minister said at a memorial service: "He eulogized the demons that plagued the body of sick society."

That was the great Lenny Bruce debate: Was it he who was sick or was it society that was sick? One thing is certain: He was ahead of his time. Today, when every bimbo would-be comic who gets on stage at comedy clubs to rant about Quaaludes and toilets and punctuates each sentence with two-dozen f-words, one is reminded even more of Bruce's courage.

DICK GREGORY — He was the first black comedian to play white nightclubs. At a sensitive time in American history, he gently ridiculed race relations. "I waited all these years to be admitted to the Woolworth lunch counter, and now I find I don't like anything on their menu!" he said. Or "The waitress said to me, 'Sorry we don't serve colored people here.' I said to her, 'That's all right, I don't want to eat any, bring me a chicken.'" Or "Wouldn't it be hell if all this was burnt cork and you people were being tolerant for nothing?"

By the mid-'60s, he began phasing out his comedy career in favor of political activism. He was beaten and arrested several times in civil-rights demonstrations in the South. He also ran for president in 1968 on the Peace and Freedom Party ticket. In 1980, he

Lenny Bruce

Mike Nichols
and Elaine May

tried, unsuccessfully, to get the American hostages released from Iran. He often goes on marathon runs and lengthy fasts to publicize his causes.

BOB NEWHART — The button-down mind, an accountant turned comic from Chicago, went on to greater fame with his '70s TV show, where he played a harried psychologist. But in the early '60s he was master of the monologue, disguised as phone dialogues. For example, phone call of a Madison Avenue type placing a call to Abraham Lincoln: "Hiya Sweetheart, how's everything going? How was Gettysburg? Abe, listen, I got your note, what seems to be the problem? You're thinking of shaving it off? Abe, you're kidding, aren't you? Don't you see that that's part of the image? It's right with a shawl and a stovepipe hat." His *Button-Down Mind* LP was one of the '60s' biggest sellers. Unlike Lenny Bruce, he was safe for TV.

MIKE NICHOLS AND ELAINE MAY — The undisputed king and queen of early '60s improvisational comedy. This tremendously talented duo, members of Chicago's Second City troupe, won

audiences with their unsentimental, sardonic, neurotic humor. Their nightclub act didn't have strict routines because most of their stuff was sheer improvisation.

They were censored from the 1960 Emmy Awards ceremony because of a sketch ridiculing home permanent waves and because they said TV was sponsor-controlled. Not coincidentally, the ceremony was sponsored by a company that manufactured home permanent-wave equipment.

In one example, Nichols and May lampooned people at a party who pretend they know everyone intimately.

N: And then there's Albert Einstein's theory.

M: Oh you mean Al. A great dancer, love his hair.

N: But of course he had to leave Germany because of Adolf Hitler.

M: Oh that Dolphie, he was a riot. I used to call him Cuddles.

N: Good God!

M: Oh, Him — a close personal friend of mine.

Nichols and May both went on to careers as film directors after they split in 1961, Nichols with *The Graduate, Catch-22* and *Who's Afraid of Virginia Woolf?;* May with the less successful *The Heartbreak Kid* and *A New Leaf.*

WOODY ALLEN — He had not yet reached the demigod status he holds today. In the early '60s, he shucked his lucrative TV comedy-writing job for the grueling, humbling life of a stand-up comic. Clubgoers at first didn't know what to make of this nervous, redheaded runt who wore his neuroses on the sleeves of his tattered sports jacket. But they later got hip to the fact that this urban angstmeister was talking about *them*. By the end of the decade, he would be a successful screenwriter, playwright, and movie star.

Sports in the '60s

The affluence of the '60s created demand for more leisure-time activities. Participant sports like bowling, golf, and tennis flourished. But most of the time was spent watch-ing sports on television — all professional leagues expanded, new leagues were formed and died, and pro football became the nation's number one spectator sport.

BOWLING: During the '50s, bowling pulled itself out of the gutter, so-to-speak, and, by the early '60s, it had recast itself as a sport for mothers

Three members of the Jefferson High School Jesters Club in Lafayette, Indiana began a 50-mile hike in a snowstorm in February, 1963, as a sign of their commitment to President Kennedy's physical fitness program. They managed to walk 17.5 miles before the snow stopped them.

(the at-home variety, not today's working mothers) and families. Alleys were brightened and automated, pinboys and seamy characters had been exiled. Said Jack Vaughan, manager of Albuquerque's Bowl-a-Drome: "Where else can a woman compete after she gets married? They need competition just like men do."

The Hart Bowl in Dallas had a piano player working the lounge. Said lane owner Larry Hart: "The women have themselves a real ball. They like it and it sure beats going home to do the dishes."

In 1962, bowling and its assorted activities accounted for expenditures of about $1.5 billion, more than the combined gross national product of Iraq and Cambodia, according to *Time.*

Many lanes provided baby-sitters and nurseries. The Futurama Bowl near San Jose had nursery facilities for 180 children, a restaurant-bar, a "Glamorama" room with a physical therapist and body-building equipment. The Bronco, a Dallas bowling alley, had a four-chair barber shop, beauty shop and dance band.

Futurama's owner observed: "These women start to take inches off their behinds, build their bust up two inches. They go insane. Then their complexions start to get clearer and they wonder why and then realize it's from the steam room melting all that junk they put on their faces."

Bowling also tried to go big time. Only die-hard bowling fans and trivia buffs remember the National Bowling League, which was born in 1961 and died a year later. The ten-team league played in huge bowling centers, some with a 3,000-seat capacity.

The league's promoters thought they would create more great sports rivalries. No such luck—but a battle between the New York Gladiators (who actually bowled in Totowa, New Jersey, alley space being at a premium in Manhattan), and the Dallas Broncos (who played in the Bronco Bowl), just didn't carry the weight as, say, a clash between the Cowboys and Giants. So fans had to bid farewell to the Gladiators, Broncos, Kansas City Stars, Detroit Thunderbirds, and the league's other six teams. The NBL will reside forever in '60s sports trivia bins along with Abe Saperstein's American Basketball League and Branch Rickey's Continental Baseball League.

BILLIARDS: Another pastime that tried to go legit, with a bit less success than bowling, was billiards. And, like bowling, billiards was a sport more associated with Ralph Kramden and Ed Norton than with mom and dad. So enterpreneurs tried spiffing up the all-male, smoky poolrooms, moving them from drab city side streets to suburban shopping malls and calling them "billiards lounges" with names like the Golden Cue. Many had wall-to-wall carpeting, pastel tabletops, and pseudo-Tiffany lamps. In 1966, about 3,000 new poolrooms opened, many of which were these "family" billiard lounges.

Entrepreneurs wanted women to play pool the same way they had taken to bowling, but these efforts didn't boom as the industry had expected. Many of the new billiard centers went out of business. Families, it seemed, preferred the cleanliness of the new-style bowling alleys instead, or else were content to play at home on pool tables in finished basements or rec rooms.

PHYSICAL FITNESS: Spurred on by JFK (who said on December 5, 1961: "The sad fact is that it looks more as if our national sport is not playing at all — but watching. We have become more and more, not a nation of athletes, but a nation of spectators"), the early '60s saw America's first wave of fitness mania. Despite his bad back, JFK played softball and touch football. Robert Kennedy took a fifty-mile hike along the Chesapeake and Ohio Canal. The goal of all this activity, said a *Look* writer, was "cornucopia without corpulence."

The good folks of Muskogee, Oklahoma — before Merle Haggard made the city famous — really took the president to heart. In the early '60s, the city was named as the pilot city for Bud Wilkinson's campaign as head of the President's Council on Physical Fitness. Muskogee schoolkids, 6,557 of them, took a physical fitness exam (pull-ups, sit-ups and squat thrusts), and 3,043 flunked.

A compulsory fitness class for grades 4 through 12 was started. But then things got out of hand; some children worked out in garages with improvised weights and muscle stretchers. YMCA classes sprouted for men, and housewives did push-ups in their living rooms. Gas stations handed out calisthenic booklets instead of road maps. A time-traveler from the '80s would probably feel right at home for that brief period in the Muskogee of 1962.

With patriotic fervor gym teachers had us grunting and groaning with "calisthenics": squat thrusts, jumping jacks, leg lifts. We hated it, but it was OK; we imagined JFK doing the same thing in the Oval Office. We needed this strength for the hand-to-hand combat against the Reds who were sure to invade our typical American suburb quicker than you could say

"Nikita Khrushchev." If you could do one hundred sit-ups and fifty push-ups, why you'd be able to take on those Russkies, no questions asked. Well, no Russians came, and the fitness boom waned. We let ourselves get soft and flabby. Who'd believe twenty years later that we'd gladly pay hundreds of dollars to do the same thing in a "health club" where these same stupid calisthenics were given a fancy name: "aerobics." This renewed fitness obsession was undertaken without a presidential decree, no less. We were now worried by an enemy far more deadly — namely, advancing age and increasing sloth.

Vic Tanny, where are you now that we really need you?

INDOOR SKIING: One of the strangest indoor sports of any decade was this one, which appeared briefly in 1962. For the skiier who couldn't wait to get to the mountain, there was Ski-Dek Center, indoor skiing. That's right—an indoor moving mountain, with hand-painted Alpine scenery and a large, carpeted escalator without steps (the "ski run"). It was a moving belt covered with white caprolan fiber, twenty-by-fifty-five feet long. The skiier wore small skis, pushing off from the top of the platform, against the moving belt, which was able to alter his balance because it could be run at many speeds. The pile in the rug was soft enough to allow the skiier to make all turns.

The brains behind this franchised operation was G. David Schine, the former aide to Senator Joseph McCarthy. The first Ski-Dek Center opened in Buffalo in a converted movie house. For $1.50 admission you got skis, poles, and boots. They're probably back to showing movies by now.

PLAYBOY ATHLETES — Before the '60s, athletes usually hewed to the straight and narrow. Oh, you'd hear about a few exceptions — Babe Ruth's appetite and the New York Yankees Copacabana brawl — but athletes mainly were still your basic Frank Merriwell characters. But in the '60s, jocks began swinging with more than bats.

Witness the profusion of Hefneresque athletes: baseball's Bo Belinsky (he pitched a no-hitter as an L.A. Angels rookie and then scored with Mamie Van Doren and playmate Jo Collins), Joe Pepitone (the first baseball player to place a hair dryer in the clubhouse), Ken Harrelson (the dandiest dugout dresser), and the coolest cat of them all, Mr. White Llama rug and Fu Manchu moustache, Joe Namath, who was signed for a $400,000 bonus in an era when such salaries still had the ability to boggle the minds of players and viewers alike.

The evolution of Joe Namath from short-haired Alabama quarterback to the swinging signal caller of the New York Jets

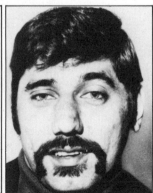

MUHAMMAD ALI — The 1960 Olympic champion, Cassius Clay, defeated Sonny Liston for the heavyweight championship in 1964 and changed his name to Muhammad Ali. His refusal to serve in Vietnam made him a hero to some, a traitor to others. Why couldn't he be like Joe Louis, polite society asked. "I am the Greatest!" answered Ali.

SONNY LISTON — Ali's adversary, a surly ex-con who Norman Mailer called "the king of hip" and "the ace of spades." So mean he made Mr. T seem like Arnold Stang, Liston was also a some-time movie star who appeared in *Harlow* and *Head.*

THE NEW YORK METS — One of two National League expansion teams formed in 1962, the Mets assembled an all-star squad. Unfortunately, it was the National League all-star team of 1955. Casey Stengel, coaxed out of retirement, managed the world's worst collection of castoffs, has-beens, and never-weres to a 40 and 120 record their first year. Seven years later, in one of those miracles that happens every thousand years or so, the Mets won the World Series.

VINCE LOMBARDI — The martinet coach of the Green Bay Packers during their glory days and the author of the phrase, "Winning isn't everything...it's the only thing." Lombardi took a ramshackle team and converted it into the most powerful NFL squad of the '60s (six western conference titles, five world championships).

SANDY KOUFAX — The best Jewish pitcher ever.

SPORTS MOVIE of the '60s — *Safe At Home* (1962), in which a little leaguer lies to his pals about his friendship with the Yankees stars, Mickey Mantle and Roger Maris, then gets to meet his crew-cut heroes in the flesh. Roger Maris was not nominated for an Oscar. This movie also features cameos by pitcher Whitey Ford and Yankee skipper Ralph Houck.

EIGHT RIDICULOUS SPORTS FRANCHISES OF THE '60S

Does anyone remember them?
1. Anaheim Amigos (ABA)
2. Chicago Zephyrs (NBA)
3. Kansas City Steers (ABL)
4. Los Angeles Jets (ABL)
5. Minnesota Muskies (ABA)
6. New York Generals (NSL)
7. New York Titans (AFL)
8. Pittsburgh Rens (ABL)

Eats

My childhood was filled with food. Forget those starving European children. Feed me! Buy me that new food they're pushing on Saturday morning TV. Eat, bubbula, eat!

They call it junk food now, but we called it snack food then, and that's what we lived on. Who cared about chemicals? They were good for you. Better eating through chemistry. Bring on the Tang, the Instant Breakfast, the cereal with dehydrated, inflatable strawberries, and the frozen sausages and eggs (TV breakfasts). Yum, yum, eat 'em up. Who knew from natural? That meant they probably put leaves and sawdust in the food. Yogurt was a communist plot.

Fast food was American, and the '60s were the dawning of the fast-food age. McDonalds, Wetsons, and Kentucky Fried Chickens appeared on the suburban horizon, mysteriously sprouting overnight on vacant lots. Hungry families could be fed for under a $1 and never have to leave the comfort of their cars. McDonald's meals were treats to be anticipated and savored. When the Big Mac was introduced in 1968, my family actually made a special expedition twenty miles away to the one franchise that was offering the item on its menu — the way gourmets today track down the latest foie gras at the trendiest gourmet food emporium.

Pancake houses became extremely popular — Aunt Jemima's was one chain. Some had thirty-seven varieties of flapjacks advertised in prose that was probably more fattening than the actual item: "Persian pancakes: delicate egg-batter crepes rolled and filled in with strawberries and peaches garnished with smooth rich whipped cream." A visit to a pancake house was almost as exotic as a trip to the Pearl of the Orient.

You knew where you stood, food-wise, in the '60s. Chocolate chip cookies meant a bag of Chips Ahoy! — not those $1.25 "all-natural" things you see today. One of those monsters is the price of two bags of Chips Ahoy. Ice cream was sold to you by some guy in a white shirt who drove a truck with bells, not hand-dipped out of some vat by a guy in a Lacoste shirt who wears bells around his neck.

But there was a price to pay for all this indulgence. Dietetic madness in the shape of Tab Cola ("the now taste of Tab," said its ad), Pepsi's less-successful Patio Cola, No-Cal cola, Diet-Rite cola, Metrecal, and Sego. There was the Stillman Diet and the Calories Don't Count diet. Or, Nutriment, if you wanted to go the other way.

Maybe this generation is now doing penance for a childhood spent gorging on Twinkies, Ring Dings, Shake-a-Puddings, Lucky Charms, Captain Crunch, pizza-flavored catsup, meatball-flavored crackers, chicken-flavored crackers, sour apple chewing gum, Bugles, Chipsters, and Whistles, washed down with Wink, a Strawberry Yoo-Hoo, or a Great Shake.

What has happened to that generation? Was it the chemicals from all that stuff that warped our minds, making us crave such foods as alfalfa sprouts, raw fish, and granola?

'60s Ads and Commercials— A Market Testing

The boys on Madison Avenue worked overtime in the '60s chasing after the youth market. ("Taste the NOW taste of Tab!") Ads proclaimed that to use a certain product would put you where the action is. This ploy was used to sell everything from deodorant to shows. Models wore miniskirts to sell aspirin. Op Art, Pop Art, real Peter Max, and fake Peter Max graced ads. What a time to be alive. There were no ads for video games, designer jeans, or discount stereo stores.

Attention members of the Pepsi Generation! You spent enough hours in front of the tube, thumbing through magazines, singing the jingles — or even using the dumb product. You must remember some of these memorable ads. Really — this isn't such a tough quiz. You're not going to get Excedrin Headache No. 5 if you take it. In fact, you can do it during a commercial break.

'60s Ads Quiz

1. Where do you meet the nicest people?
2. Ultra-Brite gives your mouth _____ .
3. Look Ma, no _____ .
4. What great item was invented in 1963 that greatly aided the efforts of beer guzzlers? What was the first beer manufacturer to use it?
5. I want my _____ !! (not MTV)
6. What flavor was Wink?
7. How much did the Polaroid Swinger originally cost?
8. When you got it, _____ . What company used this slogan?
9. Only her _____ knows for sure.
10. Name three products that used tigers in their ads.
11. What was the only brand of chewing gum to inspire a dance? What was the name of the dance?
12. Name the only hit record inspired by an Alka-Seltzer commercial.
13. Who was the cartoon character spokesman for Fritos?
14. What does Ajax clean like?
15. Let _____ put you in the Driver's seat.

Answers

1. On a Honda
2. sex appeal
3. cavities
4. The pop top. Schlitz.
5. Maypo
6. Grapefruit
7. $19.95
8. flaunt it. Braniff airlines.
9. hairdresser
10. Esso, Top Brass hair dressing (hawked by a pre-99 Barbara Feldon), and Kellogg's Sugar Frosted Flakes
11. Teaberry. The Teaberry Shuffle.
12. "No Matter What Shape Your Stomach Is In," by the T-Bones (1966)
13. The Frito Bandito
14. A white tornado
15. Hertz

HE SMOKES 'EM

The '60s was also the last decade that we were allowed to see commercials for cigarettes on television before they were banned by the FCC in 1971. Take a deep breath and see how well you recall the nicotine scene.

1. Show me a filter cigarette that really delivers taste, and I'll eat my _____ .
2. What brand was a silly millimeter longer?
3. It's what's up _____ that counts.
4. The Marlboro commercial song was based on what movie theme song?

ANSWERS

1. Hat
2. Chesterfield 101's
3. front
4. *The Magnificent Seven*

Thirteen '60s Words Now In Disuse

1. Brand X
2. Discotheque
3. Gay — as in happy
4. Girls (to be replaced by women)
5. Monoaural
6. Negro
7. Pig, heat, fuzz, the man — for policeman
8. Plastic — as in fake
9. Red China
10. Silent majority
11. Sneaker
12. Straight — as in non-drug user
13. White backlash

A Rogue's Gallery of '60s Celebs

Below are miscellaneous pop-culture heroes of the '60s who were too unimportant to have their own chapters, but are also too important to be ignored.

JANE ASHER — Paul McCartney's first love and the sister of Peter (of Peter and Gordon). Rumors of their marriage caused green waves of jealousy to hit American teenage girls in 1964. But, as we know, Paul wed Linda Eastman and, as you may not know, Jane pursued a fairly successful acting career in England.

BABY JANE HOLZER — Tom Wolfe's "girl of the year" in 1964. A Manhattan socialite who slummed in the swinging sixties and set her own fashion style, she now runs a fancy ice-cream parlor for Palm Beach swells.

VAUGHN MEADER — A $45-a-week stand-up comedian who rose to fame in the fall of 1962 with *The First Family,* an LP which poked fun at JFK, his family, and associates — and sold more than five million copies. Meader, then a 26-year-old, tousled-haired New Englander, vaguely looked like, and very much sounded like, the president. The pres said Meader sounded like Teddy; Teddy said he sounded like Bobby, and Bobby said he sounded like Sargent Shriver. But Meader's career skidded to a halt a year later on November 22, 1963 ("Nobody wanted to know from me. I was as dead as the president," he said).

By 1967, a bearded, flower-bedecked Meader was telling columnists "through LSD, I found peace." By the '70s, he became a heavy drug user, went broke, and got involved in the Jesus movement (he released a bomb LP about JC in 1972 called *The Second Coming),* and worked as a counselor in a drug-rehab clinic in Louisville. He also played Walter Winchell in the 1975 gangster film *Lepke,* did a stage show, "characterizing, not impersonating" JFK, and toured as a country-western singer.

PAT PAULSEN — He was the double-talking, deadpan comic who delivered editorials on the controversial "Smothers Brothers Comedy Hour." "We can win the war on poverty by shooting 400 beggars a day," he intoned on the show. He once branded California Governor Ronald Reagan a "known heterosexual." Paulsen ran for president in 1968 on the Straight Talking American Government (STAG) party, whose motto was "We can't stand Pat." ("With Hubert Humphrey, Richard Nixon, and George Wallace in the race, what possible harm could one more comedian do?" he reasoned.)

Humphrey claimed that votes for Paulsen cost him the election. He ran — almost on a more serious note — as a Republican in the New Hampshire primary. The FCC took him seriously; at least, they wouldn't allow a Disney special to air because they claimed Paulsen's appearance on it violated the equal-time provision. Today, Paulsen, like his comrades, the Smothers Brothers, owns a vineyard in Sonoma County, California, bottling wine under his own label.

JOE PYNE — Acid-tongued syndicated talk-show host, he did a 180 on Donahue and all those "happy talk" gabsters who would succeed him in the '70s. "Go gargle with razor blades," the one-legged ex-Marine would often advise his eccentric guests, who included hippies, homosexuals, UFO advocates, and peaceniks: "If brains were dynamite,

B aby Jane Holzer

you couldn't blow your nose." Most memorable exchange: with Paul Krassner, editor of the iconoclastic magazine, *The Realist.* Pyne: "Isn't it true that your magazine is full of homosexual material?" Krassner: "Why, Joe? Did you see something that interested you?" The heavy-smoking Pyne died of cancer in 1970.

Barry Sadler

Joe Pyne

SERGEANT BARRY SADLER — For a brief period in the spring of 1966, the Green Berets were folk heroes and Sadler, a real-life Special Forces paratrooper, was their troubadour with the Number 1 record of the year, "The Ballad of the Green Berets." Post-Vietnam life wasn't nearly as heady for Sadler. In the '70s he served time for homicide, but he also authored a series of action-adventure novels.

ALLAN SHERMAN — A bespectacled, chubby Jewish TV comedy writer and producer (he co-created "I've Got a Secret") who took traditional folk songs and substituted new lyrics with a Jewish twist to them. His parodies of the garment-center, Borscht-Circuit set captured Middle America's fancy. Thus, "Frere Jacques" became "Sarah Jackman," the story of a yenta; "Alouette" became the tale of "Al and Yetta."

His first LP, *My Son the Folksinger,* was one of the top albums of 1962. At the time of its release in October, 1962, it became the fastest selling LP in the history of the record business. Sherman's biggest hit was 1963's summer-camp parody "Hello Muddah, Hello Faddah," sung to the tune of "Dance of the Hours" from the opera *La Gioconda.* Later LPs included *My Son the Celebrity* and *My Son the Nut.* Sherman passed away in 1973.

NANCY SINATRA — Frankie's daughter wore boots that could have walked all over me anytime. She was as much a turn-on to adolescent boys in the mid-'60s as her dad had been to their moms. With her long, ash-blonde hair, slinky striped tights, and leather miniskirt, she summed up the essence of mid-'60s sexiness. She later mellowed and cut a duet with her pop, "Something Stupid," which, according to the *Saturday Evening Post,* "is called the incest song by hip teenyboppers."

TINY TIM — When Boy George really was a boy, this hook-nosed, stringy-haired, ukelele-playing character was the world's foremost androgynous entertainer. The former Herbert Khaury was a fixture of low-rent Greenwich Village nightclubs for years before he burst into the national consciousness in the summer of 1968, blowing kisses on "Laugh-In" and trilling turn-of-the-century tunes in his falsetto voice on his LP *God Bless Tiny Tim.*

But Tim's most notorious moment came on December 17, 1969 when he wed 17-year-old Miss Vicki Budinger in front of a nationwide audience on "The Tonight Show." The happy couple spent the first three nights of their honeymoon apart in keeping with Tim's bizarre sexual code. Clearly, not a marriage meant to last, they separated in 1972. Vicki took their baby daughter Tulip in hand and dis-

appeared until she hit the front pages when it was revealed that she had to work as a go-go dancer at Minnie's Lounge in Camden, New Jersey and accept welfare to support herself. Tim offered to take her back if she would undergo a test for VD. She refused, and they finally divorced in 1977.

The freak show also ended for Tiny Tim in the '70s. He toured the backwater lounges of America as part of a traveling vaudeville show whose other acts included Zippy the Chimp and a fireater, and eventually lost much of his money, moving back to his parents' New York apartment in 1980. A much chubbier Tiny Tim occasionally makes the news pages today, but younger and weirder gender-benders have eclipsed his star.

Tiny Tim

A '60s Postscript

Just so you shouldn't forget: There are some differences between the '60s and the '80s.

'60s	'80s
BAKING BREAD	MAKING BREAD
FREE LOVE	HERPES
"LET'S TRY LIVING TOGETHER"	"LET'S TRY A TRIAL SEPARATION"
RUNNING AWAY FROM HOME IN SUBURBIA	BUYING HOME IN SUBURBIA (IF YOU CAN GET A MORTGAGE)
"OFF THE PIGS!"	"MORE POLICE PROTECTION!"
FLOWERS HANGING AROUND NECK	PLANTS HANGING FROM CEILING
READING *STEAL THIS BOOK*	FALSIFYING EXPENSE ACCOUNTS
BLACK LIGHTS	TRACK LIGHTING
KRAFT'S MACARONI & CHEESE DINNER	TORTELLINI W/PESTO SAUCE
HIGH: ONE'S HEAD	HIGH: INTEREST RATES
TAKING COURSE AT "FREE UNIVERSITY" ON "AMERIKA: A PIG NATION?"	TAKING COURSE AT "NETWORK FOR LEARNING": "HOW TO MEET YOUR LOVER AND PICK A SUCCESSSFUL STOCK AT THE SAME TIME."
FAVORITE LPS: SGT. PEPPER LET IT BLEED CROSBY, STILLS & NASH	FAVORITE LPS: SGT. PEPPER LET IT BLEED CROSBY, STILLS & NASH

INDEX

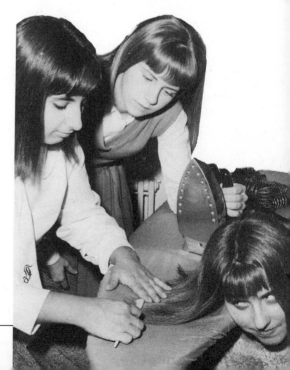

World Almanac Publications
Order Form

Quantity	ISBN	Title/Author	Unit Price	Total
	31655-X	Abracadabra! Magic and Other Tricks/Lewis	$5.95/$7.95 in Canada	
	32836-1	Africa Review 1986/Green	$24.95/$33.95 in Canada	
	32834-5	Asia & Pacific Review 1986/Green	$24.95/$33.95 in Canada	
	32632-6	Ask Shagg™/Guren	$4.95/$6.50 in Canada	
	32189-8	Big Book of Kids' Lists, The/Choron	$8.95/$11.95 in Canada	
	31033-0	Civil War Almanac, The/Bowman	$10.95/$14.75 in Canada	
	31503-0	Collector's Guide to New England, The/Bowles and Bowles	$7.95/$10.95 in Canada	
	31651-7	Complete Dr. Salk: An A-to-Z Guide to Raising Your Child, The/Salk	$8.95/$11.50 in Canada	
	32662-8	Confidence Quotient: 10 Steps to Conquer Self-Doubt, The/ Gellman and Gage	$7.95/$10.75 in Canada	
	32627-X	Cut Your Own Taxes and Save° 1986/Metz and Kess	$3.95	
	31628-2	Dieter's Almanac, The/Berland	$7.95/$10.25 in Canada	
	32835-3	Europe Review 1986/Green	$24.95/$33.95 in Canada	
	32190-1	Fire! Prevention: Protection: Escape/Cantor	$3.95/$4.95 in Canada	
	32192-8	For the Record: Women in Sports/Markel and Brooks	$8.95/$11.95 in Canada	
	32624-5	How I Photograph Wildlife and Nature/Rue	$9.95/$13.50 in Canada	
	31709-2	How to Talk Money/Crowe	$7.95/$10.25 in Canada	
	32629-6	I Do: How to Choose Your Mate and Have a Happy Marriage/ Eysenck and Kelly	$8.95	
	32660-1	Kids' World Almanac of Records and Facts, The/ McLoone-Basta and Siegel	$4.95	
	32837-X	Latin America & Caribbean Review 1986/Green	$24.95/$33.95 in Canada	
	32838-8	Middle East Review 1986/Green	$24.95/$33.95 in Canada	
	31652-5	Moonlighting with Your Personal Computer/Waxman	$7.95/$10.75 in Canada	
	32193-6	National Directory of Addresses and Telephone Numbers°,The/Sites	$24.95/$33.95 in Canada	
	31034-9	Omni Future Almanac, The/Weil	$8.95/$11.95 in Canada	
	32623-7	Pop Sixties: A Personal and Irreverent Guide, The/Edelstein	$8.95/$11.95 in Canada	
	32624-5	Singles Almanac, The/Ullman	$8.95/$11.95 in Canada	
	31492-1	Social Security and You: What's New, What's True/Kingson	$2.95	
	0-915106-19-1	Synopsis of the Law of Libel and the Right of Privacy/Sanford	$1.95	
		Twentieth Century: An Almanac, The/Ferrell		
	31708-4	Hardcover	$24.95/$33.95 in Canada	
	32630-X	Paperback	$12.95/$17.50 in Canada	
	32631-8	Vietnam War: An Almanac, The/Bowman	$24.95/$33.95 in Canada	
	32188-X	Where to Sell Anything and Everything/Hyman	$8.95/$11.95 in Canada	
	32659-8	World Almanac° & Book of Facts 1986, The/Lane	$5.95/$6.95 in Canada	
	32661-X	World Almanac Book of Inventions°, The/Giscard d'Estaing	$10.95/$14.75 in Canada	
	29775-X	World Almanac Book of World War II, The/Young	$10.95/$14.75 in Canada	
	0-911818-97-9	World Almanac Consumer Information Kit 1986, The	$2.50	
	32187-1	World Almanac Executive Appointment Book 1986, The	$17.95/$24.95 in Canada	
	32628-8	World Almanac Guide to Natural Foods, The/Ross	$8.95/$11.95 in Canada	
	32194-4	World Almanac's Puzzlink™/Considine	$2.95/$3.95 in Canada	
	32626-1	World Almanac's Puzzlink™ 2/Considine	$2.95/$3.95 in Canada	
	31654-1	World Almanac Real Puzzle™ Book, The/Rubin	$2.95/$3.95 in Canada	
	32191-X	World Almanac Real Puzzle™ Book 2, The/Rubin	$2.95/$3.95 in Canada	
	32625-3	World Almanac Real Puzzle™ Book 3, The/Rubin	$2.95/$3.95 in Canada	
		World of Information: see individual titles		

Mail order form to: **World Almanac Publications**
P.O. Box 984
Cincinnati, Ohio 45201

Orders must be prepaid by one of the following methods:

☐ Check or Money Order for _____ attached

☐ Bill my charge card (Add $5.00 processing charge for orders under $20.00)

_____
Visa Account #   Exp. Date

_____
Master Card Account #   Exp. Date

_____
Interbank #   Exp. Date

_____
Authorized Signature

Order Total_____

Ohio residents add 5.5% sales tax_____

Shipping and Handling:_____
(Add $2.50 for every purchase up to $50.00, and $1.00 for every $10.00 thereafter)

TOTAL PAYMENT_____

Ship to:

Name_____

Street address_____

City/State/Zip Code_____

Special Instructions:_____

_____
All orders will be shipped UPS unless otherwise instructed.
We cannot ship C.O.D.